SEEKING SPIRITUAL MEANING

SOCIOLOGICAL OBSERVATIONS

series editor: JOHN M. JOHNSON, *Arizona State University*

••

"This new series seeks its inspiration primarily from its subject matter and the nature of its observational setting. It draws on all academic disciplines and a wide variety of theoretical and methodological perspectives. The series has a commitment to substantive problems and issues and favors research and analysis which seek to blend actual observations of human actions in daily life with broader theoretical, comparative, and historical perspectives. SOCIOLOGICAL OBSERVATIONS aims to use all of our available intellectual resources to better understand all facets of human experience and the nature of our society."

—John M. Johnson

Volumes in this series:

SEEKING
SPIRITUAL
MEANING
THE WORLD OF VEDANTA

JOSEPH DAMRELL

 SAGE PUBLICATIONS   Beverly Hills • London

For information address:

SAGE PUBLICATIONS, INC.
275 South Beverly Drive
Beverly Hills, California 90212

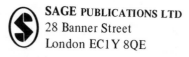

SAGE PUBLICATIONS LTD
28 Banner Street
London EC1Y 8QE

Printed in the United States of America

Library of Congress Cataloging in Publication Data

Damrell, Joseph D
   Seeking spiritual meaning.

   (Sociological observations ; 2)
    1. Cults—United States—Case studies. 2. Vedanta.
3. Religion and sociology. I. Title. II. Series.
BL2530.U6D35   181'.48   77-9145
ISBN 0-8039-0802-4
ISBN 0-8039-0803-2 pbk.

FIRST PRINTING

CONTENTS

ॐ गणेशाय नमः
ॐ सरस्वत्यै नमः
ॐ नारायणाय नमः

FOR JEAN-PAUL

ACKNOWLEDGMENTS

I am deeply indebted to the people in this study for the opportunity to be among them, and to their teacher who befriended me. My hope is that the ways in which I have benefitted from knowing them will be reflected in this presentation of their search for Truth as an understanding of Vedanta, and as a profound commitment to Self-Realization. I have learned philosophy, worship, meditation, music, art, a language, history and a way to live in the world. If any of the Spirit of Vedanta and its heroes has rubbed off on me in the process, let it find its expression here as an appreciation of the gifts given me.

Writing this book has required a special kind of solitude and social insularity that Linda Damrell helped provide. She was with me throughout the adventure, acting as a "control" on my experiment, and maintaining my role when the experiment seemed from time to time as though it might fail. Her contribution to my project is immeasurable, "and not in your Vedantic sense," as Sri Ramakrishna once said.

I also wish to thank the following friends and colleagues who contributed to this endeavor. Bennett Berger, my former sociology mentor, has aided my understanding of social life and helped me to become committed to my profession by his untiring support and friendly criticism. Bruce Hackett, another friend and former teacher, has frequently made himself available to discuss with me some of the ideas in this book, so they have taken shape under his influence. Likewise has Leonard Schatzman been a major source of inspiration and insight during our altogether too brief association as members of the same academic department. Randall Collins, Catherine Ryan and Robert Broadhead read the original draft of the book and offered me valuable criticism and encouragement. David Farmer painstakingly combed the manuscript for lapses of grammar and thought, as did Rhoda Blecker, Senior Editor for Sage Publications. Each of these persons has made a special contribution to this study and to my sociological imagination.

My sister, Anna Peschel, is owed a special debt of gratitude by me. She typed the original manuscript at considerable personal sacrifice and has been a great help throughout the project. I am grateful for her love and assistance.

Finally, I wish to thank Professor Jack D. Douglas for reading the manuscript and calling it to the attention of John Johnson, Editor of the series in which the book is being published.

–J.D.

INTRODUCTION

During the period when the author of this ethnographic quest was doing the work which produced this book, some of his friends and former teachers, myself among them, would sometimes ask (with an anxiety composed partly of incredulity and half-prurient anticipation): "What do you think? Has Joe found religion? Has cynical Joseph Damrell, that cool and abrasive veteran of the rock scene, become a Hindu?" There was precedent for the anxiety: More than one sociologist of our acquaintance had been captured by one or another of the visionary/redemptive religious movements which, like a cosmic Electrolux, had rolled into the ruins of the counter culture with a Cyclops eye seeking the crash pads of the spirit to suck up the psychological debris left by its casualties.

As it turned out, the questions themselves were problematic. I wasn't quite sure what "found religion" meant, and I certainly didn't know anything about what it was to "become a Hindu." But my concern was real enough. It was founded in what I knew were the powerful experiences religious rebirth could provide to those whose needs for transcendence were so great as to render unthinkable a purely secular life bereft of visionary devotion. It was intensified by the magnetic attractiveness of such experiences, particularly to those who had come to a crisis point or a dead end in their own lives, or for whom the rewards of everyday life had in some way irrevocably soured. And I saw the attraction of the "conversion experience" as an opportunity for the desperately unsatisfied to transform their desperation from a symptom of malady into a positive cognitive credential which sanctioned their efforts to strike through the masks of secular rationality into the epistemological unknown on the other side—those "other" realities, cleansing and intimate knowledge of which was promised by psychedelic missionaries, reborn Christians, Yaqui warriors, scientologists, teenage Divine Masters, and other gods, gurus, priests, prophets, saints, avatars, sorcerers, magicians, lords, and servants all to the yearning for a glimpse of the eternal.

So what's wrong with that, you say? Well, nothing very much perhaps, and I surely wouldn't want to be caught red-handed arguing against Seekers, who, after all, have a very good reputation indeed. But my anxiety was not so much about the Seeking as the Finding, for it seemed to me that passionate Finders frequently developed vested interests in the *mystery* of their Finding, so much so that their transfigured subjectivity withdrew from or resisted attempts at "explaining" it, as if explaining meant explaining *away*—in much the same sense that the Romanticist bias against analytic understanding is expressed in Wordsworth's warning that "to dissect is to kill."

My anxiety about religious Finders, then, became a melancholy about the potential loss of friends, analytic colleagues, fellow intellectuals, who might Find something so ineffably precious that to undertake full sociological analysis of it was a danger too great to risk, even in the mighty name of understanding. The transfiguring religious experience seemed to me too much like an initiation into an exclusive club whose members were tumbled out of a frame of reference in which meaningful dialogue could occur with the nonelect—for example, me. Attempts at rational inquiry would be shunted aside with affirmations of faith (sometimes patronizing, sometimes not) that the experience could not be understood but only undergone.

In my harsher moments, I'd think: Vested interests are vested interests, and regardless of whether it's money and property on the one hand or spiritual experience on the other, the reluctance to make "full disclosure" of their sources constitutes a mystification of their power; hence, an ultimate betrayal of the most fundamental of intellectual tasks: to make things plain. Seriously daemonic Seekers, it seemed to me, would be less circumspect, more greedy; would want it *all*—the illuminative religious experience *and* the full analytic understanding of it; would want to cradle the mystery in the palm of a hand, like a mouse, scrutinize it carefully and not be disappointed; God appraising Her first week's work and finding it Good.

That shouldn't be very hard to do, particularly for sociologists of culture who subscribe to the phenomenological persuasion that reality is "socially constructed." For to believe in "social construction" is to believe that something is *built*, and if one believes that, then the sturdiness of the construction should not be threatened by the expertise of the builders/architects/engineers present at the site. Real construction workers are not so Romantic as to believe that their real buildings may be shaken or undermined by the builders' understanding of exactly how they were put together. Quite the contrary is likely to be true; like other structures, social structures are likely to be sturdier by virtue of their builders' knowledge of exactly what they were doing all along.

It is in this sense that *Seeking Spiritual Meaning: The World of Vedanta* reveals its author to be a master builder in the reality-construction trades. Dr. Damrell undertook this work not to "study" a Vedanta church or its membership, and not to "become a Hindu" in order to do participant-observation of the religion, but to make himself available to religious experience, so that if it occurred, he would be in a position to report its phenomenology. He enters into a sort of contract with the Swami to undertake the role of devotee, to fulfill its obligations, and to practice its discipline to the extent he can. In the language of current ethnomethodology, he attempts to "become the phenomenon," to let it occur to him and in him.

One of the wonders of this text is that there is hardly a clue in it as to the author's instrumental motives for having done it. There is by now a long tradition in sociological field work of steeping oneself in the lives one studies, of attempting to get all the way into their experience for wide varieties of "in order to" reasons: to see the world from their perspective; to celebrate and affirm that perspective or to debunk or otherwise expose its claims; to render the alien familiar or the routine strange; to make prostitutes and homosexuals more respectable and sympathetic or teachers and physicians less so. There is virtually none of this egoism evident in Dr. Damrell's text. He makes no secret of the fact that he found his research experience rewarding, but he does not thereby become a partisan of Vedanta, ready to push his readers around "in order to" score ideological points in behalf of Vedanta. The author of this book got what he came for, and I take it as a measure of his gratitude and his ethnographic grace that he *respects* his subject matter sufficiently to regard as a temptation any impulse to *use* it for ideologically self-serving ends, and a betrayal actually to do so.

Whatever his motives, the temptations are powerful to "use" one's research subjects. There is much agitated talk these days in research proposals about "protection of human subjects," but the discussions have barely scratched the surface of the subtle moral problems that lie hidden underneath. It is very difficult to do extended field research without developing sympathies for or antipathies to the subjects/objects of one's study. Living among "others," particularly under relatively insulated conditions, generates strong pressures to become one of them (the "my people" thing among anthropologists), and the loyalties so engendered can motivate strong desires to speak in their behalf, to defend them against detractors, to maximize their strengths, minimize their weaknesses—to be a catcher in the rye.

The opposite occurs, too; if you don't like the people you're studying, that fact will be hard to hide, particularly if you're with them for a substantial period of time, and if the research is to continue, you'd better learn to hide it well, because groups which are busy sustaining their own lives don't have much reason for tolerating enemies (manqué or not) living among them. Probably the most familiar way of hiding dislike is the scientific posture; objectivity, detachment, and the *assertion* of theoretical interests effectively *distance* researchers from their subjects, and hence function not only to disguise negative valence but to protect researchers from being experientially affected in ways they'd prefer not to be (that is not *all* the scientific posture does, of course).

But the moral problems of "protecting human subjects" are not nearly solved by being "for" them rather than "against" them, and surely not by a ritual show of neutrality. You may be "for" them in interpretive ways which they reject, so that with friends like you they need no enemies; and you may be "against" them (say, for insufficiently living up to their professed aims) in ways that motivate them to try harder, for which they may be grateful. In either case, whether you are protecting or damaging human subjects is a subtle, elusive, perhaps imponderable question to which serious answers are not readily available.

Joseph Damrell's answer (although he does not pose the question explicitly) is almost the most impressive feature of this book, because the Vedantic posture (which I take to be a systematic beating down of reflexivity to the point where the ego is exhausted) enables him to transcend the imponderables: the empirical imponderable of who "he" is among "them" (imposter? devotee? seeker? sociologist?) and the moral imponderable of whether his presence among them does injury to either. The Vedantic posture sees such concerns as "illusions" (the Latin root of "prestige" *means* delusion) to which proper responses should be above all practical rather than spiritually ambitious. The Vedantic posture (as I came to understand it from this book) provides an answer to "the reflexivity problem" in sociological theory by permitting us to see that the "problem" of infinite regress is *merely* theoretical; in *fact,* the reflexive thinker tends simply to become tired, bored, exhausted by the regression of his or her own reflexivity. The Vedantic posture, then, becomes for Dr. Damrell a way of being a sociologist: An exhausted ego creates an almost ethereally detached researcher, attempting to get through the data of research to the lives and experience of those (including the researcher) who provide the data; getting through *without* getting "on top of" or "underneath" or "behind" or any of the other metaphors which indicate that the researcher's ego is busy being superior to, deeper than, redemptive of, solidary with, or aloof from the "others" with whom he is engaged in a joint enterprise.

I am not sure whether this achievement is an expression of Dr. Damrell's gifts as a field researcher or whether he was just very lucky with his choice of religion, or some mixture of the two. No matter. Dr. Damrell got his religious experience, both under meditation and with the aid of the Swami's special instruction. Less extreme than Castaneda's and less portentous than Jules-Rosette's, this experience is more impressive for its modesty, its matter-of-factness, and its utter indifference to the reader's suggestibility. Other reports of religious experience with which I am familiar convey awe and amazement, valuable no doubt to the person undergoing the experience but not much help to readers seeking analytic understanding. Dr. Damrell is not ready to sacrifice one to the other.

"Do the trip," said the hippies. "Take the path," said the Swami. Dr. Damrell did the trip and took the path and the journey presumably continues. I don't know whether he has "become a Hindu"; he may not know himself. In either case, the answer is not relevant to his readers; the evidence of the journey is. And what he has shown us is that religious experience is like other genuine experience; it is socially constructed, and with a modest quantum of reflexivity it can be reported and its circumstances can be described without mystification. Wisdom dictates caution in making causal inferences from circumstances to the experience; we may not yet know how to "make" religious experience "happen" (we don't know how to make "love" happen either). But the most impressive achievement of this report, at once ethnographic, autobiographical, phenomenological, is that it *makes such experience plausible and routine,* rather than awesome and amazing. By having become the phenomenon, Dr. Damrell has demonstrated that authentic experience needs no protection from analytic understanding. Like an instant replay in a football game, he "slows the spiritual machinery" so that we can see its constitutive processes. The description of it strikes a blow against mystification by making things plain. That deserves high congratulations.

San Diego   *—Bennett M. Berger*

PROLOGUE

This is a study of a Vedanta temple in America, its head, its community of monks and laypersons, and above all the perception and construction of the ultimate meanings of spiritual experience which its special ambience harbors. The only possible excuse that I can offer for engaging in such an investigation—since my aim is not to promote a pro- or anti-religion position—is that the subject matter is of special value to the pursuit of sociological knowledge about reality-construction, with special emphasis on the definitions of situated religious experience. I allowed myself to assimilate the philosophical qua spiritual frame of reference that derives from the ancient Hindu tradition, and then reflected on my experiences from the standpoint of an ethnographer.

In this account of a spiritual religion through my experiencing of some of its historical, social organizational, and mythological facets, I have intentionally reduced to a minimum the usual preoccupation with technique that characterizes much reported field research. I want to preserve the natural heterogeneity and complexity of Vedanta and of the setting in which I encountered it, so I have given an experiential interpretation to both the Vedantic tradition and its contemporary lived meanings. Rather than attempt a sociology *of* Vedanta which would place a greater emphasis on the structure of the community in which it inheres, I have attempted to remain as true to its everyday focus as possible. However, because language renders presentations into representations, my interpretations of Vedanta tend to give it an obdurate, static quality which in its adherents' everyday worlds it seemingly lacks. Thus, my account of the Vedanta phenomenon, in spite of my intentions to avoid doing so, tends to "explain it away." In recognition of this problem, I have decided to explore different facets of Vedanta on several different levels simultaneously, and in this way allow the reader to encounter it in a more or less holistic form. For the most part, my approach is phenomenological, although my prose style infuses the descriptions of Vedanta with references to structural and emergent situational factors that "explain" the members' religious "behavior." While the subject matter and the various sociological treatments it receives may interest qualitative sociologists, students of religions, social movements, and Eastern philosophy and culture, this book was written with a lay audience in mind. On the one hand, the manner in which I have done the field research and my way of presenting the subject matter are intended as a demonstration of the consequences for the discovery of sociological knowledge that flow from a researcher's intimacy with the object of study. Yet, in place of a preestablished research strategy and a set of conceptual and analytical guidelines or frames, I have absorbed my own experiencing of my participation in the world of Vedanta and have attempted to derive from interactions, thoughts and their accompanying timbre and feelings the essential meanings of the religious experience of the temple.

The chapters are organized into the following sequence: Chapter 1 is concerned with the situation of a sociologist in quest of knowledge and the Vedanta temple's situation with respect to sociologists. The second chapter concerns the Indian social movement of which the temple is a part. Chapter 3 explores the temple in Valley City and describes the rationale for the spiritual search in Vedanta, which is in turn analyzed in some detail in Chapter 4. Chapter 5 focuses on the Swami, who is the principal spiritual person in the setting. Chapters 6 and 7, respectively, emphasize the web of social life in the Valley City temple and the contexts in which tensions among members arise as they pursue spiritual goals.

Chapter 8 introduces the idea of the relationship between inner aspects of spiritual experiences and meanings for the temple's cult, and the social contexts in which these are emergent. With each succeeding chapter, the book's analytic and descriptive foci are shaped by my initiation into and participation in dynamic cultic events, each of which I use to illustrate the nature and substance of the spiritual life of Vedanta. Thus, in Chapter 9, I describe my initiation into Vedanta and my introduction to the shrine, which has a special significance for the cult and its adherents. Chapter 10 is a phenomenological reconstruction of the mythic and cognitive features of meditation, which are then portrayed in the next four chapters on the charismatic hero's birthday celebration (Chapter 11), the role of music in the cult (Chapter 12), the gospel of action (Chapter 13), and the meaning of pilgrimage (Chapter 14).

Chapter 15 summarizes the study with an outline of a cognitive socio-logical theory of spiritual identity. Chapter 16 is intended as a metaphor-ical demonstration of the altering of the consciousness of a person who has been inducted into the special life-world of the Vedanta temple cult. The epilogue, Chapter 17, analyzes an underlying experiential dimension of cult life that is the foundation for the spiritual in Vedanta as conceived by the cognitive sociological perspective.

In this book, I am concerned with presenting—in simultaneously descriptive and analytic fashion—living persons and their social worlds as I have encountered them in a mutual undertaking of a type of spiritual life. In order to give my account of spiritual life in Vedanta conceptual balance, I utilized existential and phenomenological motifs in characterizing the subjective realm of the religion, and ethnographic and social interactional modes of analysis in discovering both the situated cultic meanings and the ongoingly negotiated dimensions of the temple's multiple and overlapping social worlds.

The first part of the book (Chapters 1 through 7) is primarily concerned with Vedanta's historical, cultural, and philosophical context and contemporary social location, together with the temple's everyday life. The second part of the book (Chapters 8 through 16) is intended as a demonstration of my sociological method and theoretical perspective through an account of my study of Vedanta and my participation in the temple's spiritual experience. The last three chapters (15-17) are intended as a step in the direction of a new discovery in sociological thought. These chapters contain a dynamic synthesis of several field research approaches that is utilized to explore dimensions of human social reality and subjectively real experience that are precluded from consideration if one adheres to a single perspective within the field research tradition. My approach, it is hoped, will in the present instance yield a more accurate sociological interpretation of religious meanings.

—J.D.

1. JOINING: Becoming My Own Subject Matter

For six years I have been studying and practicing Vedanta in Valley City (a pseudonym) with a senior monk of an Indian monastic order. He agreed to accept me as a student on the condition that I would follow a specific spiritual path, but the choice of path was up to me. Since I wanted to benefit as fully as possible from my contact with him in a sociological way, if not in any other, and since I wasn't prepared to choose any particular religious personality as my "ideal" (or even a particular religion per se), I chose the path of the Vedantic seeker. My choice, and the arrangement to study and practice with the Swami of the Valley City Church Universal, were a kind of contractual agreement, inasmuch as I was required to promise to undertake the *sadhana* (spiritual inquiry)[1] in good faith and with utmost self-effort, doing what was asked of me. No behaviors were specifically forbidden, but the Swami made it clear that I should "refrain from doing whatever might jeopardize the undertaking." The course of study was free of charge, and he or I could terminate it at any time. He said: "At such time that you can learn nothing more from our association, I will inform you. Until then, you will study *bhakti yoga.* Later on, you will study *jnana yoga.*"

Bhakti is the path of "faith"; jnana is the path of "knowledge." They differ considerably in their approaches to the goal of spiritual realization, the former relying on traditional objects of religion, the latter on philosophical inquiry. However, the Swami told me two weeks after I met him that for his own Master, Sri Ramakrishna, they were identical, and in the temple it is believed that "all paths lead to the same goal."[2]

During my first two weeks, on four or five occasions I visited the temple, which was located in a fairly well-to-do suburb, to attend religious services and talks held for the "congregation." During each visit, the Swami found a moment or two to talk to me privately. I told him how I first learned about the Church Universal from a group of people I had been studying for my doctoral dissertation. They had taken me with them to a different branch of Church Universal, which, it seemed to me, much more emphasized the religion's Hindu, or at least Indian, origins than did the Valley City Church Universal. By contrast, with the Swami as "minister and teacher," Valley City's was a more traditional-seeming church, patterned after the Judeo-Christian culture into which the Indian character of the setting and the thrust of the teachings had been all but fully assimilated. I tended at the time to try to live with this by having a relationship with the Swami, not with the Church as such, because, as previously implied, I did not then nor do I now see myself as religious. But in order to gain the full benefit from association with him, I gradually recognized the need for attending group functions, including public religious services, even though I was not particularly excited by the idea.

Whenever the Swami and I talked, he would ask me questions about my occupational goals, my situation with respect to graduate school and work, my interest in Vedanta, and my family and religious background. I told him about my work at the university, my intellectual interests, and tidbits about my personal life (such as my age, where I grew up, my home life, my parents' passing interest in Christianity, and some of my experiences as a musician). I emphasized, perhaps a bit too strongly for someone in that situation, that I had an intense dislike for religion and churches but found the Vedanta temple's atmosphere—with its "presentational" and "vertical" direction—tolerable, if not downright pleasant.[3]

The Swami told me that people came to the temple out of an interest in making "God-realization" the goal of their lives, and that some, perhaps, would reach that goal. "We do not go in for displays of this and that sort," he said. "People like to wear costumes and draw attention to themselves, but we do not want anyone to notice. Vedanta says that in order to realize the highest truth, one must give up all attachments, fear and anger, name and fame, all the normal round of life's dualities. It is all right to want success in life, to have name and fame. But the time will come when these things are not enough. Then the person becomes 'restless for God,' as Sri Rama-krishna said, or, in Vedantic language, the person desires to know the highest truth within; this is the True Self, the *Atman,* God."

He went on to explain how there was room, because of Vedanta's liberalism and humanism, for diverse approaches to spiritual fulfillment and how, therefore, my intellectualism and political radicalism (I had told him I favored revolution over his idea of gradual progressive reform, and we were in agreement on a socialist goal for society) would not be a barrier to member-ship. "You must not preach to the devotees. You must attend to the learning of the Vedanta and adhere to the path of the 'Seeker of God.' Every day you must try to keep your mind in 'God,' in that highest spiritual experience that is within. You must cultivate a distaste for sense objects and enjoyments even beyond what you naturally feel as a result of your striving to be a scientist. . . .

"Even sociology has a sacred character," he added, remarking how the Weberian idea of subjective meanings and Sorokin's stages of organic development had an analogue in the Vedantic thought of Vivekananda (called Swamiji). "Swamiji was a great scientist. He tested Sri Ramakrishna, and as a result his mind became filled with that highest truth of man, that He is Infinite. But we don't go around saying, 'I am He, I am He.' No. We are taking the attitude of devotees. 'Not I but Thou,' is what the devotee says. And this is grounded in the nondual reality. The goal of the devotee is to give up his attachment to even his ideal, and merge in the absolute *Satchidananda*" [an epithet of *Brahman* meaning infinite existence, knowledge, and bliss]. He paused for a while, and then he said: "No, we don't broadcast this place. This is why I don't often wear the *gerua*" [the saffron robes of the monk].

Since I have known him, I have learned he wears the gerua usually only on ceremonial occasions. He wears a suit in public and American casual attire the rest of the time. He never asked me to cut my long hair, which he said was my "privilege" by virtue of my youth and my university affiliation. Without regard for what impact it would have on my personal style, he said I was to live the life of the "householder," a married person who is dedicated to the quest for spiritual realization. Linda Damrell was with me during the entire course of my studies with the Swami, but I will speak for the most part in the first person singular about my relationship with the Swami. The relationship with one's teacher is personal, and so I cannot speak for her; although she was with me at the temple on most of the occasions this book describes, her own experiences have followed another course.

My self-presentation to the Swami was affected by two important factors which bear on this study's organization and focus. One was that before meeting him I had learned the behaviors conducive to acceptance as a student of a *sanyasin*. The learning had taken place at the other Vedanta temple I had visited while working on my dissertation. This knowledge enabled me to present the image of a candidate potentially fit for sadhana, and particularly fit for the path prescribed by Sri Ramakrishna and his disciples. I did not consciously convey a false impression or give any erroneous information about myself, although I did—in spite of having neither belief nor disbelief in a god—agree to worship, in the fashion of as sincere a spiritual seeker as I could be, Sri Ramakrishna and his wife, Sarada Devi, as my "chosen ideals."[4]

When the Swami asked me if I accepted the Vedantic idea of the *avatara* (that the undifferentiated Brahman occasionally becomes a human form), I remember thinking that if anyone could be God in human form, Sri Ramakrishna was certainly a prime candidate for the role. I had read *The Gospel of Sri Ramakrishna*, as well as several accounts of his life and teachings, and was quite intrigued ("turned on" may be a better term) by the natural simplicity of this holy man in the context of nineteenth-century Bengali Hindu religious life.[5] Aldous Huxley's introduction to the *Gospel* says approximately what I felt at this time—namely, that Ramakrishna's life and the book in which portions of it have been "preserved" are amazing phenomena that readily invite intense scrutiny. The *Gospel* contains a complete banquet of Indian spiritual culture; it is a kind of postgraduate study in universal religion with in-depth consideration of numerous individual religions. So with my experience in the field studying the group that had become completely immersed in the *Gospel* and their teacher at another Church Universal temple, and with the *Gospel* and the Swami of Valley City having rekindled some smoldering interests in the sociology of religion, and in Max Weber's ideas about charisma and prophecy, I made the leap—which is to say that I undertook sadhana, taking a vow to make the realization described in the *Gospel* and other religious scriptures "my own," as the Swami sometimes puts it.

The second factor influencing my presentation of myself to the Swami will explain what may seem confusing in the above description. The kind of sociology I was and still am doing is called qualitative sociology, whereby a field researcher becomes personally involved in the subject matter rather than maintaining a distance from it through the use of preestablished conceptual frames and analytic techniques.[6] At the time (1970) I joined the temple, I had been doing field research by taking advantage of my student status and "drifting," open to varieties of social life, until I found something I could know sufficiently to make into a paper or book. When I secured a full-time, eight-to-five job in a number-crunch department at the university, I found my openness in jeopardy. I was no longer free to roam about studying what caught my interest. Thus, I took the opportunity to settle into the role that I found open to me at the temple, and to relieve the boredom associated with my full-time job I became engaged in a concentrated effort to absorb the Vedanta tradition, Sri Ramakrishna's legacy, and the Swami's teachings. I did not, in other words, undertake a formal study of a religious setting or religious phenomena, complete with predetermined research goals, methods, strategies, and so on—but neither did I fit the "native" category of "spiritual seeker." Despite my obvious, if unstructured, analytic interest, the Swami accepted me as a student, and I agreed to work on behalf of the goal of spiritual life as it is conceived in his tradition.

During the six years the book covers, the Swami frequently gave me private audiences, at both my own and his initiation. In these audiences, he addressed himself to the duties of the *chela* (disciple), of the *bhakta* (devotee), and of the "householder" (defined earlier)—three "roles" to which I was then accustoming myself. He advised me on all sorts of matters, from how to set a table to how to breathe while meditating. Early on, I was enjoined by him to meditate every day and to study the Vedantic scriptures (the *Upanishads,* the *Brahmasutras* and the *Bhagavad Gita*) and the lives of gods and saints (Sri Ramakrishna, Swami Vivekananda, Buddha, Christ, Mohammed, Shankaracharya, Krishna, and others) when time permitted.[7] I was to maintain a steady job and commit myself to the householder's life of sacrifice on behalf of others.

Shortly after I met him, the Swami announced that he had made me a member of the Church, but that the $2.50 per month dues need only be paid if I had the money. No one would ask for it. (I have paid only when it occurs to me.) A month later, he initiated me with *mantras* from Sri Sarada Devi's spiritual repertoire.

My interest in what the temple was all about and what was going on between the Swami and me grew more intense as my job at the university required more and more of my time and permitted little opportunity to do field research. So to keep myself and my sociology professors happy, I made the determination to keep my ethnographer's skills sharp, although officially my "job" was to cut carrots and feed people rice in the name of "consumer" science. Based on my readings and observations, I wrote a paper on Ramakrishna and the Hindu Renaissance which the sociology department accepted as a Ph.D. qualifying examination in the area of social movements. This encouraged me to discover more about contemporary Vedanta, so as my dissertation on the other religious group took shape, I used information gathered from Vedantic literature and from conversations with the Swami to illustrate features of the religious lifestyle of the group about which I was writing.

In the meantime, I allowed bhakti and Vedanta their tenuous place in my daily life. Partly out of respect for the Swami, my teacher, whom I had quickly grown to like, and partly out of the need to immerse myself in something besides eight hours a day of food texture variables and palatability scores (not to mention dissertation-writing), I tried to follow the Vedantic regime faithfully. I kept some notebooks of my studies and made recordings of talks by the Swami. I wrote down experiences I had at the temple while interacting with the devotees when the experiences had some special significance for my spiritual quest. I attended every private and public function that my schedule of work, graduate studies, and private life would allow. I changed the pattern of my life, cutting myself off from less-than-close associates, putting aside certain leisure pursuits, avocations, and pastimes, and made the temple and the special life it harbors the center of my thought and activity. During gaps in my work, I would meditate, read Vedantic literature of one type or another, or simply write about this or that observation. Evenings not spent in dissertation-writing, and even some that were, were patterned with some aspect of Vedanta or the Swami.

After receiving my Ph.D., I opted to stay in the area so that I could continue my association with the Swami and complete the study. Even now, the association continues and my inquiry goes on.

This research is not clandestine, although I have seldom directly mentioned the project to anyone at the temple except the Swami. I did not function exclusively as an observer, nor put on any more pretenses than are required of anyone else in the setting. I did not take notes in dark corners, or tape record conversations which I then submitted to meta-sociolinguistic analysis. I did not formally interview anyone. I strictly avoided getting into the frame of mind that would yield quantitative data about the scene, its history, its proportions, the dollars and cents of everyday life, and though some of this has found its way into this book, I did not look for it. I resisted as best I could the temptation to take a fragment of the collage and plug it into the theoretical constructs being promoted by my professors. I even tried to avoid making private value judgments about who the people were or what their lifestyle meant. This was more than casual neutrality; I had to maneuver out of many situations because my stance gave all the moral absolutes of various people within and without the setting a decidedly provisional character, and I was disinclined to argue about theological or scientific points, moot or not. The role I took was that of witnessing the induction of a person, myself, into a special world. Most of what I did as a role-incumbent was the specific creation of or at the direction of the Swami and the devotees. My "self," me, the personal continuous awareness of my subjectivity, remained on the sidelines casually and intermittently noting the absorption-rate, the net effect of this and that associated process, without over-sociologizing. What I am attempting to do here is not to discard the familiar tools of qualitative sociology, nor have I tricked people into letting me observe them up close or secretly spied on them after having falsified my purposes for being in their midst. Still less am I claiming an exclusive insight into a particular religion or religion in general; nor am I promoting a spiritual lifestyle. My goal in this book is to utilize a kind of reflexive native experience that will contribute to a sociological understanding of the spiritual meanings that are emergent in the Church Universal and Vedanta philosophy. I shall not resort to religious explanations of spiritual meanings, nor will I automatically discount them from a scientific or sociological point of view. In this book, I shall attempt to bring to the foreground both the sociological and the Vedantic explanations—not necessarily to fuse them and thereby come up with a "science of religion," but rather to allow the reader to encounter the everyday contexts of spiritual life as it is lived in an experiential social context.

Thus, there are several methodological and substantive issues that bear on my involvement as a field researcher in this particular setting and on my attempts to attain the experiences described in the scriptures and by the teacher. Part of my reporter's role will be to show how the relationship between the Swami and me has evolved, and from the vantage point I have attained, I will attempt to describe the experience in a way that links some of its external trappings—temple life—with Vedanta's "inner logic."[8] Again, it is primarily because I see religion (and all other constants in human experience) as presentational, as opposed to merely representational or symbolic, that the approach I utilized in this study seems the most appropriate one. Thus, I am not so much concerned with explaining the character of the affiliation, identification, and involvement of people in religion or with the variables that play upon these considerations, as I am with describing and explaining the phenomenological objects of religion per se, objects that find their expression in the Vedantic explanation and elaboration of the world as a kind of transcendental experience. I intend this study not as a mere adjunct to the usual positivistic, causal way of treating the "Hindu" religious factor, but as an altogether different kind of knowledge about the interplay between the subjective religious experience and the institutionalized version of such experience found in society and history. Thus, I am not concerned with the truth or falsity of Vedanta's religious claims, but with *the consequences in human terms of regarding certain classes of phenomena as real.*

My prescriptions for the real, for my own experience of the world, have been altered during the course of this study, but it is not because of the discoveries I made that I wrote this book. I consider myself a student of the social, and religion is considered in the Durkheimian sense the "epitome" of the social. But due to the exclusiveness of Vedantic circles and the philosophic and spiritual character of study guided by a personal tutor, I could not directly apply my sociological tools by organizing my participation into data production. What I could do (as I said earlier) was write.

Several times, at the Swami's request, I gave talks at the temple Sunday services on Vivekananda or Vedanta's spiritual life. Another time, I lectured about Gandhi and Indian independence. Finally, I began writing on the subculture of Hinduism which contained in it the social reality I had been admitted to but felt constrained not to directly look at. I ended that particular project midway, when it became apparent to me that the completion of the subculture's structure was impossible without the sort of picture I was busy *not* studying at the temple.

My purpose in this book, which I began writing in April 1975, is to show specifically an interaction between the inner dynamics of religious experience and a group's outer social arrangements and cultural circumstances. These latter come across in mundane and special occasions of social life, and I record them here as an immersed yet reflexive observer. Because it is impossible by such a method to describe everything, I have tried to consign what I couldn't describe to silence (to paraphrase Witgenstein).

As for airing the group's dirty linen, of which there has always been a commendable shortage, or telling group secrets, I haven't. My own interpretation is necessarily conditioned by my sociological frame of reference, though I intermittently suspended its use in the field and in post-research retreats, relying instead on an intuitive and more or less spontaneous grasp of situations and their function in cult life. As long as a picture of the experiential *meanings* for the actors is sought, those meanings will have to be experienced by the researcher. Thus, another field researcher using another method of observation and another participatory device might come to different conclusions.

The present study represents, to employ both sociological and Vedantic pedagogy, one way among any number of alternative ways, each of which will yield its own "kind" of knowledge. The kind yielded here is intended to lend some support to the phenomenological foundation of a cognitive sociology of religion. By means of descriptions of lifestyle elements and religious experiences, some with empirical and some with hypothetical supports, I intend to explore some of the avenues opened up by the cognitive perspective.

It is *not* a study of people and their social customs, gestures, habits, foibles, and the like, but of their spiritual experience in the sense that they refer to it. If my descriptions leave out most tangible people, their individual biographies, mannerisms, idiosyncrasies, and the like, it is because to include these would have been a violation of the pact that I made with the Swami. I don't want to assault their privacy or their being. Yet, this book rests on the assumption that other things are relevant to sociologists about this setting and my way of being in it. I concentrated in this work on roles and role-relationships and on intersubjectivity, rather than on personal biography and personality, although the latter are closer to the subjective realities of participants. Social personhood, too, is undoubtedly a feature of life in the temple, but I have reflected on it only indirectly as a result of my predilection with respect to being there. Perhaps Vedantins will one day be approached by a thoughtful person with questionnaire in hand who will ask all the right questions.

For personal as well as sociological reasons, this approach did not appear to me to be likely to generate much beyond some demographic trivialities which could then be causally linked to or disjoined from extant theory concerning religious affiliation. I was more interested in how the fabric of life was interwoven with the world view encompassed in the system of thought Max Weber once referred to as "sublime."[9]

Doing Vedanta, becoming a seeker, seemed the most efficient way of finding out what Vedantins are about, and to learn from experience Vedanta's embedded sociological lesson. So what follows is an intellectually reconstructed view of Vedantic spiritual experience discovered in a temple in America, and the outlines of a cognitive sociology of religion.

NOTES

1. The meanings of Sanskrit words and of some other concepts which will be used throughout are given in the glossary at the end of the text.

2. My decision to keep the name of the group anonymous was made in order that I might discuss freely some of its characteristics without invading privacy. Also, the group prefers its relative anonymity anyway, a preference stemming from the "exclusive," personal character of Vedantic inquiry.

3. "Vertical" refers to the direct experience of something, whereas "horizontal" refers to knowledge *about* something, a concept that has come to me from William James via Alfred Schutz (1944: 500). "Presentational" means roughly the same thing as "vertical"; its opposite, "representational," refers to objects representing or standing for something. It is a term I borrow from Ninian Smart (1973).

4. The divinity of Sri Ramakrishna and Sarada Devi is taken for granted by a large number of modern Hindu Indians. Making them my "chosen ideals," as the selection of a path is called, meant that I attempted to have a "vision" of them. The term "vision," as I will demonstrate, is one name for the central spiritual experience of Vedanta.

5. See the Further Readings at the end of the volume for information on books mentioned.

6. For a recent analysis of this kind of sociology and its trends, see Helmut R. Wagner (1975).

7. This smorgasbord of religious life is standard fare for the Vedantin, whose universal outlook equalizes spiritual personalities under the rubric of divine incarnation, with its various degrees of manifestation. The god-men the Swami told me to study are particular choices of the Ramakrishna movement—that is, are a part of that movement's development.

8. The way religion focuses on its central divine objects cannot be understood from without. We shall take a phenomenological look at the "inner logic" formed by Vedanta's various foci and thereby demonstrate how it is grounded in the experience of the religious. "Inner logic" and "phenomenological focus" are terms used by Ninian Smart. My use of them, while being guided in general by Smart's overall

direction and mode of analysis, is grounded in the discovery of the spiritual correlates of everyday life of the temple. Smart's approach is comparative, polymethodic, and structural, whereas mine is for the most part sociological and cognitive. Therefore, my use of these terms is according to my own, not Smart's, definitions.

9. Speaking of the "great Indian doctrinal systems" in general (including Vedanta, Yoga, Samkhya, etc.), Weber (1958: 176-177) said that rational striving, combined with holiness sought through contemplation, characterized people who were divorced from the "practical tasks of doers." Because of his orientation to the impact of religious ideas on economic rationalization, Weber said that he would resist the temptation to go more deeply into Vedanta, although its discoveries were "sublime in their way."

2. THE MOVEMENT

The historical antecedents of the Valley City temple are both American and Indian. The Vedanta movement in America is an outgrowth of its Indian parent, which originated with Sri Rama-krishna.[1] I believe it will be relevant to briefly discuss how the movement has been described by reporters and to present here evidence of some day-to-day correlates between Indian and American realities that affect temple life.

At the time of Ramakrishna (1836-1886), Bengal was under-going what is referred to (perhaps too lightly) as social turmoil and unrest. The British conquerors had broken down much of the traditional culture and replaced it with the Empire's indus-trial, bureaucratic, and rational power. For the Hindu people, it must surely have seemed the twilight of the gods. There appear-ed assorted movements generally explained by the relative deprivation members experienced under colonization. Millenari-anism resulted from the loss of meaningful activity by people who had been previously utterly occupied with ritual and spiri-tual practices. The very core of the society had been excised, and with it went the constitutive, integrative processes on which the continuity of society was dependent and on which people relied for their existence.

At the same time, the counterpoint to this theme of cultural deprivation and individual anomie is the renaissance of Hindu culture that flourished in the midst of the crumbling older order. Much of the energy of the renaissance was directed toward the integration of European and native culture, especially of the major religious and cultural themes. The integration had the effect of Christianizing or rationalizing the main Hindu religions.

Much energy was also directed by Indians toward the total abnegation of Hindu culture and the wholesale acceptance of rational European thinkers, such as Mill. Bohemians, literati, intellectuals, dandies, and strata of higher civil servants, the languishing royalty and *declassé* Brahmins gave Bengali public life a romantic, if occasionally decadent, flair. The theatre and several other art forms grew, including the novel, musical composition and poetry. In the meantime, the orthodox were left to view the ruin of the former holy order. The energy of Ramakrishna and his followers, it could be said, was directed toward a revival of the religious model for living in the world which had been the foundation of Hindu civilization. Based on the individual in ecstatic communion with the Divine, the gospel of Ramakrishna was clearly one of devotional salvation (Rolland, 1965: 92-146). Ample biographical records exist suggesting a sense of personal deprivation in the followers of the god-man. The breadth and scope of this sense of deprivation can be seen from the fact that the followers represented a cross-section of Bengalese society. Ramakrishna's followers included bohemians as well as "integrationists," religious, cultural and otherwise, but it did not in the beginning include Westerners.

Ramakrishna is regarded as an embodiment of all the world's religions; his special significance for India is that he proved, by parable, vision, trance, and discourse, that Hinduism, allegedly inferior, was not only the *equal* of other religions, but was their *source.* It was later said that Vedanta provided the rational basis for understanding god, while Ramakrishna revived the best method for realizing god. The method, of course, was bhakti, the religion of devotion and ecstatic love which is a prominent feature of Hindu religious culture. As an *avatara* (incarnation of the Absolute), Ramakrishna was to reestablish the hegemony of the divine order which is accessible through ecstatic devotion. Because of his humble origins, his ability to find wisdom in the homeliest of phenomena, and, of course, his exemplary life as a religious seeker and teacher, Ramakrishna gave Hindu society as much-needed, godlike hero.

Ramakrishna's principal disciple, Vivekananda, was the Vedanta movement's main architect. His transformation at the hands of Ramakrishna is perhaps classical in its proportions, for the agnostic youth became a kind of model for patriot-saints who followed. If to himself Ramakrishna's godhood was a matter of personal opinion, Vivekananda sought to establish the Master's role as objective fact. He founded the order bearing the Master's name, and he and his brother monks gave Hinduism an unusual direction. The many religions (all of which Rama-krishna had practiced and mastered), representing the varied temperaments of mankind, could and should be worshipped in *man himself.* The rationale for that worship was Vedanta, wherein the person's "soul" (atman) is identical with the "cause" of the universe *(Brahman).* By serving man, one worships god. Thus, Vivekananda's movement stressed the social reconstruction of India—charitable institutions, schools, hospitals, and relief agencies, in addition to monasteries and convents.

In a sense, Vivekananda's fame and influence in India derived from something that happened in the West. Swamiji stole the show at the Chicago World's Fair of 1893, where his addresses at the Parliament of Religions were met with wide acclaim. Afterward he toured the United States, speaking before university and church audiences. He turned down professorships Harvard and Columbia offered him, having answered what he believed was a higher calling—to uplift India and to bring her spiritual heritage to the West.

Back in India, where much clamor had been created over the new and unknown leader of India's cause before the world, Vivekananda became an instant modern savior. Owing to his efforts and to those of the order of monks, a continentwide resurgence of faith in the traditional India, couched in the rational framework of Vedanta, occurred and was to be the foundation for the later political movement that eventually expelled the colonial administration and set up the new government. Its symbol, the simple god-man, Ramakrishna, was its spiritual preceptor.

Despite the "social" facets of its origins—the loss of traditions, the need for humanitarian ministerings in India, or the simple necessities of living under British domination—Rama-krishna's movement was and is a religion. We need to under-stand the dynamics of its specifically religious content, and to explore the ways in which that religious character influenced the outcome of the movement itself. Ramakrishna's pure cha-risma was ritually "distributed" on his death, a portion going to Vivekananda and the other intimate disciples, and the rest to the order which they formed. Today, the swamis of that order are invested with a transcendent authority that derives from the original distribution. In the temple, rational and charismatic elements are evident, both in the Swami's role and in the structure of social life.

Vivekananda founded the Church Universal in the West and set up several temples and monasteries in America and Europe. His idea was that, in return for spiritual values, the West would usher India into the age of science and industry. He did not have in mind that Vedantists in the West would give India money in exchange for yoga and philosophy (although that has happened). His idea was that Indian religion would provide a solution to the problem of materialism that sensitive Westerners were bound to confront. In this way, India and the West would develop a cultural reciprocity and to the benefit of both, the world as a whole would undergo advancement.[2]

For Church Universal temples in particular, this idea has had a profound consequence. Unlike their Indian counterparts, which are service-oriented (as well as religiously so), Church Universal is limited to the cultural sphere. Vedanta books, periodicals, and other products have found wide acceptance among certain strata—particularly professional—as well as those composed of retired, upper-middle-class women. Today, al-though the Church Universal is derided by some as stuffy and conservative, its publications, particularly those on Vedanta, including the works of Vivekananda and the *Gospel of Sri Ramakrishna*, are in wide use as reference books by scholars and by people in divergent religions. Although a cult flourishes around the departed charismatic leader, Ramakrishna, and his missionary prophet, Vivekananda, the main impetus of the movement is institutionalization of the religious aims. It is a Hindu denomination for modern Indians and a kind of Chris-tianized yoga theology and Sanskrit outpost—site of the continuing evolution of Vedic thought—rolled into one. Some writers describe it as a pillar of "real" religion of the sort that Christianity was in the caves.

The Church Universal is an interesting example of a religious movement that has become institutionalized. Although it is Indian in origin and retains some trappings of formal Hindu orthodoxy, particularly with respect to the selection and elevation of candidates for monkhood, it is well assimilated into the cultural mainstream of American religious institutions. The order of monks operates as a "church," with all its structural and organizational accoutrements, and it seems to have legitimized Indian philosophy, yoga, and a particular brand of rational mysticism and scientific religion. It takes its place on the intellectual and cultural frontier of religion alongside Unitarianism and other universalistically inclined sacred ideologies that collectively move away from a formal narrow, sectarian focus of religion in the face of an increasingly scientifically rationalized and constructed world.[3]

Vedanta makes a case for the truth of all religion. Its own ancient philosophy, which is said to contain the origin as well as the essence of all religious sentiments and thought, is to be the basis on which the opposing religious and scientific views of the world can be reconciled. The "manipulationist" character of yoga and the "practical Vedanta," as modern Vedantins call their world view, gives the appearance of movement to an institution that is really quite stable and routinized. Bhakti, a devotional religion associated with medieval Indian decline in Brahmin hegemony attendant upon Moslem political conquest, pervades the Vedanta scene in the West.[4] And the cult of Ramakrishna, Sarada Devi, Vivekananda, plus *Tantra, Shakti,* and *Vaishnava* forms of Hinduism, are a central part of the religious tapestry in the Church. But the official view of such obviously arational motifs is that they are symbolic or mythological ideas from a prior period in history, when the evolution of human consciousness was at a pre-scientific stage. The Swamis often interpret *pujas* in ways reminiscent of scholarly analyses of anthropological data. Dramatic "enactments" are undertaken in modified—that is to say, streamlined—form. Meditation is sandwiched between ritualized routines. Worships are shortened and such things as clarified butter, camphor, sandalpaste, and other ingredients associated with Vedic rites are often omitted. However, such things are all known to the swamis and they *are* employed when it is convenient—which ranges from when the items are available cheaply to when the ritualized occasion appears to demand it. Music is translated into simple Western modes, the inflections and inner dynamics of the Indian style left completely out. Thus, several recordings made by Vedantic groups tend to focus on English-language devotional songs, although several Sanskrit and Bengali hymns have become institutionalized, albeit within a Western musical form. There is, moreover, little emphasis on the Indian things per se, the main emphasis rather being on the cultural pattern of the group in its Western situation. The infrequent times when members approach politicality are as conservatives and among the core in the country upholding "morality" and "goodness." They tend to deplore the ruin of the social fabric in the counter culture, and they eschew alcohol, drugs, fornication, and the "materialistic solution" (i.e., communism). At the same time, there is within the organization a liberal element, including some swamis and most of the young members who are not monastics. This element leans toward libertarian ideas on the role of women, the need for welfare to alleviate oppressive social problems, and the questionable authority of leadership, secular or religious.

This combination of rigid and fairly liberal people gives the Church Universal a somewhat ambiguous character. On the one hand, there is talk about and *to* incarnations of God (Ramakrishna, Jesus, Buddha, and so on). On the other, there is talk about how this is so much hocus-pocus, rituals and such are mere "mythological ideas" that serve to point out some principle that cannot be grasped with the intellect. Then there is the churchly flavor of Vedantic activities and social functions, albeit with improvisations on the theme derived from counter cultural definitions of what constitutes appropriate church behavior. Among the super-short haircuts and wire-rimmed glasses, the black suits and skinny black ties, there are beards and smocks and sandals and an occasional dhoti or sari. Among the wearers of feather-covered, nylon mesh, and sequined Sunday bonnets, there are women whose heads are beneath shawls, who don't wear nylons, high heels, or spray perfume.

It is, in short, an intercultural atmosphere, with an undertone of sobriety and contrivance occasioned by the Protestant control of the definition of the situation. One may listen to a lecture on the use of breathing in inducing the contemplative mood, or hear a bamboo flute and *tanpura* as the collection is being gathered by sober-looking ushers. Those who attend "church" do not have to indulge in any inner struggle to make it all seem rational, appropriate, and normal. Kookiness and spontaneous displays of religiosity, which have their place in other forms of religion, from fundamentalism to vitalism, are devalued in favor of inner ecstasy and private communion with the Divine Ideal *(ishta)*.

Thus, modern Vedanta has been described as an institutionalized Hindu social movement. The subdued, routinized character of religious events held at temples espousing Vedantic themes in the United States gives rise to the interpretation that Hinduism, in this particular form, has taken on a churchly, denominational flavor. The mysticism of the movement's charismatic leader, Sri Ramakrishna, has been superseded by the ascetic rationality of subsequent heroes. Religious experience has been transmuted into religious explanation; where the charismatic prophecy of the simple Bengali holyman once brought devotees communion with the objects of religious focus, there now remains a more or less worldly ethic which accommodates Hinduism to the forces of modern history. Thus, Vedanta's message for today, observers have said, is summed up in its "scientific" approach to religion. Vedanta temples form part of a "frontier of religion" seeking a reconciliation between traditional and modern forms of thought and social organization. Apart from this role, they remain *somewhat* marginal vis-à-vis the society.[5]

At the same time, however, sociologists and other observers of the contemporary practitioners of Vedanta have recognized a central role of the "movement" in establishing a toehold for Hinduism in the West as well as in revivifying Hinduism in India, a role that continues as increasing numbers of Hindu groups pop up in the West and as "religious" India enters the modern world.

Some observers have been fairly sensitive to the "porosity of the religious collage," as Ninian Smart (1973: 86) calls the picture of religion in society and history. Though it has not been systematically studied, it is recognized that a certain cultic elán obtains for Vedantins in this country, and some of the Swamis who head Vedantic temples have gained public recognition for their literary erudition and spiritual contributions. It is implied that a kind of charismatic quality pervades temple life despite its seemingly opposite character. Yet, so far as I have been able to discover, there is no clear picture in the scientific or even popular literature that fully describes the inner dynamics of the cult surrounding Vedanta's departed prophet, Sri Ramakrishna, nor has there been interpretation, based on Vedantic religious life, that accounts for the manner in which institutionalization of charismatic authority occurs. The predominant view of the Vedanta movement tends to isolate it from the milieu and historical context in which it inheres. I would like this book to provide some sociological ballast to that top-heavy picture. For the past 75 years in America, the Vedanta movement has been relatively cohesive, probably more due to its intellectual attractiveness than to agreement regarding its aims. Vedanta is modern religion in its mainstream form, riding on the currents of diverse movements in thought and culture.

But what makes Vedanta run? And is it running in place or moving forward? How do the Vedantins describe what they're about? It is useful to know the answers to these questions because the advent of considerable numbers of groups with an Eastern religious orientation in recent years has been viewed as a sign of our times. This phenomenon, of which Vedanta is a part, is somehow unambiguously appropriate to its context in the contemporary world. Though we don't know exactly how or why, it is becoming less incongruous to see American Sikhs, Nisei devotees, black Krishna consciousness-ites, and teenage pundits. Not that the majority of people are likely to don saffron robes and sandalwood paste in the near future, or even to sit at a Thanksgiving table repeating their "franchised" mantras (a scene I once observed). Americans have a long way to go (from McDonald's to the Sacred Cow) before there will be any wholesale adoption of Eastern customs.

But the Hindu ideas are there—universalism, individual responsibility, good health—and these are in line, if not precisely in sync, with the dominant themes of the twentieth century: humanism, scientism, individualism, and so on. Leaving aside the impact of their ideas, the multiplicity of groups that dot the social landscape contribute to the proliferation of lifestyles, customs, and manners. And one place on this landscape is firmly occupied by the Church Universal.

NOTES

1. A good historical account of the initial decades of the movement appears in Rolland (1965). A more up-to-date but in some ways less detailed account of Ramakrishna's prophecy and the movement it generated appears in Isherwood (1965).

2. The foregoing discussion was based on my reading of the biography of Swami Vivekananda (Nikhilananda, 1953). Also consulted were M (1969) and Saradananda (1963). These three works are among several that interweave history and biography with Hindu orthodoxy and Vedantic philosophy.

3. For a longer look at the "frontier of religion," see Smart (1973).

4. See Cultural Heritage of India (1936: volume II, 126-136) for a discussion of bhakti in the *Bhagavad Gita*.

5. Lawrence Veysey (1973) describes Vedanta in this manner, as does Jacob Needleman (1970: 210). The term the latter uses is "sedate," although he acknowledges that the role played by the movement's spokesmen caused "the East [to be] taken seriously here."

3. THE VALLEY CITY CHURCH UNIVERSAL

As we noted in Chapter 2, the Church Universal was founded in the early 1900s by Vivekananda, the Indian patriot-saint whose revival of Vedanta philosophy was intended as a synthesis between Eastern spiritual culture and Western material prosperity. In the East, in India, Bangladesh, Sri Lanka, Burma, Fiji, Japan, and several other countries, the order of monks he headed established schools, hospitals, and relief agencies of various sizes and kinds. In the West, particularly in the United States, but including several countries in Western Europe, branch churches dedicated to the study and practice of Vedanta were established. Currently there are some fifteen Church Universal organizations in the United States.

The branch of the church in Valley City, the site of my study, was founded in 1950 by members of branches in another city and Valley City residents who had become interested in Vedanta. It was built by volunteer labor over a period of years, with private worship and study being held in an interim locale on the grounds until the temple was completed and opened to the public in 1964. By 1977, it had 125 members, most of whom lived in Valley City but some from a nearby university town and from a larger city somewhat more distant. The temple's income derives from the dues of $2.50 paid monthly by members, and membership contributions to the general, building, retreat (garden), and monastery funds. Occasional bequests and gifts from long-time members are an additional source of monies, as are Sunday collections and proceeds from the sale of Vedantic literature (much of it published by the Ramakrishna Order), incense, and tape recordings of several of the Swami's lectures.

As in the case with other branches of the Church Universal, this one has as its head a swami. The Swami, my teacher, is about seventy years old. A native of Bengal, he entered the Ramakrishna Order in his early twenties after finishing college studies in science at the University of Calcutta. His spiritual training was under a direct disciple of Sri Ramakrishna, and he was schooled in comparative religion, Eastern and Western philosophy, psychology, and ethics in two theological seminaries of his Order. First as an apprentice and later as a *sanyasin,* he worked in various capacities in the fields of education and social services in assorted branches of the organization in India and (then) East Bengal. On taking his final vows of *sanyasa* in 1939, he was appointed secretary to the Order's president, a position he held for twelve years. For five years, from 1952 to 1957, he was the editor of a Bengali monthly journal of the Order, and in 1957 he was sent to the United States to serve as an assistant to the head minister of the Bay City (a pseudonym) branch of the Church Universal and to give classes at the new branch center in Valley City. In 1970 (the year I met him), as it became an independent organization, he became the Valley City temple's minister and teacher. The temple had operated under a different name as an extension of the Bay City branch until 1970, and by this time the Swami had already lived there for a year. The Swami has an apartment at the temple. (His lifestyle is discussed in Chapter 5.)

In addition to the Swami, three monks (one an American sanyasin), two lay workers and a half-dozen or so young apprentices live on the eight acres of the temple grounds. The Swami (in his apartment), two of the monks and the apprentices (in the monastic quarters) live in the main building complex. At the rear of the property are two houses. An older woman lives in one. The other is a kind of duplex that houses a monk and a male lay worker in separate quarters. Still another house, on a distant edge of the temple grounds, is occupied by a retired couple who are long-time associates of the temple and the Vedanta movement. In addition, several members including several women who share a residence that has been purchased for such a purpose, have found either permanent or temporary housing in the immediate and general neighborhood. Together the full-time temple and neighborhood Vedantins make up a core community of spiritual seekers.

In order to complete the picture, several other groups should be mentioned. First, there is a steady stream of students from the local universities and community colleges, and occasionally from high schools. These people on the whole tend to have erratic commitments to Vedanta, but nevertheless constitute an important segment of the temple community in that they work in the garden from time to time and spread the word about the Church Universal to others in the Valley City area. Second, there is a sizable group of Indian people who associate with the temple and the Swami but who are not active members of the church organization per se.[1] (The Swami once told me that twelve Indians are members of the Valley City church.) Several Indian women do much of the cooking for ritual celebrations and have taught a few of the American women how to prepare some foods. (Without Indian food, the Hindu imagery would suffer greatly.) Several of the men participate (assisting the Swami in some way, singing on special occasions, or otherwise engaging in the activities performed by members in various contexts of temple life), but by and large the Indian men tend not to play as highly visible a participatory role as their American counterparts. Both Indian men and women attend private encounters with the Swami when they are on the scene, but for the most part they interact among themselves or with a scant half-dozen of the Americans. Finally, there are the American householder devotees, some with close personal ties to the Swami, temple activities, or both, who frequent the place on a nearly daily basis. (They will be described in more detail throughout the succeeding chapters.)

Interaction per se is a very important feature of life around the temple. A diagram of the interaction would show it to be relatively circumscribed between members and highly concentrated on the Swami. I have discovered in the Vedanta scene few so-called "backstage areas" where people might let down their defenses against the potentially critical or negative intrusions of others. Among the members, there are many twenty-four-hour Vedantins who are by and large self-motivated in their pursuit of spiritual goals and whose main concern at the temple is with what the Swami is teaching, and only to a minor degree with what other members are up to. Also, there is an emphasis on the distinction between public events (at which the public and general membership is welcome), and private events (which can include between one and fifty or so people, plus the Swami, in a variety of contexts of both a planned and spontaneous nature), yet private and public events tend to overlap to a considerable extent.

Generally speaking, a private event is of a very intimate nature, where the Swami and the attending devotees carry on dialogues about subtle philosophical points of Vedantic thought, worship various gods and goddesses, and otherwise enact a scenario characterized by the familiarity of role-incumbents with the special situation. Public events are the Sunday lecture, the Wednesday and Saturday night classes, and the ritual worship held on religious days of celebration. Though some of the classes and rituals take on a private character in that they are more openly Hindu, the public events are orchestrated around Christian/devotional (albeit with variations on the Christ imagery) and scientific/rational (i.e., Vedantic) themes. The "public" is thus frequently exposed to a variety of situational contexts that stem from a wide assortment of values, attitudes, and beliefs inherent in the temple's overall lifestyle, and in particular in the Swami's own personality. For his part, he attempts to "tone down" the religious expressiveness of some of the younger core members. In this way, he can prevent confusion or consternation among other, staider members (or newcomers and outsiders) who may either not understand or who may disapprove of Hinduized or intensely devotional mannerisms and customs. And, on certain occasions, he invites only those who have an affinity for Indian culture to participate in functions at the temple.

Typical members define their purpose in being at the temple as "attempting to realize God," "doing spiritual life," "learning about Vedanta," "keeping holy company," and so on. Most are idealistic, believing in the infinite (read: divine) nature of man, the perfectability of society, and the rational foundation of modern thought. Many profess belief in spiritual heroes and various gods and goddesses, while others are "agnostic," and/or "cynical." Vedanta is to many members a kind of psychosocial method of self-reconstitution. It attracts intellectual types, as well, and can be a highbrow meditation-spa a few steps along an evolutionary path from 1920s parlor-religion. While among the core group of members traditional WASP values are upheld and attempts made to give the temple a public image of singular straightness and conservatism, there is a good deal of sentiment in favor of a hip, folk-rocky kind of counter cultural Hinduism—and a dash of (to me) genuine eccentricity that makes for real heterogeneity. A further glance at the more than one hundred regulars and/or members reveals businessmen, college teachers, working-class men and women, farmers, and members of a drifting group of temple-hoppers who glide from place to place for celebrations, meditations, get-togethers, and chats.

But, apart from all this, the temple contains the "holy of holies," as one visiting swami referred to it. The temple shrine, located in what is called the auditorium, has been duly consecrated according to Vedantic scriptural injunction, and it contains some of the relics considered sacred by the Ramakrishna Order in addition to the objects of daily worship. Only a chosen few are allowed to touch the shrine itself or to do worship before it, overseen by the Swami, who ensures that devotees pay strict attention when in the shrine's vicinity. Yet an ambiguity exists concerning how the shrine is to be regarded, because it is located, after all, in an "auditorium," which is hardly a holy name for a room that is ostensibly sacred. By being quiet and composed, one can be near the shrine without holding a special belief in its assorted religious meanings, even though only such a belief enables those who come to mediate and pray before it to carry on their internal relationship with the shrine's contents.

The Swami periodically assigns several women devotees to conduct morning worship in the temple. (The objects of worship are discussed in subsequent chapters.) He himself conducts the Sunday public worship and between fifteen and twenty worships on special holy days, such as Easter, Buddha's birthday, Christmas, Sri Krishna's birthday, the birthdays of Sri Ramakrishna, Swami Vivekananda, and Sarada Devi, the *Durga, Kali* and *Jagadhatri pujas, Shiva Ratri,* and (in private) the birthdays of several of Sri Ramakrishna's disciples, the day for the honoring of the guru's lineage (known as *guru purnima*), and so on.[2] Two daily meditations are led by the Swami in the auditorium, and the temple is open to the public for meditation between 9:30 a.m. and 8:00 p.m. Many members use the shrine as a place of meditation on a daily, near-daily, or simply recurrent basis. The Swami, the monks and apprentices, live-in lay persons, and faithful devotees (plus assorted persons who are members of other Eastern religious groups) define the shrine and the seeker's encounter with it as entirely sacred.

For some of these people, this experience is more "vertical" than it is for others, the point being that the temple and its shrine are central features of the religious experience itself, not just a place where the experience happens. The temple "lives" in the consciousness of those who invoke the real in its shrine. And, in a special sense, the deities there "respond" to the prayers, offerings, and entreaties of the devotees through the latter's experiencing a simultaneously immanent and evolving spirituality.

NOTES

1. By "Indian people" I mean Indian nationals, naturalized American citizens of Indian descent, Americans of Indian descent, and Americans married to Indians. Economically and occupationally, they constitute a diverse group. Moreover, they have various Indian, Christian, and secular backgrounds and display different interest in and capacity for Vedantic inquiry.

2. Most of these occasions, including the Christian and Buddhist ones, are important to Hindus in India according to my informants at the temple. The pujuas honoring the Divine Mother in various forms are discussed in Chapter 17. Shiva Ratri is an all-night worship in honor of the Hindu god of destruction, Shiva, whose significance is mentioned in Chapter 16.

4. THE IDEA OF THE RELIGIOUS:
God and Yogis

The Church Universal owes its stability and success in part to the fact that it does not recruit members. It is called by insiders "a steep path," meaning that it is a full-time, somewhat risky pursuit, though provision is made for those who cannot devote their lives in toto to meditation and scriptural study. Whether they are immersed in religious practice or not, members tend to stay with the church once they gain access to the core group—or, rather, are admitted—and there is relatively little turnover beyond a peripheral, marginal group composed of persons with an eclectic religious outlook who bounce from church to temple to synagogue.

Hence, the *metier* of Church Universal is conditioned largely by the extent to which members view their scene as an exclusive community of spiritual adepts. Many members evince a kind of self-styled status-pride and make known to others their accomplishments as amateur scholars, metaphysicians, or religious seekers. And at times the opportunity arises for individuals to utilize their talents for the good of the organization and the kind of interior spiritual life it embraces, despite the authority of the Swami which actually precludes others from adjudicating spiritual values. Thus, people become expert in decorum. Formal observance of rules of association and interaction are a prominent feature of all public functions, and conscious or accidental deviations are met with sanctions (some subtle, some otherwise) from people who use the infraction to become moral entrepreneurs. While the outlook of some members could be characterized as cosmopolitan, there are people within all the temples I have observed who are decidedly provincial. They see Church Universal as their particular church, with all the invidious exclusion of outsiders and the parochial reality-construction this implies. The Swami is to these people a "minister" on the Anglican model, who lives in and sets the religious example, but is not so extraordinarily endowed with holy power that he is inaccessible. This, of course, at times lends to Church Universal temples in general a parlor-religion atmosphere. With the rise of its reputation as "orthodox" in some communities, however, the parlor has been converted into the auditorium, as it were, and a rich old lady listening to the holy utterances of a beturbaned mystic has been supplanted by a more modern denominational-congregational, minister-parishioner arrangement with a semi-Eastern cultural timbre.

The retaining by the devout of a household or community priest, who will conduct the worship and instruct in all matters of theological and ritual propriety—in fact a timeless practice constituting a central historical fact of Brahminism—has been accommodated to the model of modern religious America. Cultured, professional monks—men of letters, arts, and in some cases, sciences, Vedic scholars, musicians, gardeners, administrators, specialists and generalists alike—live in the center of the group of neo-Hindus, teaching, ministering, amusing, and sharing with them a special kind of value arising out of that association.

That value forms the basis for a mutual reference-world. But exactly what is it? There is a technical definition of Vedanta, embracing the various schools of thought that have appeared in its history of ideas, which Hans Kohn (1965) says is remarkably well-preserved from ancient times. Then there is a historical-social definition of Vedanta, and of the Church Universal, one of Vedanta's adherents (but not the only one). Then there is the religious "definition of the situation," a perpetual emergent for the members in various social and existential contexts. All of the definitions carry the force of imperatives operating in the setting in a way that requires the members to address or come to terms with the centrality of the values in their own experience.

And, since any one of the definitions can lead us far afield, in order to keep to the immediate situation of the members, I will not present them, but rather explore the phenomena as a reconstruction of religion, a web of beliefs, values, experiences, and practices, including norms, history, and living representations of "the religious." This presentation will necessarily differ from the result that would come of describing Vedanta in entirely one-dimensional terms (for example, as a philosophy, a method of salvation or a movement, or these in combination with a system of myths, symbols, and mystical formulae).[1] When described as philosophy, Vedanta has a way of looking like something very specialized and remote. It is a thing an esthete, affecting cultural relativism, might try on. So it is assumed that Vedantins resemble philosophers or fops, or that their "look" is philosophical, highbrow, different, eclectic, but their intelligence is directionless. When it is described as an occult system of thought or as a magical, metaphysical occupation, Vedanta resembles what those who engage in such diversions look like in light of science's having stolen their thunder—namely, pretenders, or, simply, pretentious. Described as a "movement," it appears static, a successful adaptation to a hostile time and clime that will continue to serve as proof of the salience of the model of heterogeneity and pluralism on which the American culture is allegedly founded. Phenomenologically, it is none of these, but something quite other.

In order to give a clear picture of the overlapping and sometimes conflicting reference worlds that make up the church members' world view, I will undertake here a brief incursion into what might be termed the worlds of the jnana and the bhakta. Jnana, meaning wisdom, is in temple life commonly referred to as the path of the sanyasin.

In the Indian tradition, monks are people who, having renounced all claim to body, soul, hearth, home, and liberty, spend their lives in contemplation and transcendental inquiry. The philosophical summaries of the *Vedas* are the *Upanishads,* and their terse insights constitute the *Vedanta,* literally meaning the "essence" or "end" of the Vedas.[2] Freed from the religious symbolism of ritual, myth, and theology, the *Upanishads* (to-

gether with the *Brahma Sutras* and *Gita*) form the core of works
(to Hindus "revealed scripture") of the "path of wisdom"
(jnana yoga). So steep and arduous is the jnana-yogi's life-
course that it is only accessible to those who completely abandon the affairs of men and mount the "path of the gods." To
the jnani, ignorance *(avidya),* based on the perceived multiplicity and permanence of phenomena, veils the "real" from the
human being's consciousness. Phenomenal life is, hence, a kind
of illusion *(maya).* The jnani seeks to eradicate this ignorance
and illusion by reason, inference, and realization. His enlightenment or realization means he has succeeded in knowing that
reality is not two, but one. This life goal represents the oldest
and most central urge of all Eastern spiritual culture, and is the
end and essence of the major systems, whether Vedantic, Sufi,
Buddhist, Tantric, Yogic, or Taoist.[3]

In the modern Church Universal, the Vedanta forms the
cognitive and ontological basis for the bhakti religion surrounding the avatar, the disciples, and assorted gods and goddesses.
The embodiment of both the jnana and the bhakti traditions is
the Swami. His exemplary role mediates between the different
styles constructed by those on the path of wisdom and those on
the path of devotion. While on the one hand, the jnanis try to
reason out the apparent superimposition of the two onto the
one, the bhaktas cultivate religious forms of devotion. The
former are intellectual and cerebral, the latter pious and emotional. The Swami is there to remind everyone that the Master
and himself, by virtue of his sanyasa (monkhood), are endowed·
with the essence of both temperaments. As for the others,
among both monks and "householders" there is an attempt to
synthesize the two pathways or at least to remain tolerant of
the different approaches the paths represent. But it is said
the monks are primarily jnanis, while the householders are
bhaktas, and this distinction has yet a different meaning
beyond temperament.

There is no way to talk about emanations, vibrations, and
higher states of consciousness, important but obscure elements
of the spiritual reference world, without doing the devotees'
view some damage because of our preconceived ideas about
such stuff. Insofar as the effect of such states on the devotees is
concerned, we might say that their existence is at least hypo-

thetically conceivable because "consequences" arise. But are these things phenomena in the usual (common) sense? So long as we want to know about the interaction between divine beings and the members of the cult, there must be a kind of "inquiring neutrality" on our part. By neutrality, I don't mean an attitude of tolerance. With a "tolerant" point of view, we are still skeptical, albeit more or less open to the possibility of there being another kind of, or another context for, rationale behind an alternative view of reality. With "inquiring neutrality," we seek proof and open ourselves to its consequences.

Certainly Carlos Castaneda has done this in *Tales of Power*. And the consequences are spectacular, not only for him as a person qua "warrior," which he had allegedly become, but for the kind of anthropology his study created. In the beginning, he was all models and hypotheses. These later gave way to a progressive suspension of belief in his own world-constructing conventions. Ultimately, he suspended doubt in the world being shown him by his teacher, Don Juan, and took the plunge (literally off a cliff). But the way of the sorcerer is different from that of the way of the sanyasin, although both are "men of knowledge" and move in separated, if not "separate," realities.[4] And this fact has its methodological consequences.

For me, in the temple setting, it was much easier to take a less defensive and more supportive position. There are no mind-altering, ingestible substances in use, at least not in the form of psychotropic plants. The mantras are surely devices that get people "high" and are used to induce certain "experiences." It's just that the experiences seem more benign than what Castaneda encountered in his many visions. The sanyasin is not "terrific," like the sorcerer, although he produces the necessary wholesale changes in the novice's self-perception and world view. In my case, the changes were not something I was immediately aware of. It was only after several years that I found myself dissimilar to the "I" that had begun the study. This change will emerge as the study proceeds, but first the meaning of a central idea in Vedantic religious experience should be elaborated, as it bears on the nature of temple life.

The idea of the god in the Church Universal is among the first things to be considered in an inventory of cult belief and practice. And as a corollary of the idea, it is important to understand the theology of the cult, so that the interaction between the cult and the objects of its focus can be phenomenologically described and explained.

Because the idea of the god has several meanings and connotations, depending on its perceiver's intent, it is necessary to eliminate conscious or unconscious preconceptions that carry over from our modern Judeo-Christian world, where the idea of god is invariably associated with a *personality* (e.g., Jesus Christ) or the *authority* of a supreme lawgiver (e.g., Jehova). In Vedanta, the supreme cannot be said to "exist" in the sense usually conceived by human beings. The supreme is the ineffable Brahman, "One without a second," for which no attributes (including "attributelessness") obtain.

My attempt to use language to describe a concept or reality that is "beyond language" may seem to be so much "doubletalk." This is all but unavoidable; even when a metaphor or analog is employed, we have to address the subject indirectly and talk "around" it. In Vedanta, god, mythology, and philosophy represent a "degeneration" from the indivisible reality that forms a substratum on which all apparent reality rests. Strictly speaking, the notion of an indivisible reality underlying the multiplicity of forms is not *monism,* since the idea of the "one" implies the existence of an "other" from which the "one" is distinct and separate. (Such a notion of reality could thus be characterized as having the attributes of "distinctiveness" and "separateness," which, according to Vedantic reasoning, are limiting adjuncts, not positive affirmations of the essential oneness of Brahman.) Thus, Vedanta has a nondual conception of reality. The separation of the "seer and the seen" (the perceiver and the object of perception), a product of ordinary consciousness, is counteracted by the "method" of *advaita* (nondualistic Vedanta). Although it begins with a *negation* of all phenomena (a process characterized in the phrase *neti neti*—not this, not that) the Vedantic method of inquiry ends in an affirmation of the unitary existence, knowledge, and bliss (Satchidananda), which, incidentally, is the reverse of the essentially negative Buddhist characterization of reality as *nirvana,* which means "extinction." Of course, different schools of thought in Vedanta philosophy account in different ways for reality and the world (see Deutsch, 1968: 81-99). In the Church

Universal, whatever is not Brahman is maya (illusion), which has been superimposed on the "one" by a series of mental and perceptual processes. Any gods or other religious objects, conceptions, or experiences, therefore, are a part of maya, but they may be employed as provisionally real devices to aid the seeker in attempts to attain the knowledge of Brahman, a Vedantic approach developed by Shankaracharya.[5]

An important question to be raised at this point is: If Brahman (which is not God or any other "object" of knowledge) is the intended focus of a devotee's meditations and worship, in what sense is "God" involved in the religion? At the highest level of reality in the Vedantic system, there is only Brahman. At the lower levels, where the influence of maya exists, there are the gods, the cosmic powers, knowledge, spiritual life, the world, and so on. When one is worshipping, say, Sri Ramakrishna, with incense, lights, flowers, water, and food, the focus is Brahman with qualities *(Saguna Brahman)*. Not that Brahman, being the Absolute, can ever be thus limited, or encumbered, as it were, with divine characteristics. Rather, the worshipper, understanding that Brahman is unapproachable with the ordinary mind (only when it is "not mind" is the "self" capable of identifying itself with Brahman), recognizes the existence of Brahman in the object of the ritual. Put metaphorically, a particle of Brahman resides in the deity, just as a portion of Brahman as Absolute Existence resides in the existent person. A particle of Brahman as Cosmic Intelligence appears as human thought. Brahman, the Real, is reflected in the appearance of things. And so on. From the Vedantic standpoint on perception, we superimpose a perceiver and a perceived, a knower and a known, a self and an other, on that unitary reality, the "one" that we experience when not reflecting about it or focusing on particular aspects—Brahman. Moreover, Brahman is in everything, but nothing is or can be in Brahman, which renders useless all attempts to attain the knowledge of Brahman by means of the mind and senses, there being an irreconcilable difference between Brahman and mere perceptions, sensations, and objects of thought. However, the true "self," the particle of Brahman (viz. the atman) residing in the human being is *ultimately nondifferent* from Brahman. The appearance of difference between the self and Brahman must be bridged or eliminated. This is where worship and other spiritual practices come in, say the Vedantins at the Church Universal.

Their charismatic prophet, Sri Ramakrishna, is, they say, a "living" embodiment of Brahman and a testimony to the universality of the ultimate truth of Vedanta. Not only did he experience the "truths of each of the world's religions," but he showed that the way to the "absolute" was via the "relative." That is, Brahman could be known through various embodiments of the supreme. And Ramakrishna's life is clearly a life of successive discoveries and demonstrations (along Vedantic lines) of his divine selfhood. Historically, for India, Ramakrishna's discoveries established the link with a vanishing, glorious past. What was happening in nineteenth-century India could be "explained" by the Vedas. The conflicts between sects and sectors of society could be resolved through the invocation of universal principles which India herself had produced in her age of spiritual glory. The principles' discovery, presentation, and diffusion throughout India, or to be more technically accurate, their re-manifestation, amounted to the beginning of the end for British colonialism and set the stage for India's long climb into the modern era. A succession of "patriot-saints," from Vivekananda to Gandhi, gave the ancient ideas modern application (Rolland, 1965: 96-99).

These ideas of the Prophet's import are at a distance from Him as actual avatara (incarnate Brahman) whose simple, if spiritually tumultuous, life gave little indication of the above wider meanings of his embodiment of ancient, capital-T truth. And it is precisely the personality, visions, and teachings of the god-man Ramakrishna that form the nexus of ideas that the members of the Church Universal shape into god and utilize in their religious observances and practices. The god-man, though manifestly maya in his form on earth, points the way to Brahman, and, as *The Gospel of Sri Ramakrishna* and other works on his life demonstrate, he is *identical* with Brahman. His practice of the world's religions, including different branches of Hinduism, his visions, and his continual identification with Brahman throughout the better part of his "career" as a holy-man exemplify the state of consciousness to which Church Universalists aspire. At each point along the individual's religious undertaking, there is a conscious effort to achieve perpetual identity with the Absolute via the "purified relative," incarnate in the cult's hero. Through devotion to Ramakrishna, through holy works, through the paths of wisdom and psychological analysis—in a word, through a synthesis of the yogas and the truths of all religions—the devotee or yogi attains freedom.

In sum, the idea of god in the Church Universal includes both a transcendent principle, Brahman, and a personal divine object, the avatar, in which the transcendent principle is immanent. Reference to one cannot exclude the other. And whatever truth is found must be acceptable on the "higher" level. This has important consequences for the manner in which cult life is organized and how members define the situation. On the one hand, Brahman and the philosophical systematization of its attainment contained in Vedantic thought are truth that stands on its own, resting on no external supports. Its criteria are contained in its own a priori givenness. Thus, whatever is regarded as truth cannot be different from other truths, since truth is one, not two. Thus, religious visions or experiences are subjected to the most critical kind of examination. No one can claim a monopoly on truth, because Truth cannot be thus divided. Trances, superconscious states, visions, dreams, and the like may have spiritual import in the individual's life, but they are essentially maya and not to be cherished or cultivated for their own sake. Cult rules permit no attempt to induce transcendental states or to seek divine intervention on one's behalf. They allow only the most private type of spiritual experience. Gods, goddesses, (living though they may be) rituals, holy work, and the rest are "devices." One's devotion to the ideal may be the paramount factor in his or her life, and experiences of a mystic sort may come in due course, but this is understood to be a "worldly" enterprise, which molds one's life in the direction of purity and prepares one for total release from the bonds of relative existence, but is not itself the final goal.

Yet, in the cult that surrounds the prophet, the devotional response is of a character that seems to obviate the notion of Brahman. One hears only of Sri Ramakrishna, or other gods. Yet the presence of Brahman is implicit (and explicitly represented in the Sanskrit *Om* on the altar) in the conspicuous absence of claims to the avatar's grace. Any such claim would automatically, as it were, be treated as maya, and, if the person were convinced that his vision or whatever gave him special prerogatives, they would be called "delusions." This is because the meaning of the avatara's incarnation is, again, universal, and not subject to particularistic interpretation. The truth of the vision must accord with the higher unity. Hence, the cult is protected against potentially disruptive claims by would-be spiritual adepts by the trans-divine focus of the members and the structure of the inner logic of the "religion" of Brahman.

The history of the cult from the time of the prophet's incarnation as a "world-teacher" essentially effects a transformation of his charisma into a different form which in a sense institutionalizes it, but preserves elements of its arational power. Vivekananda, the prophet's principal disciple, founded the Ramakrishna Order—a kind of heirocratic association— which has carried on his teachings and applied his message of universalism and the "worship of god through service to humankind." The Church Universal is an American outpost of the organization. Its Swami is an Order-trained professional monk who is steeped in the traditions of religious India as well as skilled in the worldly art of temple administration and leadership. His training has involved (among other things) immersion in the lore of the cult surrounding the departed Master (Ramakrishna). He supplies the devotees with the meaning and interpretation, simultaneously in terms of the gospel of universalism and the life of the avatar, of spiritual life. He is in possession of a portion of the original charismatic power and represents a living link to the avatar as well as to the "rational" criteria governing the truth of Brahman. Devotion to him as the guru (which likewise must be a subjective and private attitude, as the Order recognizes only one guru, the Supreme Brahman) constitutes the means whereby one gains access to the cult and formal admission to the path to the divine that membership in it represents. One enters into a sort of contract with the swami and is guided along the path to the final goal. Whatever the swami asks one to do is considered to be a part of the overall journey to Satchidananda as well as an immediate practice that potentially gives one proximate association with the divine person, Ramakrishna.

Thus, the evolution of the spiritual community has borne the mark of the members' commitment to the teacher-disciple relationship, and the construction of the temple, the maintenance of the grounds, the operation of the temple organization, and the ongoing spiritual life contained therein is an outcome of that relationship. While the outer face of the religion takes on the character of a church, the subjective attitude of members, particularly those of long association with the cult, is determined by the trans-divine focus and its secondary divine objects. Externally, the church is a part of a movement and an institutionalized religious body. Internally, it is a cult based on the worship of the avatar and guided by a successor to his charisma, the swami. In a word, its subdued and rational appearance is its outer face. Within lies the religious dynamic that animates the cult and sustains the organization over time.

This makes the rational character of Vedanta understandable, as well as the manner in which the cult becomes a church during public celebrations. Cult priorities are masked, as it were, by the churchly character of events. The swami is the minister. Different devotees do the ushering or provide music. People sit on chairs in perfect equipoise, betraying no emotional involvement with gods. In the sermons, Sri Ramakrishna is billed as the equivalent of Jesus Christ, Buddha, Mohammed, Krishna, etc. "All religions are the same," the Swami often says from the pulpit. "Only the means to the end differ." How to live in the world as a spiritual person is the general theme of sermons. In the cult, flight from the world to the divine defines the ongoing process of involvement.

Such bifurcation of the religious focus can account for the stability of the Vedantic movement and its success. And, Hinduism was made to order for the qualities it displays in its modern, Vedantic form. As Weber (1958: 6) said, Hinduism is a church "con-joined to sect-like exclusiveness." The church is the rational, institutionalized core of social life. Its theology emphasizes reason, scientific analysis, and performance of duty. The cult is the arational complement to the externalized church body. Its doctrine is derived from the life of the prophet and the personality of the swami, who has made a portion of that life his own. While the external is animated by the cult, the church regulates the cult and prevents excesses. What this all has to do with "realizing God" can be seen in the next section.

THE YOGIS IN THE TEMPLE CULT

It is something of a contradiction to speak of the world view of the yogi. By definition, a yogi has directed the focus of attention "elsewhere." For him or her, the status of the world has lost its given character, consciousness having resolved its multiplicity and mutability into one. However, though the one *is*, from the standpoint of the yogi there is a sense in which a kind of provisional status is granted to everyday concerns. The yogi, in spite of being otherworldly—or because of it—is also by definition immensely practical.

As I have already explained, from the outside looking in, the Church Universal displays all the signs of religiosity normally equated with Christianity, but with an apparent Indian motif. But the full-time personnel of the Church collectively hold a world view that guides and reformulates the definition of the situation. For some, Sunday services are "church"—for others, they are "experiences" of a different kind.

Externally, it is not apparent what kind of experiences these are, though their effect would appear to be related to the degree of the person's involvement in religious practice. To define them is not a matter of dividing up people on the basis of how often they meditate. Most members do it daily. Nor is it simply a procedure whereby the more gods one worships or the more stories one can relate, the more involved one is. Quite a few members don't worship gods, and a few profess no belief in a deity. Some of them are involved; others are not.

In other words, who the yogis are is not easy to know because there is no external sign. What someone is *doing* may be defined as yoga, but *being* a yogi is something else.

At first I believed that it would be possible to divide the group of members into an inner and outer circle. In fact, this division was suggested to me by several members, who, of course, saw themselves as belonging to the former. Yet there is no discernible social line of demarkation between groups of members, at least insofar as it relates to centrality of participation in the cult of Sri Ramakrishna. Over the years, I have utilized the inner- and outer-circle concept to try to keep track of the ebb and flow of persons in and out of the setting. I even tried on the conception myself and did observations from the point of view of a member of an inner circle of devotees surrounding the Swami. It seemed fairly easy to discriminate between those who viewed the whole thing as a kind of Indian unitarianism and those who laid claim to a spiritual path. Moreover, it was clear that even among long-time members, there were people who knew next to nothing of the rudiments of Indian thought and culture, but who nevertheless seemed to be totally occupied by religious concerns. Occasionally people whom I assumed to be "inner" would suddenly be in the "outer circle," while still other insiders would leave the Church altogether. More than once people who I thought were marginal members would wind up performing some central role or other. And each time an anomalous case would appear I would, so to speak, sort the deck, looking for another dependent variable.

But no combination of variables explains who the yogis are, or what identifies them. Finally I reasoned that perhaps inaccessibility is the clue. Those who are most remote, who seem the most spaced out, or who are somehow ambiguous, must be the yogis. But most of these people are simply a part of the marginal social fields and bounce from religion to religion, occasionally landing someplace. A few of them are, however, central, but they are different from those in the cult.

But within the Church there are distinct subworlds recognized by quite a few (forty or so) members. One subworld is formed of the older Vedantins who saw the temple built, and in a few cases, actually helped build it. Some of these are the disciples of a deceased swami who inaugurated the project. They include adherents to their teacher's advaitism (nondualism) as well as bhaktas (devotees of Ramakrishna). As a group, associated with the movement an average of twenty years, their numbers include three old monks and the older lay men and women who live in houses apart from the temple, but on or near the Church property. Their full-time work at the temple includes gardening, carpentry, ritual duties, serving the Swami and the devotees, cleaning, etc. Many are retired, living on small pensions, the pooled resources from which enable them to maintain their respective quarters supplemented by occasional donations from other members. They interact with one another and the Swami on a daily basis and are usually present at every temple event.

Another subworld includes around fifteen or twenty people who are somewhat younger, ranging in age from their twenties to their early forties. Together with some of the longtime Vedantins, they were initiated by the Swami in the first such ritual ever conducted by him at the temple. These people are all householders, and most have children. They come to the temple as often as possible. If they live nearby, their contact with the Swami is on a daily basis. If they live farther away or have "worldly duties" (e.g., jobs or studies), their contact is less frequent. For the most part, their contact among themselves generally takes place within a religious context. They seldom, for example, go to a movie together, unless it is on a religious topic, although they might do such things alone (or as a couple). They work together in the garden, perform various services for the Swami, such as driving him to pujas in Bay City, sing together, eat occasional dinners together, and otherwise interact and commingle—though always, so far as I have been able to determine, in contexts that are defined in part by the rules laid down by the Swami and by the priorities of sadhana. It is not that this group is not characterized by substantial cohesion or that the group does not form a predominant part of each member's personal reference world. In fact, the members of this group occasionally refer to their scene as a "community," with the temple and the Swami as the core of that community. However, they do not share a common economic situation. All of them are employed in jobs ranging from counselor to maid to librarian to planner to sociologist (myself plus one other) to art teacher, and so on. And they display various amounts of preoccupation with the struggle for survival in the world along with that relating to the quest for spiritual wisdom. They donate their labor and some money to the temple, of course, and in their apartments and houses there are shrines and other accoutrements of the religious life with which they undertake the practices taught by the Swami and/or improvised by themselves.

In contrast to the first subworld, composed of retired, full-time members who have "left the world" (and in some cases have *formally* renounced it), the younger group is "in the world," although as they are quick to point out, not of it. Their main focus is *dharma* (duty), while that of the full-time religionists is *vairagya* (renunciation). Bhakti, as a devotional religion, transforms dharma into mysticism and vairagya into asceticism. Tantra, the underlying methodology, as it were, of dualistic bhakti, balances devotion with renunciation, making the two groups religiously interdependent, and making one path out of the two polar modes of Vedantic spiritual life.

Thus, in addition to age, involvement in temple history, and economics, the differences between the two subworlds are exemplified in their differential religious orientations. The older group has come to associate the divine with the gradual development of communion with the spiritual Ideal (whether Brahman or Ramakrishna) and its manifestation in the temple life. Hard work, self-sacrifice, and self-abnegation, plus dedication to the spiritual life have been watchwords over their long association with the Order. Moreover, they have been conscious all along of the place of the temple in the community and the society, and they have struggled with the problem of fit between themselves and the potentially unaccepting outside world. Austerity, simplicity, and loving attention paid to nearly every nook, cranny, and detail, as well as the detached approach to work are features of their involvement. They converse little among themselves while engaged in mutual activities, berate one another occasionally, complain the usual amount and otherwise relate to everyday phenomena in a commonsense, matter-of-fact manner that is probably understandable to Hindus and non-Hindus alike. For the most part, there are no active theologians among them. They are fairly nonverbal, having conditioned themselves to the indrawn nature of life in a meditative setting. As regards their view of public worship, they tend to believe that no ostentation, no display, no oddity should confront the unwary. Thus, they interpret Vivekananda's message to mean that they, as his spokespersons, should assimilate Vedantic ideas as far as possible into the mainstream of the Western world, and neither try to become "Hindus" nor try to turn anybody else into one. Some profess belief in a god and perform various practices ostensibly aimed at attaining "realization." Interestingly enough, some are Christians, others profess various degrees of faith in Hindu gods and goddesses, and still others have created admixtures of several religions to suit their own religious purposes and temperaments. And some believe in no gods at all, but do study Hindu scriptures. Most, I think, whether they are Christians, Hindus, non-dualist Vedantins, or whatever, work at being yogis in one way or another.

The second group, consisting of relative newcomers to Vedanta, has a mystical religious orientation. Because most of them are married, they are defined as "householders." Perhaps their display of interest in the vertical side of religion and the cult-side of the movement featuring devotion to the Master and the Swami is a compensation for their worldly entanglements. They do not have access to the solitary life of the monk or nun, so they tend to value the less sedate aspects of the religious experience. In the main, they are more likely to initiate their own ritual practices than are the older, veteran members, the latter having become accustomed to attending the Swami's pujas in the temple. Included in their talk is reference to being "saved" by the Master or Swami, of having traveled a perilous road before winding up at the temple, of having been transformed from a "nothing" into a "devotee of God." They relate to the Swami in the customary manner of old, wherein the guru's word was taken as final. They seek his advice on all manner of topics, worldly and otherwise, and after enjoying an audience with him, whether private or in a group, sing his praises to all who will listen. As one told me, "He [the Swami] makes it living religion; he is a real holyman."

In addition to the recognition of each other as subgroups, most members of the two groups have a conception of an inner circle, of which they are a part, which includes their idea of the most "intimate" devotees. The conceptual size of the inner circle varies with the person's perceived distance from the Swami; the closer one perceives that one is to the Swami, the fewer are the number of others who share in the relationship. Moreover, perceived closeness and distance may vary with each contact with the Swami. For example, occasionally, if he relates a personal matter to someone, that person will readjust his or her conception of who is within and who without, and, by eliminating others, place himself or herself closer. Taking others into account in this fashion is a means of establishing social space for the self.

This also implies the scarcity of the religious experience, or, put another way, raises its value in the marketplace of everyday temple life. Since the knowledge of Brahman is reserved for departed heroes and the Swami—at least in the sense that they can be discussed as experiences—proximity is the next best thing. Thus, one negotiates a place that is proximate to the experience. A "place" might be a specific chair in the temple auditorium, or a seat on the platform before the shrine, a station at the door, a function to perform at an event, such as passing out *prasad* to the devotees after a puja, or an encounter with the Swami. Where one sits during the eating of prasad, or where one hangs one's work clothes in the changing-rooms adjacent to the garden, or where one shovels and plants the soil signify a placement of the person in both the spiritual and social fabric of temple life.

NOTES

1. The source book of greatest value to my Vedantic inquiry has been Nikhila-nanda (1953). In addition to containing the main writings of Vivekananda, the biography of Vivekananda is authoritative both in style and substance, weaving as it does the personal lives of modern heroes with the spiritual bases and philosophic directions of Hindu culture.

2. The *Vedas*, India's most ancient scriptures, are said to extend back to 4,000 B.C. The books that comprise the *Vedanta* (*viz.*, the *Upanishads*) were composed mainly in the second millennium B.C.

3. Zimmer (1951). A more expanded and complete reference work for Vedantic philosophy is *The Cultural Heritage of India* (1936). See also, for a philosophic treatise employing phenomenological methods, Deutsch (1968).

4. See Castaneda (1974: 147-163).

5. Works by Shankaracharya (c. 8th century A.D.) consulted for this study include his *Self-Knowledge* (1967). His introduction to the work is an excellent, detailed excursion into the de-ontological reaches of advaitic philosophy. Two other works consulted can be found in the list of Further Readings.

5. THE SWAMI

To complete the picture, it is necessary to know the Swami. It is his personality, coming through his actions and his world view, that prevails in everyday temple life. His word is authority; his manner, demeanor, and conduct, models of exemplary behavior. What the devotees know of Indian religion, of Sri Ramakrishna, the Holy Mother, gods and goddesses, meditation, and the rest, they have learned from the Swami. He embodies the ideal *yogin,* and he is loved and revered like "the Lord himself."[1]

The Swami is a charismatic figure. Yet, the popular imagery of the guru—the bearded, flower-decked, berobed holyman, seated on a throne-like dais in the lotus position, dispensing abstruse piety to his enthralled disciples—has no place in the Church Universal. I have a photograph of the Swami, taken sometime in the middle or late sixties, which shows him standing near a rosebush wearing a blue cardigan sweater and gray slacks, his tortoiseshell glasses reflecting a bit of the sunlight. The look on his face is ministerial, somewhere between that of a Unitarian minister and a university professor. Another photograph shows him in his gerua, rapt in meditation, the example par excellence of the Hindu inner life.

The Swami is approaching old age, but is in relatively good health. He is strongly built, with gray hair, balding on top. He easily breaks into laughter; not of the giggly, high-pitched variety associated by the media with gurus, but a full, hearty laugh. He is something of an expert on Abraham Lincoln, is a writer of articles for various Eastern and Western publications, and has written seven books in his native Bengali. His order has been home for forty-some years; he has lived full-time at the temple in Valley City since 1970.

The Swami lives in an "apartment" that is attached to the temple complex, by the library and two offices, one his, the other that of the Church. His quarters are austere but warm. In his living room is a couch, two semi-stuffed chairs, and numerous bookcases containing Hindu works and Western books on religion, psychology, medicine, anthropology, race relations, etc. Here and there are religious pictures of Shiva, Krishna, and personalities associated with the life of Sri Ramakrishna. His kitchen is tiny, holding a waist-high refrigerator, a stove and sink, a few cupboards, and a small table. On one wall is a picture of Sarada Devi, the Holy Mother. On another is a picture of Krishna as a flute-player. Besides the bathroom, there is one other room in the apartment, the Swami's bedroom.

His single bed is along one wall. At one end is a small shrine. On the shrine his gurus, Sri Ramakrishna and the Holy Mother, are represented in small, framed photographs before which there are usually small offerings of flowers and incense. A large rolltop desk covered with papers and books is at the opposite end of the room. Along the wall under the windows there is a kind of built-in bureau. *Ganesha,* the elephant-headed god of wisdom, is portrayed in a museum photograph above the door. More bookcases contain works in Sanskrit.

I have not lived with the Swami, so I cannot exactly describe his customary daily actions, but from tidbits gathered from him and some of the devotees, and from a few inferences I drew, I can put forth the following sketch of his everyday routine.

The Swami's day begins, from what I can gather, in the wee hours of the morning with a shower and a shave, spiritual practices, and some *hatha yoga.* Breakfast with the monks takes place around eight, following meditation and worship in the temple. After breakfast, he usually tours the temple grounds directing the work of the devotees and monks and goes into his office, where, surrounded by his books, a calendar, and correspondence, he writes. Between letters, he calls and is called by various people—and people call on him. A little before noon, he repairs to his shower and afterwards changes into the gerua, the ochre robe of the sanyasin. Then he goes to the temple and sits for meditation with devotees and monks. After meditation, he changes clothes and eats lunch with the monks in their kitchen. Following lunch, he looks after a bit of business or work, or talks to a devotee. His nap usually begins at around 2:30 p.m. At four o'clock he arises and, in his kitchen, has tea prepared by women devotees. Usually tea is attended by members or guests who come to have an audience with him. After tea, he returns to his office and interacts with various people in person, by letter, and by phone concerning all matters of temple business, both spiritual and worldly. Evening meditation in the temple, for which he once again changes from slacks and sports shirt into the gerua, precedes supper with the monks. After supper, he prepares for the evening class lecture and/or a round of visitors. After everyone has gone home and the monks have retired to their quarters, he continues work at his desk or perhaps spends his time in meditation or study of the Hindu scriptures. After a late hour period of meditation, he retires, to rise again in the early morning.

In this way the Swami accomplishes quite a lot. He lectures forty-five Sundays per year. He holds classes on Sanskrit, the *Gita* (or *Upanishads*), and the teachings of Sri Ramakrishna three nights a week, forty-five weeks a year. Often he travels to towns outside Valley City to hold forth for devotees there. On an average of once a month, he visits other Church Universal temples to officiate at pujas or to give spiritual talks. Local colleges invariably invite him to give discourses several times a year on Hinduism for classes in psychology, sociology, and religion. For several years he held a meditation class once every month at a prison near Valley City. Since he was once the editor of an international journal published by his order, he regularly receives manuscripts from the Order which he edits and criticizes. And he answers correspondence from several hundred people in India who seek his advice and/or blessings. In the course of a year, he receives numerous guests, including visiting Swamis from other centers. And, as increasing interest in the Hindu religion per se has resulted in the addition of Hindu ceremonies to the religious calendar, the Swami conducts about seventeen such ritual events a year (including ten or so in Bay City). On top of this is continual, usually daily, work with those in his immediate charge—namely, the monks, lay workers, and the close devotees (about twenty people). He has less, but still considerable, contact with the other members (around one hundred more people), plus the "public."

During his vacation, which generally runs from late July to mid-September, he is often traveling to other parts of the country or the world to give lectures and discourses for people interested in Vedanta. When he doesn't travel during the vacation, he carries on classes as usual with the Sanskrit students, the temple musicians, and other close devotees, conducts worship and meditation classes, and visits devotees' homes.

None of which is to say much about the Swami's understanding or his depth of character, although I find both to be considerable. This is a matter more for the biographer to take up, or the critic of values. As a reporter of an event and its context, I am less inclined to judge the merit of the Swami's lifestyle—if indeed it can be called "style," as unfashionable and rooted in tradition as it appears to be—than I am to simply try to show how the Vedantic religious "collage" is arranged. Simply because I have purposely put myself under the tutelage of this man does not qualify me to rate his self-realization. The structure of the Church Universal and the rationale of his philosophy have together spared him from having to make claims for his knowledge, so he appears noble, at minimum, not devalued or "sold out." He is required to solicit no one, yet he feels the strain of maintaining the devotees' expectations. The fixed and recurrent patterns of his life are not blatantly obvious, yet he seldom varies his routine. He intellectually forearms himself against the dogmatism into which religion must of necessity sink when a creed attains concrete significance in the minds of its adherents, by taking refuge in the peculiar tenuousness of his situation.

As a man, he is in but not of American culture. As a sanyasin, he is in but not of the world. In the first instance, he can remain his initially socialized self—the older-generation Bengali, essentially a traditionalist, but, in keeping with the independent temperament of the intellectual and spiritual culture of Bengal, a free thinker whose ideas in another context might strike one as revolutionary. He professes a belief in the necessity of socialism, but there are obstacles to freedom, he feels, within the very human apparatus. This latter idea reflects his Vedantic world view and thought process, his yogin's vertical (and cosmic) view of reality, and human consciousness. There is, in addition to this, an undercurrent of the very Vedas within the man, which is expressed in his sanyasa. I suspect that he thinks in Sanskrit concepts and relates to his perceptions accordingly a good part of the time, and that his meditation or worship, or teaching (including lecturing) are done from the point of view which one would call the Vedantic world view.

He is passing down some of his knowledge of the Vedas, of the lives of the saints of his order, and of some of his culture's spiritual practices to several students, but his *understanding* of these things, and of the situation he encounters in his world, are less likely to be preserved. The students, myself included, are absorbing what they can of the Vedanta, but the learning of Sanskrit, studying the *Upanishads* or the lives of saints, the building of a Hindu musical repertoire, the selection of habits or customs in re-creating one's life—these things are likely to become mere specializations (or worse still, "souvenirs") rather than ultimate concerns, which religion says they must be.

There are many Swamis on the scene today, not a few of them standing on thin ice when it comes to backing up their claims to self-realization. Others appear to have taken their wisdom from counterparts in the free enterprise system. Theirs is the "business of religion," to use Mencken's phrase. A highly specialized few, like the Swami of Valley City, are self-contained, if not entirely self-realized, persons. Theirs is a simple lifestyle that, paradoxically, displays a surface complexity which makes them ambiguous and socially marginal. Yet, from their side of the world, they are without vested interests that such obscurity promotes in less self-effaced persons. They do not benefit from the class alliances of their fellow professional priests. In fact, the company men among them, who keep the faith, instill dogma in the novices, label and prosecute heresies, and prop up the pedagogical model of the guru, are threatened by their realization of the futility of words and office and outside authority. The Puranic stories of Shiva as the despised ascetic vividly portray the social cost of ascending the yogic path. They are perhaps loved by those who are close to them, but even this is outside the realm of what is "normal" in social relations. Brahminhood itself is a step, if not several steps, below the path of complete renunciation. The sacrifices, the rituals, the practices designed to liberate, indeed, the liberation itself, are all given up. What is bound to bring merit or praise is to be eschewed. Thus, relationships with them are at best difficult to maintain. One must ultimately give them up altogether. I will try to explain, without explaining it away.

The Swami has always been open with me. On the other hand, he is like a large house with self-opening doors. If I happen to be in the place where a door is opened, I can choose whether to see what is behind it. If I am somewhere else, then the door is closed and nothing I can do will open it. This is the price paid for complete equanimity. Creating balance in one's life requires manipulation of external stimuli, and for a sanyasin these stimuli come mainly, I think, in the form of social contacts. When I overcame the barriers that he contrives between himself and all others, or rather, acknowledged them without endorsing them, and allowed the world view which they support to guide my definition of the unfolding situation, I found I had a "relationship" with him, and was in line to receive whatever was being transmitted at the time. To be a recipient of his yogic doctrine does not necessarily ensure assimilation of it, because it is not done, contrary to popular belief, in pedagogical style. Although the style varies with the personality and temperament (not to mention the spiritual attainment) of the teacher, there is a mutuality, a reciprocity between teacher and disciple which is obscured by the apparently formal definitions of roles and the terseness of the "religious" content of the teaching. The social paradox here is that in order to have a spontaneous and natural relationship, an epic contrivance with rather gothic formalities must be adopted, and even though the adoption is a mere "ritual," as it were, it has considerable bulk which must be borne by the interactants. At this point in my explanation there appears to be something excessively abstract about what is ostensibly a matter of a dyadic, dominant-submissive relationship. Surely the interactants move less strenuously through the social apparatus, and the burden of this "abstraction" is borne by the conceptual framework of the analyst. In reality—that is, in the constituted world I have shared with the Swami—there is *no* relationship at all. Statistically the correlation between social contact and shared meanings between us is so low as to call into question the very foundation of our original agreement. I really have nothing to give him in exchange, except the rudimentary skills required to perform the immediate task at hand, such as carrying the sack of used flowers from the shrines in his apartment to the appropriate compost heap. Yet my unquestioning understanding of his wishes is essential to the maintenance of "our" naturalness. If I have to ask where the compost heap is or why the flowers can't simply be put in the trash, it "breaks the mood," as he is likely to put it. Not that this mood-thing is a glass house and Americans admitted inside it compulsive stone-throwers. As the Swami has told me, supreme knowledge itself is simply a "mood of knowing," which enters into the mind without any particular effort on the part of the individual. But if one *says* one knows, then one doesn't.

> He by whom *Brahman* is not known knows It.
> He by whom It is known knows It not.
> It is not known by those who know It;
> It is known by those who do not know It [Swami Sharvananda,
> *Kenopanishad,* Mylapore, Madras: Sri Ramakrishna Math, 1960, Chapter II, Verse 3].

This is not just more of what from the intellectual edifice of sociology or comparative religion appears to be a kind of word-magic. First of all the word "It" is used because the truth for which it stands is impersonal. "It" is used as a reminder that the formalism and ritualism of the exchange is not the entire meaning of the "guru-disciple relationship." My job is to know the truth about *myself,* as the Vedantic tradition prescribes, although superimposed over the truth is my "knowing"; hence, the belief that I do *not* know, which is a result of my knowledge being fragmented. If I "know" something by virtue of the Swami, this man with whom I have a "relationship," then it is not "It," the real truth. Brahman is known only by Brahman, which is neither a knowing subject nor an object of knowledge, and my knowing means that this truth is evident to me even though I don't know it, by virtue of "knowing" it. What this means in the context of the present discussion is that the subjective meanings that have arisen in the course of our contact are infinitely more complex than they would appear on first glance, and that the topography of the relationship must be continually retraced and boundaries negotiated. There is no taken-for-granted common sense which we can deploy to ease the tensions that accumulate from the undirected energies released by interaction.

Never one to forego attempting cloture on a grounded datum, believing him to be a warehouse of yogic character traits, I once asked the Swami if he would consult the Hindu astrological almanac and choose the time for "leaving the body" (a euphemism for dying). "I am a devotee of God," he said. "I have no need of almanacs." This is, of course, a surprising answer if one subscribes, as I unwittingly did, to the popular misconception of the yogin being totally immersed in occult formulae and mystic practices. He told me that his guru, a direct disciple of Ramakrishna, had given him *shraddha,* so he was never in doubt about the meaning and direction of his life, and therefore needed no such devices. By shraddha he did not mean "inner faith," as the term is often translated into English. "Shraddha is a force by which one is propelled in sadhana," he once said. "It is not belief in God, but rather a certainty that the nature of the Self is essentially divine. Its effect on my life is that I am made to feel like my whole purpose is to offer the fruits of this shraddha to Him, Sri Ramakrishna."

I shall try to illustrate this "mood."

My arrival at the temple is unannounced. I am there to see the Swami about some library books on Vedanta he told me I could borrow. My first stop is the restroom, where I wash my hands. Then I go to the auditorium and approach the shrine. It is a little after noon, so the Swami is there sitting in meditation. He is alone. I take a seat on the platform after touching my forehead to the floor (an act called "making *pranam*"). The temple is quiet and my mind accepts the peaceful atmosphere as I get into the meditation. The meditation lasts about forty-five minutes. I feel tremendously buoyant in the quiet, seeing through my half-closed eyes the ochre-clad, stone-still sanyasin silently orchestrating the inner symphony. He puts out the candles on the altar, and exits via the side door. I wait a few minutes, and then back down the platform steps. I exit and meet Ms. _____ at the door. She averts her eyes. Super shy, she has not spoken to anyone so far as I know. However, everyone says she is the ideal devotee. Her mother is dying and she has to leave this afternoon on a plane for back East. She is going in to pray that her sadhana stays together, or so the Swami tells me as we meet at the door to the flower room.

A few hours later, after some gardening, we are drinking tea and eating *sandesh,* talking about Swami's guru. A young couple is received at the kitchen door by one of the young women devotees. The Swami says from his chair, "Well. You have come? Go to the shrine. I will see you in my office later." They bow with clasped hands and go toward the auditorium. We finish tea and put away the cups. The Swami tells me to find out where the couple has gone. "Tell them I will see them now," he says. "Then go home and return at seven-thirty for class." "Okay," I tell him.

In the shrine, the couple are totally absorbed, meditating on the platform. How should I call them? A few other devotees, having finished their gardening for the day, are meditating as well. Theoretically, I could walk up to the shrine and say aloud, though softly, "Swami wants you to come to his office now." But whom would I be addressing? I don't know their names. Conceivably all five could assume I mean them, and I would have a small-scale breakdown on my hands, which one wants especially to avoid in the temple, if only out of respect for the culture, values and beliefs of the people involved, not to mention out of fear of earning the wrath of the gods enshrined therein. Therefore I say nothing, instead going outside again to ponder the situation. At the door I meet the Swami. "I will tell them," he says, seeing me empty-handed. He walks up to the platform and says, "I will see you now in my office." The couple immediately make pranam and accompany him out of the temple. The others stay put. "You will come at seven-thirty?" the Swami says to me as he passes through the door I am holding for his procession. "Yes," I answer. He says, "You should not say 'yes,' but rather, 'I shall try.'" "I shall try," I tell him. *"Accha,"* (affirmative) he says, and marches off to his office, followed briskly by the young couple.

That night the Swami tells me the couple have come from afar to meditate in the temple. "They are very much drawn to Sri Ramakrishna, but they are very poor and work cannot be found nearby. I told them to meditate in the shrine, but not to pray for worldly things. It will be all right for them. Surely they have the Master's blessing. Have you talked with him?" I answer that we chatted briefly before the Sunday lecture on a few occasions. He struck me as being sincere, and not particularly ego-involved. The Swami says that Sri Ramakrishna used to say that many were willing to be gurus, but few wanted to be disciples. "They are the 'children of immortal Bliss' of Swamiji," the Swami says, referring to Swami Vivekananda's evocation of a Vedic phrase in reference to the Indian masses. The thing is, they are hippies, or at least counter culture denizens of one kind or another. He has shoulder-length hair and a beard. She wears her hair in a single braid after the fashion of the Hindu wives. Usually she is wearing an Earth-Mother type dress, the handmade variety fashionable in the rural communes of California. She is barefoot. He wears moccasins and a Mexican peasant's white cotton pants and shirt, super-wrinkled and baggy. Pachouli oil essences pervade the air immediately around them. A few minutes later, the young man tells me, "This is a power place; a place where we can get off the planet, and out the other end of the universe. I'm going in there [in the shrine] to conquer death." "With Sri Ramakrishna's grace," adds the woman accompanying him. *"Jai* Ramakrishna," he says. *"Vijai,"* she says. They enter the temple just as Mrs. _____ is leaving. "I don't see any reason why they can't cut the lawn at an hour when people are not trying to meditate. I have come over here hoping to recharge my batteries and that lawn mower has been going constantly." She is twenty feet away, and talking to no one in particular, but I am the apparent focus of her monologue, so I say, "There, it has stopped," which it had, as she was talking. She takes notice, shrugs, and says, "Well, I guess you have to watch out what you wish for," and heads for the parking lot.

People have varying degrees of attraction to the divine focus surrounding the shrine, as these interactional segments point out. But more importantly, they show, albeit in a somewhat elliptical fashion, just what meditation is "used" for. Members go to the temple to meditate, which means in part that they partake of a certain atmosphere and allow themselves to be put into a mood, a particular sort of cognitive/affective state. To them, such states are special, but to the Swami I suspect that they are natural. I will give some more illustrations of this.

About three days before our son was born, my wife and I were in our living room talking to a friend. When the doorbell rang I was surprised to find a devotee at the door. (Since we lived thirty miles from the temple in a nearby university town, unannounced visits were unlikely.) I was more surprised when she said excitedly, "Swami is here to see you. He's outside. You have to come out and invite him in." As we scurried around cleaning up some dessert plates, I heard him at the door. "Are you in *samadhi*?" he asked, and addressed me by my Sanskrit name.[2] Four or five people, two of whom I had never seen before, accompanied him. He was wearing the gerua under his overcoat and scarf. On his head was the saffron-colored cap worn by the Order. I invited everyone in, and he led the procession. But it stopped in its tracks just inside the door. The Swami seemed to hesitate momentarily, and I couldn't figure out what I was required to do. Then I saw him looking at his shoes. I asked myself: "Should I take them off or tell him it's all right to wear them, or what?" One of the people whom I didn't know said to me: "He wants to know what to do with his shoes. Why don't you take them from him?" I got down on hands and knees to do so. Meanwhile, the Swami asked where the child was, and seemed somewhat taken aback when told that things appeared to be a few days past due. "Then this visit by a *sadhu* no doubt is a sign that all is well," he said matter-of-factly. I finally got his shoes off and laid them aside. His coat sort of fell off his shoulders, the hat trailing not far behind. "I shall go to this ashrama's shrine, but first let me wash my hands. Mother [addressed to my wife], let the husband get me some water." I thought he wanted a drink, so I started for the kitchen. Mr. _____ said, "He wants to rinse his hands in the bathroom. Show him to the bathroom." People were still standing up and the living room was positively crowded. The Swami disappeared into the room where the shrine was, saying something about how even householders could preserve the feeling of bliss. "This place," he told me, "has accumulated a strong current from your meditations and devotions. The Master [meaning Sri Ramakrishna] is pleased with you." As we came out of the room, I was introduced to everyone by the Swami. "We were singing, were we not?" he said to his entourage. "Were we ever!" said one, and they gestured their exclamatory assent. They were on their way back from Bay City where a puja had taken place and had decided to stop in. The Swami explained that he had to risk disturbing our meditation to see whether the child had been born yet. After sitting us all down for a twenty-minute meditation, he abruptly jumped up, gleefully announcing, "We shall go," and out they went, ending a forty-minute visit I shall not soon forget. This is Swami's power, manifested in his most exuberant, natural self.

The first time the Swami visited us, he came in his suit. I went to the temple to pick him up and we drove to our house. He was engaging, bright. We casually talked about my studies in graduate school, about living in a university town, and so forth. Once in our home, he settled into a very polite and somewhat disarmingly "nice" role. We sort of tensely faced each other across the living room and answered each other's lightweight questions. Finally, as if sensing that the balance of the situation was threatened by the awkwardness of the moment, an awkwardness my culture had taught me to pretend was not there, he said: "Let us just sit for a while. Then perhaps we shall meditate." The silence that followed for the next twenty or so minutes was so engrossing that the time passed by without an accompanying feeling of duration. We didn't close our eyes or assume a meditative posture, but rather just sat, looking at nothing in particular, with only the prescriptions governing the situation that I have mentioned. What the Swami did next was stand up and say, "Let us go to your shrine now." We showed it to him and made pranam with him before it. He removed a plastic bottle from his suit-coat side-pocket that proved to contain Ganges water, which he sprinkled on the shrine and on our heads. He lit incense and candles, and then we sat there in meditation for a long time. Finally, he said, "All right, dinner should be prepared." My wife excused herself and went into the kitchen.

"You have the tape recorder ready?" he asked me. I had previously requested that when he visited me he allow me to tape some songs and chants that I had heard him sing at the temple. "Yes," I said, and turned it on. From his inside coat pocket he produced a sheaf of papers containing numerous songs and chants in transliterated Sanskrit, and gave it to me. I followed it silently for the next hour as he accompanied his voice with a pair of finger cymbals I provided, singing songs associated with his order and the wider Hindu historical stream with which he is familiar. At the end, he looked at me and said very quietly and tenderly, "You know, this has been very nice." Then, arm in arm, we went in to eat dinner, which he accomplished with astounding speed and gusto. Nothing was left over. He demanded that we eat it all, and he himself had thirds of everything. Afterwards, he put on the nearest apron and did the dishes with such dispatch and abandon that water practically flooded the drain and sink and soaked his slacks. I recall his saying that this was his way of "paying" for the meal. After some spiritual discussion in which he described the attitude which the devotee should have toward meditation (viz., that it should be regular and intense), he asked me to drive him back to the temple, where we parted without my getting out of the car. "Go home," he said, getting out of his seatbelt. "Come back next Saturday." "Okay," I said. This is the Swami who is the minister, allowing the yogi to surface.

Another face. Word had come about the job I had applied for in Bay City. We were going to move in one month. Some devotees thought it would be nice to give us a sendoff, although it was known that we were not going to be completely out of touch. The Swami agreed to the party, and said he would attend. About eight to ten people were invited to the devotee's apartment. The devotees arrived before the Swami, and we got in the mood by meditating and listening to recordings of Indian classical music. One of the devotees, to whom the Swami was teaching tabla (a set of drums), had brought them along in case the opportunity arose for a lesson. When the Swami came, we immediately sensed his alert and vivacious mood. He began by sitting us all down to meditate. Then we consumed sweets and drank coffee and tea until the groans of pleasure could not be distinguished from those resulting from stuffing ourselves. It was suggested that we sing, whereupon the group formed a rousing chorus around the Swami's vocal improvisations. He was working out on the tabla. I was taking pictures. My son, then not yet two, was leaping about, yelling at the top of his lungs. Devotees were maintaining multiple conversations with over-lapping topics in between the songs. The Swami stood up and said, "We shall now do Indian dancing. You shall see, it is wonderful." He twirled and pranced, his gerua trailing ochre after-images. We were as amazed at his display almost as much as at the fact that the dancing was simply and beautifully executed, as though he had secretly practiced classical steps from one of the Hindu forms of dance in order to spring it on us in this sudden outburst of expressivity. It was much like the manner in which his tabla-playing skills had come to our atten-tion, and his knowledge of music, and sacred Vedic lore. Where previously there had not been the slightest trace of it, now the thing seemed to spontaneously manifest itself. We all danced in a circle, stepping, clapping, and chanting in a syncopated pat-tern that he set, while the form of his dance took shape. As we circled around him, he used his entire body, and his voice, to create a finely woven tapestry of rhythms, sounds, and moving forms. At the end of a timeless performance (which actually lasted nearly an hour), we collapsed exhausted and ludicrously happy. This is the Swami who is his own at his own pace, whom we occasionally catch glimpses of, but who is difficult to locate.

Another time, as my wife and I were weeding a walkway leading to a small statue of Krishna in the temple garden, the Swami came on the scene wearing khakis, t-shirt, straw hat, and sandals. I thought to myself, "Now what will happen?" A special attire always corresponds to a special job to be done. This time it was the lotuses. He had mentioned coming out to pick lotuses, but it didn't occur to me at the time that the lotuses are not accessible from the Krishna Pond's bank, or at least not since the ones nearest the bank had been thinned out. In one hand was a pair of clippers; in the other a basket used to carry the flower offerings from the garden to the shrine's flower room. With a laugh, he summoned my (then) two-and-a-half-year-old son, who eagerly mounted the Swami's shoulders.

Into the pond stepped the Swami, his rolled-up khakis getting soaked to the waist, and my son with both arms wrapped tightly around the Swami's head, holding on for dear life.

Around the leaf-crowded pond they went, cutting the long-stemmed lotuses. By the time about ten had been picked, my son hollered that he wanted to get down, so he was brought back to the edge of the pond. Then the Swami surveyed the weed-cutting I had been doing with the sickle. "Don't chop. Cut. Like this." And he went around the edge of the pond in a display of great speed and efficiency. With his left hand he gathered a batch of weeds, and with the right sliced them off with a lightning stroke of the sickle's blade. All I could do was follow him around and receive the cut weeds, which I put in a wheelbarrow. Finally, I went for another sickle. At the tool shed I stopped to talk to a young woman who attends him on occasion. "Is he getting too tired?" she asked me. "Anyway, it's time for a coffee break," she added. Once back at the pond I waited a few minutes before suggesting that we go inside, watching him at work. "What time is it?" he asked me. "Eleven," I answered after locating my watch in a pocket. "Let us take coffee and sandesh," he said.

Back in his office, from behind his desk, he is alternately casual, stern, indifferent, and consoling. People who have been around him learn not to try to predict his next move, or, for that matter, to interpret it post hoc. Perhaps this is where an economy of words can be most illuminating. Having his company for extended periods, even for an hour at a time, is a great luxury, given his commitment to serving all his students. Even during his so-called vacation, the temple is awash with society's religious tide, and driftwood floats into the place at all hours. Whoever and whatever he is, he seems a far cry from those corny metal boxes found next to the jukebox coin slot in booths of hamburger stands in the fifties (and probably later). Done up in plastic and chrome, a beturbaned figure represented on the front with "mystic eyes" offers to answer any "yes or no" question for a penny. Should one order a vanilla milkshake and some fries? On a pink strip of paper, the answer: "Swami says—The stars are in your favor."

This analysis/description has come full circle. I've tried to evoke the flavor of the Swami as a member of a social reference world that characterizes itself as religious. In this world, his role is that of teacher and exemplar. His function is not to prophesy, but to help aspirants in their search for what his tradition calls "self-knowledge." He "mediates" between gods and ordinary human beings, and appears to enact the role of "medium" through which a specially preserved form of "holy power" is transmitted and injected into the total context, as well as into specific situations in temple life and the religious experiences of the devotees. His entire presentation of self is dramatic, but not in the sense that this might immediately imply; that is, in the form of "pretense." His drama is, rather, the effect of culture and his sadhana; his personality and mannerisms form the particular way in which the drama is made to be enacted by his being-in-the-world. And the meanings drawn from those instances in which the man is the teaching—in the sense that he has become one with the putative role of sadhu (holyman)—are mediated by the student's capacity to be in the right place at the right time in the right frame of mind. Those who come to "church" find a "minister" to fill them with a dogma, albeit one which is fiercely anti-dogmatic. Those who suspend their expectations about what religious life must be partake of a wider offering.

NOTES

1. That the Swami is loved and revered like the Lord is not to say "worshipped" or so regarded in his presence. The Ramakrishna Order specifically disavows *guru bada,* as the practice of worshipping the living guru is called.

2. He has given several devotees Sanskrit names. The significance of the practice is discussed in Chapter 9.

6. THE NETWORK OF TEMPLE INTERSUBJECTIVITY

In the Swami's absence, devotees utilize a number of strategies in their relations with one another. First, there is the strategy of claiming closeness to Swami and thereby deriving a bit of authority from him. This is sometimes used to manipulate others, as, say, in the case of someone who wants a particular thing to be done in the garden and lets others know that it is really what the Swami wants. Another strategy is to lay claim to a fund of spiritual knowledge, accumulated either from the Swami or from long association with Vedanta. This is most frequently employed by the older members, who claim to have a greater understanding of the needs of the temple and the interpretation of Vedanta. Still another strategy is that of withholding approval or even acknowledgment of the claims of another. This is the most subtle interactional strategy and in some ways the most pervasive; thus I will discuss it here.

As Vedanta does not seek converts and shows only one side to the public, those who have attached themselves to it see themselves as a somewhat elite group, although the theology of pluralism frowns on one's making invidious comparisons with other sects or religious creeds. Rather, an integrative and assimilative attitude is cultivated, to the extent that Buddhism and Christianity, to mention only two religions, become, via the Vedantic word-magic, aspects of the higher Vedantic unity.

Hence, Vedantins, at least the more sophisticated ones, refrain from putting down people who come to Vedanta with values, attitudes, and opinions that differ from their own. But, at the same time, they are cool toward them, as to those who claim Vedanta as their own without having participated in temple life. Some longtime adherents seem downright snobbish because their indifference has a cultivated air to it. A few people have come to the temple on several occasions and have not been spoken to at all by any member. The Swami, of course, usually greets each person individually when he is not involved in something else, but for the members anything more than the most cursory sort of interaction is considered unnecessary.

"If people are attracted here, then they will stay. If not, they will leave before too long," one longtime member told me. Other members don't appreciate the efforts of a few to attract others to Vedanta and consider showing overt interest in new-comers to be contrary to the exclusivity that underlies spiritual practice. In short, most members are conscientious in protecting the image of Vedanta as a "steep" religious path. Most will not, at the same time, claim to have found the way, and, as I said, refutation of other paths (i.e., religions) is not considered proper Vedantic behavior. Nevertheless, these members reveal little to strangers and regard the individual's persistent presence as an index of his or her fitness for membership.

A few people have come who have not been well-liked. Although no overt avoidance or other signs of discrimination were practiced—indeed, such people were encouraged to partake of spiritual life—the message of their incompatibility was probably finally clarified, and they left. Clarification might come in the form of a recommendation from the Swami, but more often it is a kind of recognition that there is no place at the temple which one can occupy. Pretenders to spiritual insight are dealt with in the usual fashion. They are humored, if necessary, or perhaps put down in some light fashion, but usually just toler-ated until they realize that no one is listening to them, where-upon they exit.

This is not to say that among the general membership there is a homogeneous community of like-minded believers. One por-tion of the membership consists of persons who are either preachers and religious teachers of one sort or another, or else counselors, therapists, and the like. A few occasionally try to play guru, but only the unsuspecting newcomers, likely to see them as important persons in the scene, get caught up in their word-games.

Because of my university affiliation, a number of people have sought out my opinion on various current topics, such as the economy. And, because I am not one to forego a discussion, even with a non-sociologist, I got into exchanges with devotees and more marginal temple affiliates, sometimes at the expense of my sociology and the sadhana. Once a woman kept trying to strike up a conversation with me while the assembled devotees awaited the appearance of the Swami during the Wednesday morning class. Each time for three Wednesdays she would find something to tell me about this or that thing she had read in the news, and would ask my sociological opinion about it. I didn't feel much like talking, particularly in view of the explicit instruction that silence be practiced at that time and in view of the fifteen other people present who were maintaining absolute quiet. Yet I didn't know how to shut her up, and found myself trying to talk and be quiet at the same time, resulting in neither. The Swami had even reminded the group at one of these classes that the group was not there to engage in worldly conversation, but to find realization. The woman did her thing anyway.

On a particular morning, when the Swami entered the library and found this going on, he had heard enough, and could see my pained expression. He said to her in a most serious, yet kindly fashion: "You are not to bother Dr. Damrell. He has not come here to entertain you. Nor should you have come to be entertained. This is a spiritual assembly, you will please refrain from discussing these things with the devotees." I was at once relieved and horrified. The woman literally recoiled (perhaps shrank is a better word) in instant contrition. The Swami greeted the group and the class began. For a long time after that, my conversations with members of the group were limited to the immediate instrumental exchanges bearing on some situational requirement.

The Swami deals with other "deviations" as he encounters them. Occasionally people under severe stress or suffering from various maladies, some imagined and some real, find their way to Vedanta, but they probably find little comfort in the description of suffering as an inevitable consequence of having lived in the body. Healing, auras, astral traveling, and other fare of psychics, mediums, and so on are considered to be expressions of the occult powers by which the unwary might be distracted in the initial stages of the sadhana and lose sight of the goal. Powers are to be shunned and hatha yoga practices are seldom mentioned except in their spiritual (i.e., nonphysical) aspects. It might be added, too, in this context, that although the conversion phenomenon is not entirely absent, there are few who express a break with the past or display the "after-I-came-to-Vedanta-things-have-been-perfect" sort of change. The savior, Sri Ramakrishna, is not, after all, a giver of blood for the sins of the devotees, at least not in the sense that "Jesus died for your sins." (Gurus are said to take on karma and suffer pain in place of their disciples.) Rather, the savior is the embodiment of a *spiritual* knowledge, which is a decidedly more *vertical* approach to the divine than is implied in the demonstration of suffering aimed at redeeming sinners found in the Western concept of Jesus. Vedanta, in fact, grounds the Jesus of the Sermon on the Mount in the Hindu idea of the identity of atman (as soul) with Brahman (as God). And to paraphrase a Vedantic maxim, spiritual knowledge is unconcerned with the operations required to bring it about. (Vedanta is the discovery of Brahman, not an explanation of maya; Deutsch, 1968: 27-47). Yet, a person needing conversion *may* be accommodated. Numerous westerners practice a variety of Indian customs (from various Indian cultures) and though they are not discouraged from doing so, there are certain limits beyond which this ostentation will not go.

The emphasis on practical and utilitarian application of the experiences of the spiritual life acts as a check on drastic transformative episodes. The community, with its dynamic cult on the one hand, and the static social movement on the other, is, after all, stable. In no territory of interpersonal behavior are the boundaries undefined, yet opportunity for improvisation exists and persons fashion for themselves, albeit with the

Swami's concerted attention, a place in a social world of spiritual seekers.

As I said earlier, there are distinctive cohorts and strata among the templegoing people. There is evidence of an inner and outer circle of devotees, but its boundaries I have not been able to distinguish clearly as they vary situationally. There are the full-time monastics. There is the older group of longtime associates of the temple who live householder lives in the area. There is another group of longtime associates who lead celibate lives on or near the grounds, but who are not officially monastics. There are several groups of hippies numbering about six each, plus assorted children, who attend Sunday services and occasionally special functions such as pujas and the like. I have heard them claim divers gurus as their own, ranging from Maharishi Mahesh Yogi, Sai Baba, or Swami Satchidananda to Gurdjieff and other Western religious figures. Apparently they receive instruction from the Swami side by side with their practices of other disciplines and paths. Another subgroup in temple life consists of several men, who more or less share the view that relief agencies, hospitals, and schools operated by the Order might do good outside India as well. Still another group consists in the children of those who attend services. They are more or less allowed to run free on the temple grounds while a young girl babysits for them. Once, an attempt was made to harass them into Sunday school classes by a member who is the head of a prominent Valley City private school, and who even volunteered to teach the children, but few parents enrolled their kids. Later on, some of the women devotees who are teachers began to hold classes at the Swami's request. The children who frequent the place have a clearly defined routine for establishing, engaging in, and breakingoff play, and games go on over numerous Sundays.

GETTING TOGETHER WITH DEVOTEES

One of the main things devotees do with one another is what they loosely term "getting together." This usually involves sharing a meal, but may include other activities, such as going on an outing together (e.g., camping or to a spiritual event away from the temple), or informally sharing some mutual involvement, which may be either of a "spiritual" or "worldly" nature. Although shared activities outside the temple are for the most part unstructured, arising as they do out of the interests of the devotees at the time, a sort of basic pattern to these get-togethers has emerged.

As I have said elsewhere, persons classified as "devotees" live *in the world;* that is, they are not members of the temple community proper or of the order, although they may be leading full-time spiritual lives. Some of the young people who live at the temple hold part-time jobs on the outside, so it is not appropriate to describe a "householder" as one who is employed in a secular occupation. The criteria used to classify people as monastics or householders are somewhat fuzzy, because for the most part it is a subjective classification. (Even at Valley City temple, there are full-time live-in persons who are not in the Order.)

I am a householder, though I have more contact with monastic members of the temple than with other householders by virtue of my frequent association with the Swami, my work in the temple garden, and my participation in the chorus. One way to characterize temple denizens is according to their outside-the-temple interaction with one another; what the frequency of such interaction is, and whether it influences their behavior as members of the Church (or as spiritual seekers), and how such interaction is defined.

For the most part, interhouseholder relations are limited· to what takes place at the temple. This undoubtedly has to do with the fact that the Swami discourages people from interacting or carrying on socially together. If any spare time is available to a person, he or she should spend it in spiritual enquiry. At the same time, however, "keeping the company of the holy" is prescribed for the spiritual seeker, although when this edict is invoked by the Swami, he means it in the sense of keeping company with himself or other temple personnel, not with other householders. He does not forbid them from "getting together," although he has made it known that he considers such goings-on to be less than desirable pastimes. Thus, the devotees nearly always try to make the occasion for their socializing a "spiritual" one either by getting the Swami's approval beforehand or by structuring the interaction event along the lines of the sacred.

Getting together is practiced more among those who are interested in Indian culture per se than among those who are not. Since food is a branch of study that combines ritual, religious observance, social custom, and culinary practice, Indian meals are fairly common. At such meals, guests are likely to engage in listening to music, talking about some aspect of spiritual life, meditating, singing devotional songs in a group, or some other activity ostensibly Indian or temple-related. Most devotees, including monastics, keep mementos in the form of scrapbooks. As people examine pictures of the Swami and devotees, or items acquired as a result of attending a function (such as a worship), they discuss the highlights of the event and describe in somewhat indirect testimonial fashion what they got out of it. Music sung by the group may function in the same way. Songs evoke reminiscences and nostalgic memories of temple life.

Aside from enhancing the purely expressive side of the religion, these get-togethers provide younger members with the opportunity to receive feedback from others concerning their interpretations of the religious experience. Partly this has to do with the fact that the Swami is the only source of feedback. Since only he is qualified to discuss the person's sadhana in terms of its obstacles, needs, or attainments, one does not talk idly about such things with him. A younger member is likely to turn to those who are sharing—to what extent is never precisely clear—the same path. But the Swami continually warns against hanging around together, and forbids revealing one's experiences in the spiritual realm to another person. Thus, the need to perform as a spiritual seeker in some other context beside the religious one at the temple or in the home, is met in a somewhat indirect way—by improvising religious events without the Swami being present.

Let us consider why the Swami would object to something as "innocent" and possibly productive of collective solidarity as a friendly social gathering made up of devotees. He says that when devotees get together they are likely to engage in "idle chitchat" or behaviors associated with "ego-enhancement." This likelihood arises, he maintains, because they are not yet far enough along the spiritual path to be able to completely control their worldly involvements, which are a necessity, to be sure, but which are nevertheless worldly. His sanyasin's world view, with its emphasis on the inner life of solitary contemplation, no doubt influences his perception of interdevotee relations, but he is also "liberal-minded" on the issue: "Of course, contemplation is only one way. There are several paths to God which one can combine." (This is a reference to the four yogas—jnana, bhakti, karma, and raja—which Vivekananda, the Order's founder, says must be synthesized by the spiritual aspirant.) I asked him once whether his discouraging relations between devotees might not be interpreted as a means of assuring his own control of the situation.

"Of course," he said, looking at me as if I was slightly crazy for having thought there would be any other answer. "I am responsible for them. I have taken on a load. It increases every time they talk among themselves. I hear, 'Oh, Swami, she has been taught the worship; why won't you teach me the worship!' Or someone says, 'Please let me cook for you. You let *her*. And she does not know what a monk eats. All simple food. But she is so elaborate!' Or that fellow Mr. _____ says, '_____ thinks we shouldn't build a wing on the monastery, but I think we should, don't you?' I want to fly away from such things, but I cannot. They are tugging at my sleeve, 'Please tell me what I should do.' I want to say to them, 'Go ask her, she is your guru. Leave me alone.' All this comes from devotees talking among themselves and becoming confused about why they are here. But let them do it; what is the harm? The Master will guide them. There is no hurry. They have these tendencies, and until they are exhausted such will be their sadhana's course. Others know that social life is unnecessary. We have social life here that is also religious life. Don't go with them if they ask you. Well, go ahead. You are a 'doctor.' "

I answered that I was not really interested in very many of the devotees, although some are quite close. "Then be with them, there is no harm in that. It is good that you feel this way about Thakur's children. Let there be love among you. The main thing is that you carry on your life according to your dharma. Too much socializing will distract a man from his duty. You have a job; you are a sociologist at the university; you have a wife to support. There is no need to get rich or to chase after worldly things, but perform your dharma and there will be adequate things in life. Your dharma includes meditation and some study of Vedantic scriptures. You should be keenly attached to these things. There is no need to make drastic changes. Undesirable traits will fall away in due time by the Master's grace."

Getting together, at least among those with whom I have gotten together, is done with words to the same effect as those quoted above in mind. We are invited to the _____s for dinner after the lecture. Three other devotees, plus the _____s, will be there. Our arrival at two o'clock coincides with that of the others. Mr. _____ greets us and asks us if we would like to freshen up and then salute at the household shrine. We say, "Of course," and are shown to the bathroom where fresh towels have been laid. As I am washing up, I hear people exchanging greetings like *"Namo Narayanaya," "Jai Sri Ramakrishna,"* and *"Namaskar,"* greetings usually used by *sadhus* at the CU temples and in general use among various "denominations" of devotees in the West and in India. A line forms outside the bathroom. I emerge and go into the shrine room and make pranam. Incense and matches are next to the shrine. I light about half of the dozen or so candles thereon. Then I light some incense. A last pranam follows, and I pause to look at the pictures and statues before making way for the next person. Mr. _____ says that we shall all meditate later, that we should just salute the Master and Divine Mother now.

This shrine is exciting to behold and the devotees are anxious, as always, to sit before it. There are numerous Indian religious posters in the room and assorted holy articles, including photographs of the Holy Mother's feet, the hundred-and-eight names of Mother written in English and Sanskrit by the Swami, etc., which are arranged about the multitiered shrine on which flowers are piled so densely that the pictures and statues are practically buried underneath. Their fragrance is overpoweringly sweet. A multicolored light pierces loosely woven batik curtains. In spite of the clamor of visitors making their obligatory (though spontaneously initiated) appearance, the room has a kind of peaceful self-preservation about it, perhaps as much due to the fixed poses of the divine personae in the shrine as to the definition of the place that gives direction to our situation. No object is extraneous to the overall spiritual design. Each photograph or likeness is specially situated and given individual attention.

The _____ s have obviously brought the Hindu definition of the situation to bear on the level of their everyday life, since there is a continuity to the appearance of their household. It is a kind of continuity that appears consistent with where they are. They have created a Vedantic lifesyle. (They call themselves "Vedantins.") In their shrine, of course, are the temple cult's sacred objects, including photographs of the god-man and his wife, Holy Mother. But in addition there are pictures of Hanuman, Shiva, Rama and Sita, Krishna, Kali, Buddha, Ganesha, Vishnu, Sri Shankaracharya, and assorted living gurus from various branches of Hinduism. Jesus occupies a less prominent place in the shrine room in a special alcove on a shelf. His likeness is a photograph of an oil painting depicting a sort of mystic-looking, long-haired, bearded Anglo-Saxon.

The presence of all of these religious objects cannot be explained by the Swami's influence; at least not directly. While he is an important force in their lives, the specific imagery beyond that surrounding Sri Ramakrishna and Holy Mother is of the devotee couple's own choosing. What I am getting at is the basis for the selection. One opens oneself to the experience and plumbs the currents of Indian mythology and culture for objects that stand for ideational representations of spiritual selfhood. In other words, the couple has identifications with the various gods and other religious objects, and these identifications themselves express meanings and enter into dialogue with the couple. Our being there allows us to take in the atmosphere and be lifted to its "spiritual" heights.

Not that there is a great deal of piety, as we might call a lot of reverential attention or inordinate focus. After all, this is not church, although devotees' homes are called "ashramas" by the Swami on occasion. And the definition of the situation, while grounded in the fact that what they share in common is the Swami, by whom they indeed come to know one another, is nevertheless social. Here the cultic focus is broadened somewhat to allow the immediacy of the spiritual experience to be postponed, as it were, and the religious situation to broaden to include the world of work, family, and pastimes of an intellectual, recreational, or political sort.

After I come out of the shrine, I am asked if I would like some sparkling apple juice. Alcohol and other drugs are, of course, forbidden according to Hindu custom, although persons are not above making references to their personal acquaintance with mind-altering substances. Out on the patio, the host, another male guest, and I talk about Gerald Berreman's (1972) book on India. "It was ridiculous for him to use a Muslim as his principal informant," says _____. I venture that one does not have to be one to know one, and for Berreman's purpose the arrangement proved satisfactory. _____ says I am defending him because he is a fellow social scientist.

We three are each students of Indian culture after our own fashion. The host is a psychologist and has spent a dozen years drawing parallels between various schools of psychology and psychiatry and yoga psychology and spiritual disciplines prescribed by different traditions within Hinduism. The other guest is a philosophy student, studying the interrelations between Vedanta and schools of Western philosophy. I am the participant-observer, allowing myself to be buffeted by the currents of Hinduism in the West. Only our intellectual apparatus differs in various places. We have the same reflexive attitude toward our participation and what effect it appears to have. The host says that my defense of Berreman is not really my own doing: "Sociology is called the 'Mother of the social sciences,' so he is only doing the Mother's bidding." "Jai Ma," (Victory to Mother

Durga) says the other guest. The host suggests we all go in to the shrine to meditate. The hostess stays in the kitchen.

Dinner is an elegant affair, preceded by five hours of cooking, and then followed by the singing of a verse from the *Gita* and a communal digging-in. We serve ourselves buffet style and then sit in the living room. Most of the furniture is low, and pillows are stacked into piles to support the half-reclining guests, who partake of the food with their fingers, Indian fashion. Various secular and spiritual topics come and go. When everyone has had sufficient food, including dessert and coffee or tea, talk invariably turns spiritual before people depart. After one last visit to the shrine, a bow to the host and hostess with clasped hands, the guests, including myself and my wife, depart. "We shall have you over soon," we say as we leave. "Groovy," says the host. "Jai Thakur." "Vijay."

Other get-togethers of less formal status, such as taking in a movie (usually on some topic of religious or Hindu interest), have some of the same features as those like the dinner described above. It is considered proper—not only out of courtesy but out of self-interest—to visit the shrine whenever one goes to a devotee's home. One acknowledges the effort made by the owner of the shrine, as well as having the *darshan* (the presence or sight) of the deity (or deities) therein. Hands are washed and shoes removed before entering. All in all, the devotees I have visited in their homes take care to preserve the religious meaning-structure embedded in the encounter. Secular topics are usually broached using the framework of the Hindu ideology as a guide. The degree of Hinduization of the devotees varies with a person's desire and capacity to integrate the religious experience into his or her life in the everyday world of work in the American institutional sphere. Some are out-front Vedantins, letting nonbelievers know they belong to the Hindu religion, while others are "closet-yogins," with their involvement hidden from the view of outsiders. There is, however, a common seriousness of purpose, particularly as regards maintaining the spiritual practices enjoined by the Swami and those that have been undertaken voluntarily. Social intercourse usually amounts to a sharing of the religious foci and experience, as well as the events that give a grounding to that experience.

HASSLES

It is easy to understate the intensity of the involvement and the strenuous effort undertaken in behalf of participation, but invariably clashes occur and controversies develop which make it clear. Here I want briefly to mention how interpersonal troubles arise in temple life, albeit without describing why they occur or giving particulars that would constitute an invasion of privacy. The main conflicts arise from the high value placed on interaction with the Swami and on those actions which are deemed by the temple community to be central to the religious experience. Petty rivalries and jealousies are hunted down and squelched by the Swami, but a few manage to persist, despite efforts on all sides to eliminate them.

One "class" of such conflicts concerns propriety in temple comportment. Once I entered the temple to meditate. About halfway through my seven-step meditation I heard a voice saying: "You can't be here now. Please leave the temple." One of the old monks had said this to me from the doorway leading to the flower room. I came completely unglued. Not only was I snapped rather abruptly out of a rather delicate state of contemplation, but the action was, from what I had been taught, entirely inappropriate. But I didn't think it was appropriate to argue the matter either, so I got up and went out of the temple. About a month later—the next time I had an opportunity to sit alone in the temple—the same thing happened. I was into my meditation and the monk appeared at the door telling me to leave. This time I complained to the Swami, who said, "I asked him to do the worship and he is shy about people watching him. Don't be angry with him. He means no harm." Nevertheless, it was a while before I could reconcile the monk's shyness with his willingness on two occasions to break the mood of my meditation and the silence of the shrine with his demand that I leave so he could have *his* privacy.

The above perhaps is not the best example. Another more poignant one occurred when I turned off the tape-recorded music that was playing before a Sunday lecture so that the tanpura could be tuned. "Why did you do that?" a monk demanded. "So that the tanpura could be tuned," I answered.

"People are meditating. You should do your tuning beforehand," he retorted, with a raised voice. The church's president
was in agreement. I was angry at their apparent intransigence on
the matter. How could the tanpura be tuned with music playing
in the background? It had to be tuned then and there because
the earlier attempt to tune it (in the foyer) had not succeeded. I
said: "I really don't think I have earned this," and walked out.
Meanwhile, the monk scolded the other members of the chorus
for disrupting the meditation with their tuning, but one devotee
said, "We have to tune it; it's out. Listen. And we have to sing
in five minutes. It isn't anyone's fault." When I came back in,
the monk grabbed me by the arm and said, "I was only being
stern. I'm not angry with you. _____ explained what was
happening."

Holy striving necessarily sets up tensions between members
who are working at maintaining a continuity in their consciousness of the divine foci. Another example of this tension surfaced
when a woman devotee complained to others that a certain
newcomer was borrowing all the tools she customarily used in
working the flower beds where altar flowers are grown. "I have
always used that cultivator, and I always try to do it the same
way each time. Who does she think she is coming in here and
just using any old tool and digging wherever she likes with it?"
Apparently the woman complained to the Swami as well, for I
later heard him gently explaining to the newcomer that
Mrs. _____ was a faithful devotee who wanted things just so,
and that she should be accommodated just this once. "Here,"
he said, handing her another cultivator, "You use this one."

"Shiva!" he exclaimed, walking away.

USHERING

Sunday lecture celebration is to begin in fifteen minutes. The
time is called "coffee break" and comes between the puja and
the lecture. People cluster in the library, around the coffee urn
manned by two long-time devotees. A sociologist who is a Sikh
has brought his television camera and is interviewing members
outside as they approach the coffee stand. I skulk semi-obtru-
sively in the background, shadowing the proceedings. The Sikh

approaches Mrs. _____. She is a relative newcomer (two years) whose son usually accompanies her. They are avid Ramakrishna-ites and have become central in the cultic scene at the temple, and they are very close to the Swami. The sociologist asks her to tell how she got there.

"Well, it was just one of those things; we just happened to hear about it, but, you know, it is simply wonderful to be here." She smiles cheerfully. He asks her to describe whether she does any Hindu practices, such as abstaining from eating meat or wearing Indian costumes. "No," she says. "We do meditate, however, and study holy books. And of course, just try to come here to be with Swami and everyone as often as we can." She smiles again, waiting for the next question. The camera is now on the sociologist, who is saying into the microphone, "So the Church Universal doesn't advocate any abandonment of American culture as do some other groups." Mrs. _____ sort of engages me visually then, and we go into the library together. I hold the door open for her and she thanks me. We are served coffee. "Wasn't that a wonderful worship?" she asks me. "Amazing," I say. "Swami was really high today." "Yes."

People are standing around looking alternately casual, nervous, pious, somber, friendly, or just plain ambiguous. Some are sleepy, having just made it there in time for the coffee. Others are still feeling the effects of the ritual and flower offering that follows it. Indian women with children in tow hunt down the babysitter. Most Indian kids are all Western haircuts, toy airplanes, and chewing gum. The women wear saris, the men casual clothes a la Macy's double-knit stay-press. Some hippies in various ad hoc costumes lend the event a little more atmosphere. Many children accompany them, as do assorted single males of varying hirsuteness and fashion. Straight Vedantists from other temples or from the Valley City one are identifiably black-suited, although the Swami is known to be less strict about such things than his brother monks in a few other temples. So full-time monks wear sports coats and even an occasional sweater. People browse through the rather decently stocked library, containing authors from Sorokin to Allport to Buddha to Aurobindo. Others do their best to get Swami aside for some conversation about everything from lentil soup to macadamia nuts. And he turns now to this and now to that person, between passing out pieces of candy (prasad) and introducing himself to newcomers, inquiring after so-and-so's mother's near-fatal stroke, etc. My turn finally comes. It is the first Sunday in some weeks that I have been addressed during coffee break. I am accessible at other times, so usually he ignores me at public gatherings. "You have no tie, Dr.?" he asks in a provoking manner. "Yes, but not with me at the moment," I answer. "Well, that is all right. You are a Dr., eh, Dr.? Mr. _____ is not here, so will you please take collection with Mr. _____?" An involuntary "arghhh" issues from my throat. "It is that I *must* ask you to do this, so you will please do it, eh?" he says matter-of-factly. "Okay," I say. "Accha," he says, and walks away.

My quasi-ambivalence has suddenly lost its slack. If there is one thing that has bothered me about the scene it is the bizarre little offering of the collection plates. People customarily (because they are "cheap" and paper money "looks better," I was told by one on-the-scene student of this ritual) put a dollar bill into the plate as it is passed to them by a black-suited usher. Once the audience has been covered, the ushers approach the shrine, stoop in unison to one knee, and set the wooden plates (shaped sort of like walnut hats) on the platform before the shrine. They sit there like two piles of cabbage that sometimes have to be tamped down with the hand to get the offerings to stay in. It is awkward and not a little pretentious, it seems to me, to stick this bit of Americana into an otherwise tastefully written and edited script. Rabindranath Tagore poems rendered for folk guitar are quite tastefully done by Mrs. _____, but money "pies" plopped onto the shrine were not my idea of appropriate transcendental fare. It's my hang-up, though. Now I was going to have to put my money where my mouth (or at least my *head*) was. The ushers always "set the example" by digging in their pockets and producing the first dollars. I went to find my wife to get my dollar.

Doing the collection was easy enough. People know how to pass the plate between rows, so I just kind of followed it to the back of the auditorium. A few indicated surprise that I was doing the collecting, by making a face, which I responded to by kind of rolling my eyes and shrugging, a futile effort to communicate the complete emptiness of the act and my utter lack of participation in it. Others seemed to acknowledge that collection was occurring only when the plate was in the hand next to them, whereupon they deftly plopped in the buck and passed the plate to their neighbor, all with spine erect and eyes mostly closed. Checks and change and slough-offs all elicited gestures deployed through facial expressions or body movements. Mostly there is a kind of tension that had me coursing through its current with stiff, unspontaneous motions. By this time I was in front of the shrine, the one-knee stretch deposited the plate in its place, and propelled me back to my place in the rear of the auditorium. I felt everybody was watching me, and assumed that because they were not looking at me when my eyes found theirs they were avoiding looking at me because they sensed my *dis*-ease. I *was* righteously cured, however; I was not the only one who was sensitive to the incongruity of this most Christian of practices, and what made people seem mechanical in doing it was that it was a part of the script that had normative underpinnings. It is simply something that is done because it was decided long ago that this is how it should be done—how else to put some pin-money into the church coffers than to pass the plate? It simply would not do, as some see it, to have devotees leaving money on the shrine willy-nilly, as some of the Indians do at pujas. So, the opening of pocketbooks, the jingle of quarters and the rustle of dollar bills occur after every lecture, sometimes with musical accompaniment.

After the lecture was over and the auditorium was empty, the Swami asked me to carry the plates to the church office for the counting. I did so, and got to see how the records were kept. Very simple. The seventy-eight people had donated roughly sixty dollars. A few people had written checks for ten or twenty dollars, but these were counted as "dues" and credited to their "account." The Swami came into the office after the counting was over and I told him the amount collected. "You see," he said, turning to me, "We are not rich after all." "I didn't think the temple was rich, Swami," I answered. "Yes, yes," was his reply. And as he turned to leave the room, he said over his shoulder: "Many people think that we *are* rich, and their dollar entitles them to a portion of Uncle's will. Do you think the lecture is worth one dollar?" "It's worth at least two, Maharaj,"

I replied, and we laughed until my sides ached. Caught again, as they say, taking the worldly role, the role of the doubter.

A TALK AT THE TEMPLE

I was at home, reading some of Weber's stuff on prophecy. The phone rang. It was the Swami. "I must give you some very bad news," he said. "There is no way that I can get this person whom I intended to ask to speak on the temple anniversary. I asked Mr. _____, who is in the Indian Consulate, to speak, but he cannot give a long talk. So one more speaker is needed. Can you think of anyone?" There was a pause as I tried to figure out who could give a talk. Surely there was someone, but no name came to mind. "What about Dr. Damrell?" he asked, when I didn't bite. "Oh, no," I think I said, so he assured me it would be all right, and that I would have to talk for just twenty minutes on "India's Spiritual Contribution to the West." The date was in three weeks. He told me I would do well to prepare the talk in advance.

I read about ten books, from Erikson to Nehru, on the subject, but didn't reach any sort of cloture on the topic and couldn't really figure out what I should say. There was a lot to be said on the matter, but in my view, it was all sociological. I was going to be talking in a "church," not to a panel of conventioneers. I finally decided to do a civil rights ploy and evoke the image of Gandhi, Martin Luther King, John F. Kennedy, and Vivekananda. Not an eyelash batted during my whole talk, though I was ready to collapse afterward from the tension. Fortunately, I followed the consular official, who was not exactly eloquent, and so I at least felt that there was no real disgrace in having done it. Besides, I tried to think of it as reciprocity. I had partaken of my share of pujas and had wasted the Swami's time on numerous occasions with my chitchat, so it seemed only fitting that I do my Doctor thing for him and do it well. People seemed to like it, and he said I did a "fine job." Someone cut out the newspaper ad announcing the temple anniversary and handed it to me at the temple door. I recall worrying about whether my colleagues in town might have seen it, but there was little chance of that. They tended not to look at the religion page.

After the talk, the Swami, the Consul and his family (a wife and two college-age kids), myself and my wife were invited to a devotee's house for lunch. Our participation in this commensal occasion typifies, by way of contrast, the relations devotees have in the Swami's presence.

It is a Bengali feast. I count fifteen main courses and assorted side dishes. We lay people anxiously await the Swami's arrival with the Consul. When he comes, we help him remove his shoes and follow him as he goes to the household shrine. "Let us wash our hands and meditate before we eat," he says. We all do so, excepting the women, who work out in the kitchen. The Consul's son and daughter join us in the shrine room where we all make pranam and take the yogic posture. The Swami lights some candles and incense. Then he chants a few mantras which I recognize as belonging to the series he uses in the worship at the temple. A few moments later we are meditating in a profound silence. The Swami is completely motionless, unconcerned about the concrete floor and the overabundance of incense in the room. Thirty minutes pass. Finally the Swami puts away his *japa* beads, bows before the shrine, and says, "Let us go now." We all make pranam and exit the shrine room. The hostess invites us to gather around the table to sing a verse from the *Bhagavad-Gita* that is used as a kind of saying of grace. The Swami's Sanskrit, like that of the Indians present, is beautifully intoned and enunciated:

> The process is Brahman, the clarified butter is Brahman, offered by Brahman into the fire of Brahman; by performing actions with the consciousness of Brahman, one attains Brahman in samadhi [quoted freely from: Swami Swaru pananda, *Shrimad Bhagavodgita*, Mayavati, Pithoragarh, Himalayas; Advaita Ashrama, 1972, Chapter IV, verse 24].

The eating is anticlimactic, with the exception that a whole chili finds its way down my throat and I begin to emit loud hiccoughs from deep in the diaphragm. The hostess hands me a glass of buttermilk, saying, "This is the only thing that will put out the fire." Much to my relief, the cure-all works. The Indian youths are finding me amusing. The father scolds the son, telling him that one who does not obey his father should not make light of others' misfortunes. The Swami asks, "He does not obey his father? How so?" The Consul answers, "He has refused to cut off that silly beard." The Swami seems a little annoyed at this. "He is young. Let him have a beard. See the Dr.'s [my] hair. Yet he is a member of the university faculty. You should not bother him about his beard." That said about all there was to say on the topic. There ensued a seven-minute silence.

Later, the host and I are looking at some pictures of Bangladesh that have been saved from the newspaper. The Swami had been in Calcutta at the height of the people's flight from the pogrom and our talking seemed to bring back some memories of this event. He addressed the Consul in Bengali, and before long he was severely scolding the officials he felt were not doing enough to help those affected by the situation. All the Consul could do was sit and take it, as he was not about to defend the government, particularly in the company of an angry holyman.

The hostess, sensing the tension, suggested we all sing, but the Swami said, "No, you sing. I must go. Take me back to the temple; there is much work to be done. You all stay and enjoy this day of celebration." Before anyone could object or otherwise delay the unfolding drama, he was in the shrine room making final pranam before leaving. The Consul drove him back and returned a short while later. Over coffee and dessert we talked about the meaning of our being together.

The final commentary on the subject was drawn from my talk by the Consul: "This is the *satyagraha*, the 'truth power' of Vedanta that brings us into contact with Sri Ramakrishna and the swamis. Let us cherish these moments together like no others." We talked quietly into the night, and, after meditating again, went our separate ways, somewhat the wiser about what makes a sanyasin run. "He has renounced the world, but his compassion is endless," said the host as we parted at the door.

7. MUNDANE PROBLEMS OF THE COSMIC LIFESTYLE

It is an oft-repeated Vedantic maxim that the teacher will bend over backwards to make the student feel happy and satisfied about his or her progress in the spiritual life. Indeed, the *Upanishads* imply such liberality on the part of the preceptor that students of the great seers frequently went away happily with what they took for the highest knowledge, only to return the wiser many years later to have another go at it.[1] On the surface, this may seem like an irresponsible attitude of the gurus, that they will coat the fate of man (viz., death) with a honey-sweetened transcendental wisdom. However, it is really a feature of the overall Hindu cosmology that gives rise to the practices. The idea of dharma (religion, law, duty) carries with it the notion that the *sadhaka* (spiritual seeker) must undergo whatever trials result from his or her *samskaras* (inherent tendencies arising out of actions in this or past lives). In other words, realization will not come until karma (action) is exhausted. Thus, if the student is satisfied with only a preliminary understanding, then there is nothing for the guru to do but support the student's life course. The teachers of the Ramakrishna Order in particular take as their reference the Master's practice of noninterference with his disciple's spiritual tendencies and moods. The Swami is no exception.[2]

Among the members of the cult of Sri Ramakrishna at the temple, sadhana is of a particularly intense sort. Its continuity is a perpetual consideration, as evidenced by the members' frequent reference to the need to constantly "remember God." This means that attitudes, impressions, experiences, and perceptions are translated continually into the spiritual quest. People try to remain constantly in harmony with their goal of realization of their divine ideal.

But what is the measure of realization? References to visions, heightened moods, and transcendental experiences are all regarded with understandable suspicion and are considered secondary to the main goal of spiritual insight. One is left with a single measure, the relationship with the teacher, the Swami. Every encounter with the Swami is an attempt to manifest some evidence of progress in the sadhana, and, from his actions, one can assess one's own degree of attainment.

This means that the definition of the situation when any of the devotees comes into contact with the Swami is one of assessment of their understanding of the goals of spiritual life and of their assimilation of the teachings he has imparted to them. I will describe several typical encounters and thereby shed some light on the kinds of problems faced by devotees which sadhana appears to solve.

My own situation is a case in point. As I said, my role has been far from inconspicuous, as the Swami and I developed a close relationship over the years. Now that I no longer live in Valley City, but in Bay City, some ninety miles away, my trips to the temple are less frequent, but have become more characterized by the aforementioned adjudicative situational definition. On these visits, the Swami routinely discusses with me my work and in what manner I regard it, the frequency and depth of my meditation, and assorted things from child-rearing to temple business, all of which he assesses from the standpoint of my sadhana. At the beginning of our friendship I resolved never to discuss my day-to-day problems with him, as these, according to the Hindu literature, are inappropriate topics to take up with a sadhu. Thus, I inevitably answer his questions about my situation and my spiritual practice in straightforward fashion, to allow the encounter to form itself into the teacher-disciple relationship.

Quite often he will ask only about how hard I am working, about my health, and so on, or he will talk to me about building construction going on at the temple, the problem of root-rot in the walnut orchard, or some other such "worldly" thing. If I try to discuss some aspect of Vedanta, or make a point about what we are discussing by referring to a Vedantic idea or something the Master said, I usually meet with little success. After long years of trying to find a middle ground where we can meet in conversation, I have decided that there isn't any so long as I persist in trying to define the situation. Sometimes I have gone to Swami with a head brimming over with Vedantic ideas or notions of the meaning of one of the Master's parables, only to be instructed in the fine art of extracting crabgrass from the Joshua patch in the garden. At other times, the Swami has listened patiently as I attempt an intricate explanation of why I couldn't come the previous weekend as I had promised, and has given me encouragement to do exactly as I must, which, of course, causes me to wonder what had gone wrong.

The expectations I build up about the visits and the encounters with Swami are seldom fulfilled; rather, they undergo a sometimes profound shock. As close as I am to him and to the scene at the temple, it moves, as it were, according to its own dictates. The Swami is always compassionate and hospitable, but he is not swayed by the vicissitudes and highlights of my fortune. He never interferes, even when I expect him to, although occasionally he lets me know that he had not given his explicit approval for a course of action I have chosen.

One such example of an encounter appears to be sufficiently trivial on the surface, but is nevertheless illustrative of the Swami's relationship with his "disciples." On a recent visit to the temple, I learned of plans devotees were making to attend the dedication of a house in Creighton where some Vedantins were to set up a kind of private retreat for members. Since Valley City devotees would be required to pass fairly near to where I live, I seized upon the opportunity to put into practice the "keeping of holy company" and offer something in return for meals served us by the devotees. Arrangements were made for me to travel to the function with another member, while my wife and son would forego the trip to Creighton and go straight home to Bay City instead. My wife would prepare a light supper for the six or so people who would stop over on their way back home. As I reported to Swami to take my leave, he asked me what arrangements I had made, and whether I would be attending the Creighton function the next day. I described the hows and wherefores of the plan, and, to my surprise, was told by him, "Of course, you are a doctor and may do as you wish."

Knowing that this was a disapproving remark, I asked him, "Should I not have arranged for the devotees to come to my house?"

"You may do as you wish," was his reply.

"Because I am a doctor?" I asked.

"Yes," he answered.

"I thought it would be nice to have the devotees come over and have some light refreshment before going home," I said. "It's reciprocity."

"The purpose is not spiritual. You are likely to engage in idle talk, and the others will be tired for the long drive home. Householders should not approach such things lightly or they will find themselves entangled in maya. But you have a restlessness to do this, so I will not interfere. I am not a doctor." He said this in a manner so somber, as he looked into his teacup and stirred the leaves with his spoon, that I felt very much nonplussed. I left after trying to get out of having the devotees over. I pleaded for his permission to cancel the get-together without avail. The trip to Creighton filled me with apprehension. Once there, he refused to look at me or speak, beyond saying hello.

That night, once the devotees arrived at my house, I was afforded a full-fledged demonstration of my own and the devotees' "worldliness." It was an ordinary social call. Outside the context of the temple, our definition of the situation changed and we sought the common ground of our experiences as members of a wider reference world than that of Vedanta. I was the sociologist, entertaining people with other professional claims. We talked into the night about war, social psychology, the oil depletion allowance, only occasionally finding a place to interject a spiritual matter. When it was over, I felt drained and exhausted, not to mention utterly embarrassed that my motives were so transparent to Swami. At our next encounter, he made no mention of the affair, but did dwell for some time on the fact that all eyes were on us and that we had to, for our own sakes, be the ideal householders. "This is your sanyasa [the stage of renunciation] and you must fulfill it with all your capacity. There can be no slackening or you will fall."

As I said, this is a seemingly trivial incident, but it was serious to the parties involved. Spiritual life, while it involves the unfolding of natural propensities, must be intensified. Heat is applied, as it were, by the teacher, and the ego melts and is transformed into another, more refined, object. I offer the following as another illustration of the kinds of pressures those leading the spiritual life are under, and the ways they have for dealing with it.

A young woman showed up unannounced at a Saturday night class two years ago and was immediately questioned by the Swami about her reasons for coming there. She told him that she had heard of Vedanta and wanted to apply what she could of it to her life to make it more fulfilling. She was a student, working her way through a business course at the state university as a librarian. She had no plan to marry and no boyfriend on the scene.

I recall how, several times in her absence, the Swami wondered aloud about whether she would stay, and if her stay would yield spiritual things. "Most of you," he told us, sweeping his arm before the array of devotees gathered around, "are more concerned with your pet dogs than with sadhana. People are always coming to me saying, 'Oh, Swami, my cat died.' I wonder if this young woman has a cat? Who knows what samskaras are there?"

"She seems very *satvic* [self-possessed in a spiritual sense]," one devotee offered. Another agreed.

"We shall see what happens. I told her to come here and do some work for me," the Swami said. "You will teach her about the kitchen, yes?"

"Yes, Swami," a woman answered.

"We shall see what happens," he said again. "She is searching for something and she feels the need for vairagya (renunciation), but many come who are like this."

Swami may have been referring, in part, to one young woman who had been his closest student, and, he hoped, his first offering to the monastic order's convent. After she had lived with several older women devotees in their house near the temple, a dispute arose and she moved back home. Much to Swami's unhappiness, the young woman refused to attend any function where devotees were present. Although she maintains a relationship with the Swami, seeing him alone on regular occasions and receiving instruction from him, he regards the situation as an example of a spiritual life having taken a wrong turn. And it would seem that he has become cautious about developing hopes for young people to enter the Order, or "renouncing," as this is called.

To continue with the present topic, the young woman was scrutinized in such a fashion for some time, and as the devotees became aware of the Swami's hopes for her, a number of them confided to her that her "place" would be assured by her uncompromising commitment to leading a spiritual life.

Almost immediately after the woman first came to the temple, she was given the responsibility of taking care of Swami's needs, such as stocking the kitchen and tending to its maintenance. Later, Swami taught her the morning worship, which she performs in the temple on certain weekdays. I learned recently (1975) that she had moved into a house near the temple grounds occupied by several women devotees and so is nearing the decision to renounce altogether in favor of the monastic (or convent) life. This progressive involvement in temple activities and her close proximity to the Swami have earned her a certain amount of enmity from devotees protective of the Swami, and, perhaps, of their own self-image as important persons. She is privy to information regarding temple management and an interpreter of the Swami's wishes, which frequently puts her into conflict with those who doubt the validity of her word or assume that she is overstepping her "authority."

An unhappy illustration of the stress experienced by this young woman appears in the following account of a visit I made to the temple in early June 1975. Two householder devotees who normally arrange instruments and music for the Sunday service were away, and I was asked to sing with several others: a householder couple, a young man considering whether to renounce, and the young woman, Swami's helper. On Friday night, our rehearsal went fairly well, and the Swami decided which songs would be sung, their order, and so on, during the flower worship and the lecture.

On Sunday morning, I entered the temple foyer to find the young woman tuning the tanpura to the harmonium. I lent a hand and we sat there tuning up as others arrived. When I suggested we practice a song I was not too familiar with but which I understood we were to sing, the young woman questioned whether we were to sing it, since only the couple who were not present had sung it in the past. I assured her, as did the others, that Swami had told us we were to sing it, not knowing that he had told her otherwise. We went on practicing it, but noticed that she had left. When it became clear that something was amiss, I suggested to my wife that she find her and bring her back, as her voice was missing and songs could not be done well without her. My wife found her in a state reduced to tears. When the Swami approached them, the young woman cursed the couple who had contradicted her suggestion about the song, and said in effect that she could no longer stand anything to do with them. She went on and on about how people harassed her because of her role and the misery it caused her. Finally, the Swami dismissed her, telling her that her outburst was inappropriate no matter what wrong she felt she had suffered.

Then, when the woman of the householder couple heard what was going on, she, too, burst into tears and went home.

"She is a little dictator," said the other woman in reference to the first, as she left. "This is always happening. Just because she spends a lot of time with Swami, she thinks she can manipulate us to do her bidding."

This left three male voices to carry on the singing, and we weren't up to it. The husband went off to phone his wife and coax her into coming back. My wife and I consoled the young woman. By the time the hymns were to be sung, we were all in place. But what had happened turned the music into a struggle. Our voices clashed and were off-key. Swami ended the service without giving us the opportunity to sing the last hymn. Later he said it had slipped by without his notice, and he had ended the service before he remembered we were to sing. To say otherwise would have made us more unhappy than we already

were, and it was probably easy to forget something that
sounded so unpleasant. At any rate, we all were relieved that we
weren't obliged to torture others with our cacophonous sound.

What these illustrations show, I think, is the degree to which
members relate to the Swami as people trying to demonstrate
that they have made progress since the last encounter with him,
which may have been a few minutes, or a few days or weeks,
earlier. This is a central feature of life in the temple and
conditions most other elements of that mode of living. Each
person, of course, brings his or her own unique disposition to
the situation, so there is wide variation in the type of relation
that evolves between the individual and the Swami. Still, the
relation is characterized by an experimental or therapeutic
intensity that focuses on the very being of the person. Am I a
spiritual person? Have I satisfactorily applied the truths imparted to me by the Swami to various facets of my life? Is my
real nature unfolding? Am I deluding myself? These questions
continually confront the conscientious devotee, and form the
basis for participation in temple activities.

Religious life surrounding the temple involves considerable
improvisation and self-direction, albeit within the framework
provided by Vedanta. One does not learn the arts of ritual and
worship without a need to know them, and merely asking to be
initiated into special practices does not assure that it will
happen. Moreover, the Swami is quick to point out that the
worships he performs are not strictly orthodox, but are his own
improvisations on the traditions they come from. Thus, while
erudition in the scripture is rewarded to a certain extent, "mere
knowledge of the Vedas and sacrifices" is not the equivalent of
spiritual realization. Some of the members perform no rituals
and know little about the Vedantic philosophy beyond some
essential points they have picked up over the years. Still, their
lives are considered appropriate to the stated purposes of "realizing God." Each is given what he or she needs and is expected
to follow the teaching to the letter, and one develops self-ana-
lytic schemes to determine how well or poorly one is doing in
the conduct of the sadhana.

NOTES

1. See Swahananda (1965: Chapter 8, Verses 7-12).

2. "Noninterference" means that no conversion is sought. The Swami frequently describes his role as that of "helping the person to attain, through Vedanta, an understanding of his or her own religion."

8. CULTIC CONTEXT AND CORRELATES OF RELIGIOUS EXPERIENCE

In this section, I will describe the inner life of the temple. Thus far I have demonstrated how the members of the Church Universal constitute a mutual reference world. Having shown how the religious definition of the situation is a fundamental part of a constitutive process, I will now turn to the social construction of reality itself by way of an analysis and description of the temple's cultic dimension.

The temple is, on one level, an ongoing organization with a stable structure and a recurrent schedule of events. Its organization consists of a spiritual head, a governing body that handles membership, business, and finances, and a general membership that includes both central and peripheral temple habitués. On another level, the temple is a spiritual order for people pursuing a full-time religious life. Besides the monastic quarters for monks and apprentices located on the premises, other full-time spiritual aspirants, including men and women, some married and some single, frequent the temple and participate regularly in its activities.

Public events at the temple carried out by the membership form one array of social contexts. Sunday flower worship, followed by the Swami's lecture, Wednesday night class on Vedanta, and the Saturday night class on the teachings of Sri Ramakrishna and his disciples contain their own modes of social reality, and the members define them in special ways that create a particular mood and ambience. The image I see in the socially projected definition of the public events is one of a neo-Hindu church, which has succeeded in being assimilated into the American cultural stream. There is a high degree of stylized and situationally enacted social consciousness evidenced in the talk of members about what others will think if "Hindu" religious themes are displayed too prominently. At public events, the decorum is low-key and the intellectual tone rational. In terms of the religious presentation, there is a kind of cultural universalist framework that supports the Vedantic claim to be the philosophical and theological home of all religions.

This image of normalcy and institutional solidity enables the temple inhabitants and members to coexist with the middle-class residential neighborhood in which the temple is located. Its neatly trimmed lawns, the rows of linden trees, and the architectural styling of the buildings gives the temple a park- or campus-like appearance from inside the grounds and a residential appearance from without. Members dress fairly conservatively, if informally. The monastic inhabitants themselves project a singular image of straightness, while there is a fair cross-section of social images and types represented among the general membership. These would include, again, hippies, Indians, working-class people, young middle-class couples, older middle-class couples, and older single women. Their interaction at public events is governed by the definition of the situation as "church," so those in attendance can draw on familiar cultural practices to guide their participation. Care is taken to present Vedanta in a way that will make it seem relevant to the general public, and to avoid shocking the unwary with references to peculiarly non-American ideas and motifs.

Which is not to say that the shared reference world of temple denizens and friends is middle-class in its entirety, with adherence to social convention a prominent feature of situational performances by actors. Another array of social contexts, the semi-formal, nonpublic events, focus more intently on Hindu spiritual culture and its themes and traditions. Again, these events include a Vespers service on Sunday evenings, a Wednesday morning class in the temple library, and special worships conducted on the holy days of Christianity, Buddhism, and

Hinduism. Building dedications and celebrations like the Swami's birthday are included in this class of contexts.

Semi-formal private events are attended by a self-selected subgroup of the general membership, consisting of, at the most, twenty out of a total of one hundred twenty-five. At these events the situation is relatively free from the self-imposed incumbrances of integrative, rational thought, so a more "vertical" direction to religious behavior emerges. At these events, people are more likely to sit cross-legged on the floor (especially in the temple), or to display emotions, such as "happiness" or "love" (as evidenced in the laughter and exchanges between and among Swami and the devotees). In these contexts, the mood is much more clearly that of celebration, albeit within a meditative framework. Devotion is more prominently displayed, as are tales and lore of India. Sometimes, though, these semi-formal private events don't appear too different in character from the more subdued public events, and, occasionally, public events (specifically Wednesday and Saturday classes) are transformed into contexts whose dramatic valence is Hindu and mystical.

There is a good deal of "porosity"[1] between these two general types of contexts, and I have attempted to differentiate them only so that the picture of multiple overlapping reference worlds and situational definitions can be given its proper shading. On the one hand, there is the theme of cultural pluralism, represented by the Hindu/American religious institution. Its integrative theology seeks a meeting ground between Eastern and Western values and thought. Members who subscribe to such ideas still can define getting exposed to them as "attending church." Such contexts have a specific time and place with well-defined parameters.

On the other hand, the less-formal contexts are cultic, and contain most of the non-Western aspects of religion. Here the members emphasize the immediate experience of events that take place outside public view. But since members of the larger "public" congregation are occasionally present, there remains a distinctive interplay between the rational and the arational (or "other" rational), an interplay which is articulated through the ongoing construction of the event.

Such "contexts" are really nothing more than spontaneous interactions between and among the Swami and his intimate devotees in everyday life at the temple. The recurrent patterns of the interactions, and the degree of sharing of a mutual religious experience among the interactants, together form the basis of the temple's cult, which can be viewed as an "event."

The cult has very unspecific social parameters. Different people who seldom interact can be cult adherents. Moreover, some who by virtue of proximity appear to be members of the cult (for instance, several of the monks) are not, while some who claim membership in an inner circle (for instance, newcomers who come to regard themselves as the Swami's favorite disciples) are only provisional members of recognized novice status. Some cult members have asocial attitudes toward the others, relating as much as possible to the Swami alone. Others vacillate between membership and nonmembership. Indeed, membership may be an inappropriate category into which to place participation, so it will be of sociological value to examine how the cult views itself and what it is from the standpoint of its central focus. To do this will require a discussion of the inner logic of the Vedantic religious experience as it is expressed by devotees and the Swami in the cultic context. In the course of highlighting the elements of belief and value, together with the normative features of cult life, I will show how other contexts (the aforementioned public and private events) inhere in the cultic definition of the situation and vice versa. My purpose in describing the inventory of religious life in the inner temple is sociological inasmuch as I am concerned with showing how the inner dynamics of the religion in dialogue with outer structural forms create what Vedanta essentially is. Through my own participation in the cult, I will attempt to set forth a cognitive sociology of the temple's social reality and its relation to the human experience termed "spiritual."

THE RATIONALE OF THE EXPERIENCE

If the search for spiritual meaning is about any one thing in Vedanta, it is meditation. In the temple, the term "meditation" carries with it a dual meaning. First, there is the process of sitting down and doing the act (or a series of similar ones) which I will presently describe. This is what people are normally referring to when they use the term. "That was a good meditation," or "Let's go meditate," or "I wasn't able to meditate last night due to my cold," etc., are statements that make it an *act or process.* Meditation is also a *state,* a particular attainment, a special kind of reality, which is the outcome of a long process of spiritual inquiry. The Sanskrit term *dhyana* is a reference to this state of attainment of another reality, although not an *other* one. The phrase, "To be in meditation" means having "ascended that loftiest spiritual height described in the Vedanta and in the lives of spiritual giants," as I've heard members say. Only the Swami is qualified to speak in terms of meditation's higher meaning, although others allude to it, as the *outcome* of the process, or the act, of meditating. Of course, the Swami makes no direct, formal claims for himself, either, because he is a sanyasin and that claim is not for himself but for the Self. Concomitantly, anyone making claims for having attained to dhyana is automatically assumed to be exaggerating one's worth, because to say "I" is to deny the Self.

In the temple cult, a person is "dead to the world," and indeed this probably applies to the wider church-associated group: All acts, whether mundane or extraordinarily spiritual, are intentionally meditative in the sense of its second, occult meaning. People try to keep themselves in a "higher state" even when they are, say, working or doing ordinary tasks; thus they seem to comport themselves in a special manner. The Swami calls this comportment by a number of names including "Satvica" (possessed of the quality of *sattva,* or spirituality), "indrawn" (unaroused by external phenomena, including thoughts extraneous to the religious focus), "deep" (not prone to surface agitations), "high" (above worldly matters), and so on. Needless to say, perhaps, these terms are highly charged with value and affect and so contain the force of an imperative, both moral—in the sense of being what one should do—and existential—in the sense of being what one is ostensibly doing by being in the temple's and the Swami's spiritual orbit in the first place.

While this does not explain how the devotees and other members of the spiritual community present themselves in everyday life, it does place a valence on my observations of them, a valence that I can use to illustrate "where someone is at," though their specific "place" and how they got there are not known. I have mentioned how people sit erect at Sunday lectures with their eyes closed or else fixed on the shrine or on the speaker; how they attempt to exclude from their repertoire of responses any that would betray a concern on their part for anything other than spiritual reality itself; how, indeed, their holiness is something that they have cultivated into a posture vis-à-vis others and the specific contexts in which others are encountered. I have variously characterized this as sober, meditative, withdrawn, and so on. However, none of these terms quite describes it, so I will attempt the description from another angle.

Perhaps meditation can be likened to a kind of therapeutic practice that is ongoing. Even when one is not "meditating" (in the sense of performing the act) one is between meditations, as it were. Meditation is the reference point for whatever locus experience has at any given time, since it is through the meditative state (in the sense of dhyana) that spiritual reality becomes known to the meditator.

All of the Swami's classes, lectures, and private instructions are full of references, both direct and indirect, to meditation (as action and as a particular level of spiritual attainment). And members of the temple cult meditate as much as possible. In addition, though, during such times as they are not actually sitting down and going through the step-by-step process taught them by the Swami, they relate to everyday life as though the phenomena which inhere in it are extraordinary. In other words, to employ the language of phenomenology, they suspend belief in commonsense aspects of everyday life and treat things in a special way. Part of this treatment involves construction of a spiritual edifice out of their lives' epiphanies, and in part it involves a systematic disavowal of anything that seems out of place. There are several methods in Indian religion. One involves systematically negating the world and its effects. Another involves spiritualizing the world. Still another involves combining these "negative" and "positive" approaches and achieving what the Swami calls "harmony." This latter "method" is the way of the cult.

THE CULT

A member usually enters into the cultic focus of the Church Universal through the religious movement which its exemplars established and presently maintain. By attending meetings and lectures, and by communicating with the Swami about one's interest in the pursuit of the type of religious life promoted by the Vedanta movement, one can acquire a basic understanding of the immediate concerns of the people in the temple who are involved in everyday spiritual practices. To gain access to the cult, one's orientation to spiritual life must be more developed than, say, mere intellectual or natural curiosity, for in order to "do" yoga, a person must connect "studying" it with practicing its core value, which is that yoga must exclude whatever the aspirant hopes to gain from doing it. Yoga must, in other words, be motiveless in order to bring spiritual results; its ultimate misuse, according to the Swami, being embodied in the pursuit of physical health, beauty, wealth, occult powers, and the rest.

In the cult, yoga practice serves cognitively, existentially, and socially to insulate its adherents against the irony that is implicit in doing spiritual (yogic) practices without thought of a reward. For the adept, yoga is no mere *device* for keeping the body trim or the mind fit for whatever life, from the everyday to the cosmic levels, holds in store for one; rather, yoga *is* life. And it is simultaneously the vehicle by which life is borne, the encoding device through which the perceiving of life is accomplished, and the accumulated effect of its own manifestation in the person, for better or worse. This latter aspect is vital, as it alludes to the yogic way of being-in-the-world. How to be a yogi . . . the way is the cult and its teaching.

At the beginning of the spiritual search, the focus of the devotee is that of bhakti yoga. From the standpoint of the Vedantic movement, bhakti is defined as devotion to God by means of serving humankind. God is in man, so service to man is devotion to God. The more one serves man, the closer one is to God. The rationale for this approach is contained in the Vedanta (by serving the atman in the individual, one can attain the cosmic consciousness, Brahman), the *Bhagavad-Gita* (by serving man one serves Krishna), and in the teachings of Vivekananda (who emphasized the pluralism, universalism and humanism of religions when he brought yoga to the West at the turn of the century).[2] From the standpoint of the cult in the temple, bhakti means the "love of God" and service to the cult heroes Sri Ramakrishna, Holy Mother Sarada Devi, Swami Vivekananda, and their disciples, along with *other* gods, goddesses, and the sacred knowledge their "presence" symbolizes. Within the cult, the deities are *living* reality. Their continuous worship—an ongoing process since the period of Sri Ramakrishna's preceptorship (1870-1886)—provides continuity in the form of a living link to the ancient Hindu past (inasmuch as Ramakrishna had visions of various Hindu deities), and hence access to the *devas* and *devis* (gods and goddesses) that give Hinduism its mythic character. The power of the cult's definition of the situation, then, is a by-product of the *continuity of worship,* and of the *dynamic interaction,* in special contexts, between the worshippers and the object of their focus. In the cult, bhakti loses its instrumental character; the adherents have succeeded in making bhakti something that is done for its own sake. The "instruments" of worship, from camphor to the enshrined portraits of the cult's incarnate gods, endowed as they are with the collectively objectified sacred means to spiritual realization, *act on* the worshippers. If He (or She) is so disposed, the object of religious focus "accepts" the devotees' offering; there is no mechanical certainty in bhakti. The cultic idea is that in one's own yogic power lies strength to adhere to the path, but it is through the power of the religious object that one reaches the path's end.

That the end—the goal of religion—is always at hand in the cultic context is given in the inner logic of Hindu religious experience. The gods, the objects of ritual, and the devotees are Brahman. But, as the Swami often says, "God is in everything but nothing is in God," which in the cultic context has a special meaning. This, the vivid presence of our experience, especially when involving infusion of the felt sense of the co-presence of the divine through worship, *is* the God-consciousness already there—that is, *here.* To enter into the cult means, phenomenologically, to share in the experience of bhakti, the simultaneous devotion to and infusion of the power of the divine focus. To outsiders, bhakti appears to be a "method," or a theology requiring positive affirmation in experience via "moods," "psychic-emotional states," and the like. But from inside the cult, bhakti is God, transformed into an interaction between the worshipper and the object of worship, and the feelings and experiences (the "spirit") which that interaction evokes.

The principles of Vedanta, the anecdotes, stories, and parables told by the Swami, and important constituents of the cultic focus, are translated into principles, precepts, and logic by the religious adepts. The sum of these principles is in dynamic tension with the cult. By rationalizing the cult, they subdue it; by relying on the cult for direction, they help animate it. The net effect is a kind of static movement that is perpetually impelled forward but remains in place. The verbal articulation of the movement, though ostensibly scientific, is in terms of the dynamic of the cultic response, so it remains fundamentally arational. Without the cult of its practice, Vedanta is another system among systems, a dry philosophy, as they say. To be sure it is universal, nearly presuppositionless and synthetic. Considering Vedanta as a movement, however, these characteristic features are obviated by the cult's power to evoke the particular. As a philosophical system, Vedanta has a trans-divine focus, Brahman.[3] As a movement, it has a divine focus, bhakti.

To enter the cult, to know the meaning of the Vedanta movement, requires initiation. Preparation for initiation, the outcome of initiation, and the initiation itself are themselves part of the religious experience.

I mentioned that curiosity was insufficient grounds to be admitted to the cult. Nor can one purchase a ticket. One's candidacy is approved or disapproved by the Swami, who, by a series of questions and tests, adjudicates the performance of the aspirant. In some branches of the Church Universal, I have heard of people who have waited years for initiation only to be told, in one case, that it would never happen, and in another, that it already had happened in a dream the person had. By inquiring about the situation at hand during public events, one can learn how to be considered for initiation. Sometimes people will even inquire of one whose presence at public events has been noticed whether initiation has taken place, whereupon the person can find out what initiation means if he or she doesn't already know.[4]

So far as I can tell, the decision to initiate the person is an adjudicated one, but the Swami's criteria are known only to him. Getting to know the Swami usually happens after one has caught his attention by being present. One shakes hands with the Swami and gives his name. Perhaps he will be asked his occupation, or whether he has been to the Church Universal before. He might be invited into the Swami's office for a chat, although this usually happens some time after the introduction has taken place. If the person is unkempt or acts in a manner unbecoming the temperate timbre of the monastic surroundings, he will be given, in the Swami's inimitable Bengali pointedness, some basic instruction in the ideals of cleanliness and manners. This sometimes constitutes a test. If the person gets uptight, and, as once happened, feels miniskirts are okay to wear around the temple grounds, or argues with members about proper Vedantic comportment, the Swami simply ignores the person until he or she goes away, or encourages them to try religious life elsewhere, in which case the effect is the same. Others might be asked why they are there. If the answer sounds like something the Swami can deal with, then the conversation may go further, or the person may simply be encouraged to come again. Perhaps the Swami will take down their name and telephone number and give them a call. In the monthly bulletin, people are encouraged to contact the Swami about spiritual instruction. Many do so.

The initial encounters with the Swami are a kind of test of the newcomer's interest in Vedanta and in personal spiritual growth. If the person resists the Swami's questioning or objects to rules of decorum, then he fails the test. Some hang around to try again. A few come to define the temple (and Vedanta) as the final stop on the road to God. People usually begin their quest in some other religious atmosphere and then, after becoming disillusioned or dissatisfied, they land on the temple's doorstep, in a manner of speaking. By this time they may have an inkling of what spiritual religion is, or what Vedanta is about, or how to approach a sanyasin for instruction. At the temple, in exchange for instruction in Vedanta and spiritual inquiry, they must vow to stick with the search. Even if they are wholly ignorant of Hindu culture, it doesn't matter. The Vedantic plurality of religious paths will allow them to plug in from where they are. Gradually, they will see that there is something more to it than this and will petition the Swami to give them individual instruction.

In the dialogue with the Swami, he adjudicates the aspirant's qualifications for initiation into the study of Vedanta. From verbal rebuffs, being ignored, being teased, getting encouragement, or engaging in apparently innocuous discussions about seemingly worldly matters, one learns the terms of the arrangement.

NOTES

1. Smart (1973) justifies the use of phenomenology on the basis of the "porosity" of the total picture of religion.

2. Rolland (1965) has an analysis of the movement's service ideal as arising out of bhakti yoga.

3. *Brahman* is discussed in Chapter 10.

4. The terms of sadhana are never made publicly known because it is believed that each person's capacities and inclinations are variable and unique.

9. THE SHRINE AND AN INITIATION

The Swami told us to construct a small shrine—preferably, though not necessarily, in a room where only meditating and devotional acts would be performed. We were instructed to view the shrine as a place where God resides and where we were to witness the unfolding of our true divine identities. "The shrine is a representation," he said, "of the throne of one's *ishta-nista* which resides in the devotee's heart. But it is not merely symbolical. A vibration of spirituality remains there and the devotee may partake of it whenever spiritual practices are going on."

I had seen—indeed, observed—over a three-year period, how some devotees relate to their shrine and what the shrine contains, and so on. Temple shrines, of course, are much more massive, though not necessarily more elaborate. Household shrines are usually small, portable affairs, perhaps containing tiers, which are structured in some sort of hierarchical, symmetrical fashion. Pictures, statues, water container, incense holder, flowers in vases, plates and bowls, food containers, and assorted personal items valued by the devotee are carefully arranged on the usually wooden, sometimes cloth-over-wood surface areas of the construction. Quite a lot of shrines I have seen were actually built by devotees—that is, sketched and assembled. It also seems customary to simply procure a suitable

table, shelf, chest, or other piece of furniture that is then adapted to the purpose of representing the meaning of the spiritual undertaking.

The Swami told us that the shrine is closely associated with the undertaking of the bhakta. One worships divine forms there; the shrine is a kind of stage on which the interaction between the Chosen Ideal and the devotee—Bhagavan and bhakta—is an ongoing phenomenon, from which one aspires to spiritual perfection.

We would travel the path of bhakti, he had told us previously when we informed him of our choice for our spiritual ideal. Now he gave us a framed photograph of an avatara—God in human form—for whom the shrine was to be constructed. The Swami said he would later on initiate us into a special form of meditation, giving us the mantra (sound form) of our ideal. This meditation and mantra would be with us so long as we were on the path of the devotee. Using it in conjunction with the shrine, we would attain our divine natures. The Swami admonished us to follow his instructions in spirit and letter, adding that one could not treat the matter of the shrine—ideal and devotee in intimate contact with one another—lightly and succeed in attaining anything. Renunciation was required, though not external renunciation consisting in "flight from the world." We were to keep the company of the holy, avoiding contact, if possible, with those who viewed spiritual life with suspicion or disgust. Our lives were to be arranged so that we cultivated a feeling of love toward our ideal. "The Chosean Ideal is your constant companion, your mother, father, friend and spouse. You must look after the ideal once God is invited into your home."

The shrine, he pointed out, is both a thing and a place. It is an object of special importance, but it is also where something resides, where something recurs. We were enjoined to undertake an examination of that "something" through the private study of Vedanta and attending lectures and classes. Simultaneously, work in the world was to be undertaken without thought of reward. Our dharma as householders was clear: "Life's duties must be met with cheerfulness and efficiency," he said. "Understand them to be of the same spiritual substance as the shrine in your home."

We had seen and more or less become familiar with how the shrine, as the center of home life around which the daily routine revolves, is always treated in a special manner by devotees. In temples (we are talking about temples in America), various degrees of relation to the shrine as a manifestation of some form of divinity, or as a place where a living deity resides, exist. The attitudes and feelings associated with the bhakti religion are continually cultivated in the context of such "representations," as the Swami called them. In some places, the enshrined divinity is fed, clothed, bathed, and otherwise treated as living in addition to being worshipped as a "divine symbol." In homes, considerable variations on the theme of worship exist. Some of these variations are surely extemporizations, in the sense of being actions conditioned by involvement in Hindu religion, but not necessarily Hindu. They are Hindu-like or neo-Hindu, coming as they do in the context of bhakti, and they make for considerable heterogeneity in the overall American Hindu stream when coupled with the various forms of bhakti religion that have been transplanted from India. In all, much attention is focused on shrines by people who are into Indian religion. Interaction between devotee and enshrined deity transforms homes into ashramas (religious hermitages), and the shrine thus serves its purpose of providing the gateway through which the seeker is to enter the "City of Brahman."

If there were space enough in the house, the Swami told us, a shrine room should be set up. A room devoted solely to spiritual practices is preferable to one that the shrine must share with some worldly activity that goes on there. In addition he told us that the *asana* before the shrine is an important place of spiritual power and must not be subjected to nonspiritual contamination, lest the vibrations established there by the devotee during his practice be disturbed. We were also told that in selecting a place we should attend to how well we were able to meditate there, and how it felt to us. If it was heavily trafficked, it would not do: "The shrine should not be seen by those who are not devotees."

The Swami went on to say that there is an "instrumental" reason for having the shrine. It facilitates the devotee's reorganization of his life around spiritual practices which lead him to the goal, the "Supreme," as he put it. "And what is the goal?"

he asked, rhetorically. "To realize God," he answered. "But
God is not just one's own personal conception of the Divine,
although different moods and temperaments associate different
imagery with God. God is Brahman, and you are not different
from That. Your ideal is a manifestation of that Brahman. Cling
to the lotus feet of your ideal and you will be led to that
experience, first of intimacy with Bhagavan, and then to the
highest nondual experience of the Absolute."

The Swami spoke to us in the most endearing fashion. "If
you are not now doing so regularly, you should begin meditating twice a day, an hour or so each time. Morning and
evening. You will be initiated soon. In the meantime cultivate
love for the Lord. Attachments to worldly things will fall away
naturally. Concentrate now on organizing your sadhana. Attend
worship here when you can. Join one of the classes, on the
Uphanishads or on the teachings of the Master. Nothing need be
forced. There is no hurry. You can't make the experience come
any faster than is natural for yourselves. Already you have
become weary of the impermanent things of this world, and
you have been awakened to the possibility of discovering something else, more permanent. The path you undertake is no
mechanical device. Your own *shraddha* [inner conviction] can
carry you without your having to do anything extraordinary.
The shrine should be simple. Put a flower there; burn an
incense; light a candle. Then sit quietly and think of the Master.
He will come into your shrine."

I understood the shrine to be simultaneously immanent and
transcendant. God was there, but neither in the sense that the
picture was god, nor in the sense that the picture represents or
stood for the idea of God. The picture of the avatar—that is, the
photograph—is a likeness that harbors in the devotee's lexicon
evocative and provocative meaning. On the one hand, the focus
of religious attention is on the object of worship. But at the
same time the focus is moving in the direction, as it were, of a
trans-divine object, one for which no object exists or idea stands
as such, not even "symbolically," as it were. The divine object
(God with attributes—such as law-giver, savior, playmate, and so
on) and the trans-divine object (God without attributes—e.g.,
Brahman), interplay with one another and create in the bhakta's

consciousness a simultaneous microscopic and macro-*cosmic* awareness of his place in between these two polar religious tensions. On one level, the images are a device to help the aspirant to arouse spiritual feelings of "love" for the ideal. On another level, the images are "living gods," particles of the ideal toward which one maintains a continuous attitude of devotion. On still another level, the shrine, its deities, and the aspirant are themselves Brahman, the one without a second, as the *Veda* says.

This is the integrative approach, that of the Master, Sri Ramakrishna, who evoked classical Hindu practices by declaring the fundamental plurality of religious paths, the Swami informed me. There is no need for ostentation, whether by yours or anyone else's conversion. "The path of bhakti is ideally suited to the fundamentally emotional temperament of man," the Swami said, "but the paths of wisdom, work, and yoga are there, too. When the devotee loves God to perfection, he possesses wisdom, works with detachment, and practices communion with God." And so on.

AN INITIATION

We were told to spend the day meditating and fasting. At around four we were to shower, put on clean clothes and trundle off to the temple with fruit offering and *chadar* in hand for our seven o'clock rendezvous. It had been explained to us by the Swami that the auspiciousness of the occasion was such that he should like to initiate us. The date, December 20, 1970, was the birthday of Sri Sarada Devi, the wife of Sri Ramakrishna. We arrived at six-thirty and were greeted in front of the temple by the Swami. He told us to hand him the fruit and remove our wraps. After doing so, we were ushered into the temple library, where a few other persons were standing about. After a moment's absence the Swami returned and escorted us to the foyer of the temple auditorium, where two rows of folding chairs had been arranged to face the auditorium doors and where six or so people sat looking straight ahead, shoulders draped with their white shawls. The Swami showed us to two seats he had apparently intended us to sit in beforehand. He admonished us to sit quietly and think of the spiritual nature of the occasion.

After sitting about ten or fifteen minutes, the Swami instructed the group to enter the temple auditorium through the double doors, and sit in the same relative position as in the foyer on the platform in front of the temple shrine. I was seated immediately to his left, cross-legged, holding a list he had given me containing seven items. He had told me to say one to him each time he signaled during the ceremony.

The Swami lit candles on the shrine after sprinkling Ganges water on his head, and said a few mantras. Then he meditated. At the end of his meditation, he sang a Sanskrit hymn. Complete quiet pervaded the temple. The normally fidgety devotees were still. The Swami appeared engrossed in his act. As he explained at length the spiritual meaning of receiving a mantra, what the mantra is, he periodically signaled me to read the next item on the list. The items corresponded to the parts of the meditation process he was teaching us. After explaining the entire process two or three times (using exactly the same words each time, or so it seemed to me), he asked us to return to our seats in the foyer and continue meditating until we were called by him to receive the mantra proper.

Several of the older members whom I recognized as having been long associates of the temple were called first. After a wait of around fifteen minutes I was called, together with my wife, to enter the shrine.

We padded quietly toward the altar and made pranam. Then we sat cross-legged on the carpet in front of the shrine next to the Swami's seat. He uttered Vedic mantras, and we listened in silence. Then he spoke to us for a few moments in quiet tones about the need for persistence in the practice of sadhana, and encouraged us with kind words about our latent spirituality. Then he told us to prepare our minds for the receiving of the mantra. We were to try to experience the divine nature of the event and suspend all doubts we may have about any aspect of our undertaking.

I had been meditating in this way for perhaps two minutes when he uttered several sounds into my ear. At first I was not fully cognizant of the fact that it had been the mantra. I had drifted off into a somnambulent mood watching the candlelight illumine the lower lashes of my eyes. But at the same time, there was no doubt. And I had the distinct impression that it was something extraordinary, but at the same time appropriate to that particular mood at that occasion, which had a familiar "ring."

He repeated the mantra three times, pausing between each utterance and looking intently at me. Then with a gesture he indicated he wanted me to repeat it back to him, which I did. He seemed pleased and undertook the same process with my wife.

Then he told us that it was part of his dharma as a sanyasin to take on the karma of the initiates. After chanting again, he leaned forward and clasped my head with his hands. When he had done so to my wife, he told us to offer the fruit and flowers we had brought for the occasion to him as a "representative" of the Supreme Guru, Brahman.[1] When we had finished, he told us to sit quietly for a few moments, make pranam, and return to the foyer where we were to continue to repeat the mantra.

I didn't realize how high I was until I tried to walk. In about ten minutes, I had gotten as high as I've ever been on the several ritual events I've seen since. I wasn't exactly sure where I was, or whether I still had a body. Swami's words telling me to call in the next two initiates helped me to get oriented. I clung to chairs and rocked somewhat precariously down the central aisle of the temple to the foyer. Once there, I had forgotten the names of the next people. Fortunately they knew who they were, because someone went into the shrine. For the next hour or so I drifted in and out of this feeling of being high, repeating the mantra until something distracted me from concentrating on it.

The point of receiving a mantra and being "zapped," as some call it, by the Swami is the ready access it provides to the religious experience. As a semi-therapeutic device, it is intended to help "clear away the dust from the shining mirror of the atman within." The devotee repeats it until it becomes a habit and is "going on" without conscious effort or thought. The mantra is the essence of the guru's teaching of the disciple; the rest is considered ancillary and dispensable.

The primal mantra in Hinduism and Vedanta is Om, the sound form of the attributeless Brahman. Om is said to contain everything; it is the *logos* and the *noumena* in one. Other mantras include portions of the *Vedas;* still others, sounds and words "arising out of the contemplation of saints, sages and seers."

Not only does receiving a mantra provide one with a means to a "vertical" sort of experience which can be had on command, but it represents a commitment to the teacher, who, having assumed responsibility for the disciple's actions, stands to be harmed by misdeeds and backsliding. The contour of the initiation event plainly displayed the contractual character of the exchange. A dramatic representation of commitment and responsibility, together with a peek at the meaning of religious life (i.e., getting high on the intensity), together with the devotee's disposition of receptivity and acceptance, produce in him or her the full effect of transformation. In the course of sadhana, the teacher explains what the transformation means as it more fully evolves.

SPIRITUAL IDENTITY

To see the transformation in its manifest form is to see enactments of special values and attitudes. The swamis of the Ramakrishna Order, as do the swamis with other roots, frequently give their devotees Sanskrit names. Receiving a name is a sort of bonus given to the initiate. It enables the person to give new meaning to the self in religious milieu and mental set. The name, the Swami says, is not something he just gives out. Rather, it comes to him in meditation, when he thinks about the inclinations of the person and some of his traits. Its conferral requires no ritualization of the act, though its significance is far-reaching. I received mine over the phone shortly after the Swami had returned from a six-month trip through Europe to India. In the Himalayas, he said, he had an "intuition" about my spiritual identity and had come up with one of the names of Shiva. My Sanskrit name is a kind of ill-kept secret, used by the Swami and by a few of the people close to him, unless "the public" is around, in which case I am "Dr." Others use both their given names and their Sanskrit names, depending on who is around. Indeed, the name confers upon the devotee an identity that is ready-made in the myths and legends surrounding the god or goddess to whom the name belongs. In other religious settings, I have observed the use of the name as a device for claiming a distinctive status, particularly when one has gone through a kind of "conversion." In the Valley City temple, however, the name is a part of the expressive symbolism that the devotee takes with him or her into the cultic focus, or dons during private practices, or in the Swami-devotee interaction. Since Vedantins are actively discouraged from affecting the *accoutrement* of Hindu lifestyles (particularly dress), and are instead enjoined to carry out such practices as are directly relevant to the sadhana, "the name should not be used casually," and *is not* used, as far as I have been able to find out, by members when they are not in the company of other devotees, or otherwise outside their "private" social worlds. Still, the meaning of the name has a social property because it helps the person to insulate his or her perceived separateness and distinctiveness from the world, and through cultivation of the mythic and yogic chracteristics associated with it, enables the devotee to remain firm in the commitment to the spiritual search.

Thus, using the name, one enters into the meditative life and simultaneously divests oneself of the commonsense awareness that accompanies the development of the biographic subjectivity in one's ordinary, named identity. Spiritual personhood has been acknowledged in the naming. One has a new identity. So being named marks a transition point, a step further along the way from the mantra initiation on which the naming more or less establishes cloture.

More will be said about identity later on. Now I will attempt a description of a meditation, preceded by a reduction of the main themes that appear in it.

NOTE

1. This part of the ceremony is known as *guru dakshina*.

10. PHENOMENOLOGY OF MEDITATION

The idea of Brahman is essentially that of primordial givenness, and the idea of maya is that of the contrivance, a facsimile of Brahman that is constructed once the spontaneous living fulfillment of this insight into the transcendent ground of Being is past. In all its fullness—of meaning, of being, of consciousness— Brahman is embodied as maya, and the "de-ontological" mode of returning to the original self-evident state lies in a phenomenological reduction, a return to that state which can be no object for any other thing.[1]

The advaitic neti neti is no mere *method* which has as the object of its outcome the attainment of a thing called a "goal." It veritably *is* the outcome, method, object, and its own attainment—simultaneously. It forms the groundless ground of givenness, uttered in exclamatory profundity, at the dawn of the original insight into the thing itself, that unconstituted, transcendent, Absolute "one without a second."

Its axio-neotic discovery is that we dwell in absolute, spontaneous Being, with or without the capital B, and in this fundamental state lies the constitutive subjectivity known as self. Though we did not have to try to get here, we are always moving in that direction. We are already here, but we experience coming and going in order to get to where here is. I am here now, but did not come from anywhere else. I may go over there, but I am always here. This "place," the here-and-now, is the one experience of myself that defies "subration."[2] When thus reduced to the self-evident givenness of the here-and-now, my consciousness appears filled with the mere play of its own intentionality. There is nothing else, or, rather, there need not be because Being is, and I cannot escape that solitary fact.

But the very fact of Being imprisons consciousness within the "I" of my experience of myself, for in experiencing myself as my *self*, I negate Being (because the self cannot be an object of my consciousness and still remain *my* self). Thus, the "I" of experience, that intimate "me" of all my thoughts, feelings and desires, of my biography and my essential existence, remains an untranscendable transcendent, and herein lies the infinite "anxiety" of my world-experiencing life, an anxiety escapable only through the negation of my negated being.

Selfhood as the Being of negated being—my ego—has both a positive and negative existence (or a positive nonexistence and a negative nonexistence), and the struggle between the two is the essence of my life-world. Once this essence has been encoded and distilled into a series of archetypal objects of consciousness (such as form the images and symbols during meditation), it has attained the status in my new existence that "common sense" had in my old one. It is the new, *seeming* familiar of my everyday life, the enzyme that digests the world and permeates my personal existence. It is also a potential new source of anxiety. Thus, one literally needs a guide.

It is said that to practice correctly one whit of the *sanatana dharma* (Eternal Religion—i.e., Hinduism) would be to realize the ultimate goal of all life. A single glimpse of Brahman brings instant, total illumination, since Brahman is never only partly known. As limitless knowledge, it is the "thought beyond the thought of thoughtlessness," so all is subrated by it. This groundless ground is that reality connecting the ends of this time/space/matter/energy (maya) to our mind, senses and experience.

According to Vedanta I am that "Om," that primordial assent, the one. But the "I" that recognizes this becomes, in the very process of recognition, separated (a dweller in a body). Somehow the world has my body to the same degree that I have it, and at times there is contention. The interplay of inertia, intellect, and intuition form the screen of my maya, and I see myself animated thereupon as a projection. I follow its images through samsara (relative existence) to Satchidananda—existence-consciousness-bliss—the All in All. Put Vedantically, therein there is not *this*, nor *that*, nor maya nor perception of "consciousness."

In sum, human being, given even odds, is still a tricky business. It arises, say the modern phenomenologists and existentialists in various fields of psychology, psychiatry, social and political theory, etc., from the primal consciousness of at once being and having a body while in the womb, but then being unable after birth to return to that state of nondual self-sufficiency. Once recognition of nonduality is attained, one is "ripe" for initiation into the practice of sadhana. And as I have shown, Vedanta has an analogue in these modern conceptions of self and world and is the matrix of their interrelation.

A DRAMATURGICAL PORTRAIT OF THE REDUCED RITUAL ENACTMENT

I approach the shrine for meditation, having done the necessary preliminaries. I touch my forehead to the platform. I take the asana. Sitting cross-legged, I mentally call forth "peace" and send it to all quarters. I mentally salute the absolute Brahman, all the incarnations, saints, sages, and seers, the chosen ideal, the devotees, believers in truth, the atman, and again Brahman, "wherein all truths meet." I mentally pray to those deities assembled on the shrine. The prayer sometimes goes, Om, may this meditation set before me the truth. May I realize my highest nature in this meditation. May I enter into the Lord's abode by this meditation. May the Lord grant me, the devotee, a glimpse at the highest reality.

I breathe in through the right nostril, repeating Om a number of times. Then I exhale through the left nostril with an equal repetition. As I breathe in, I engage the *prana* flowing through my right nostril and send a "vibration of purity" through the nervous systems of the body as the prana enters. As I breathe out, I cleanse the body of "impurities" through another vibration. After the mind has begun to settle down and the body is relaxed, the inner world is filled with a projection on the screen of being, the indivisible Satchidananada. I often utilize the

Om-kara (sound Brahman) and the mental image of an ocean in the initial stage of this process. Then I drift somewhat according to the currents that arise in the mental stream. The dross of the mind, images, minutia, fade out into the macrocosm losing their form. Borne by Om, eventually, automatically, I am doing *japa,* repeating the mantras given me by the Swami. The nondual has become a reflexive duality. The mind repeats the mantra. As I look on the mantra turns *on* the mind, and feelings become "uplifted," as it were. There is visualization involved here, too. The shrine, whether, in one's home, in the temple or in Belur Math (the Order's headquarters) is the ground of the whole experience. In front of one's shrine one enacts the essential identity between the devotee and the deity. "The shrine is more than a likeness. It is a representation endowed with independent consciousness of that which the devotee encounters in his own self," said the Swami. Thus, while meditating on the heart center I visualize my ideal, variously surrounded by flowers, food, or other offerings in various postures and engaged in assorted actions. All the while I repeat the mantra, I turn the *mala* (rosary). I count each revolution with the left hand, occasionally opening my eyes and looking at the image on the shrine. Any desires or thoughts extraneous to the moment I attempt to counter with a greater desire for an attainment of the aim of sadhana.

Sandwiched between and comprising potential foci for my thoughts is a greatly compressed universe of images of friends, relationships, fleeting mental phenomena, ideas about this and that—the mental stream of my everyday waking consciousness which somehow goes on without my attending to it. The aim is given its "utilitarian" meaning in the meditation's last phase. The accumulated good, the exhilarating passivity and regenerated wakefulness, the physical energy and subjective power of discrimination and compassion, the freedom inherent in attempts to *realize* God, are all *given back* to the world, as it were. The knowledge, devotion, action, and insight "bestowed on" one in meditation are not his or her own according to temple thought. *They must be given in service to humanity,* in whose present age the pursuit is being undertaken.

Thus, at the end of the meditation, a "prayer" is offered for the benefit of friends, the teacher, relatives, and humanity in general. For a few moments I sit with my eyes open trying to bring the mind "back" to the everyday here and now from whence it has sojourned. A few thoughts about the day, about work or life in general are allowed to enter in. There is a noticeable sense of reentry, occasioned by the rise in pulse rate, the tingling of the legs, which I uncross gradually, and by the feeling of being brought back, or of bringing myself back, to the normal, waking consciousness. Actually I allow the world to "take" me back. This "decompression period" follows by about five minutes the previous hour.

In the next few pages I want to describe some of the correlates between this meditation, modern Hindu thought, and the social organization of the Church Universal. There are seven steps in the meditation which can be analyzed in turn. I will attempt to show how the interplay among thought, structure and focus of meditation, and the dialectic between the inner logic of bhakti and the existential context of the event—how these two generic features of the religious life in question— together create the manifest pattern of evolution in the temple's everyday life.

The big question, or at least the often-asked first one, is: Why does one meditate? The *purpose* of meditation is difficult to explain. It is a kind of "behavior" that can be considered both social and asocial. Put another way, it is simultaneously instrumental and expressive. Meditation in a group is often a highly structured social event of import to the feeling of solidarity shared by members of the Church. On the other hand, solitary meditation removes people from everyday social contacts, conferring a kind of temporary marginal status of inchoate propensities on the meditator. So far as I have been able to determine, nearly everyone in the setting utilizes their meditation in a social way—that is, as an instrument in social relations. But rather than get into too abstract a discussion, it is enough to say that the Church Universalists *distinguish* between those who meditate and those who don't, since meditation makes up a substantial portion of every day in the Hindu's life. Perhaps "discriminate against" is a better term. Meditation is the foundation of the religious life, they would say. It would even be true to say that some would even claim meditation is the *final aim* of religious life. Since meditation is something people do whenever they can, then it is instrumental in limiting inter-action with non-meditators. That meditation is the thing many want to do together makes it productive of a specifically social process of cohesion, but without communal propensities. Medi-tation is discussed, and, under the Swami's guidance, practiced— two, four, eight, eighteen hours a day (it varies with person, mood, situation).

From the standpoint of the Swami, it is how *deeply* one meditates, *not* how much, that matters most, although twice a day is prescribed for householders, three times a day for appren-tices and monks. The Swami meditates many hours per day sometimes, fewer than three some days, and sometimes only an hour per day. He guides and counsels those who seek him out for spiritual instruction (which is always centered around medi-tation). The aim of the meditator is often described by him as final release from the bonds of relative existence. In bhakti, these bonds are broken by the ideal, the personalized divinity of one's meditation. Meditation, utilizing a practice of that divine focus, infuses the mental processes with its vertical link to its ultimate transcendent ground. The linkage particle is, of course, the mantra, which, again, constitutes the essential and instru-mental teaching given the disciple by the guru. It is both the means *and* the end of the spiritual undertaking. One does not merely say the mantra or silently repeat it. One expresses it to oneself from *within* oneself and filters one's perceptions through it.

Each stage of the meditation described in some detail above has its analogue in the *Tantra Shastra* system. The successive actions of the meditator bring about changes in his awareness and in his relation to the divine. The asana, peace vibration, and the salutations mark the creation of the magic circle, within which the sadhaka, surrounded by the protecting gods and goddesses, can carry out the ritual without fear of being misled or otherwise assailed by malevolent forces. Pranayam, the rhythmic, meditative breathing, arouses the *kundalini,* the pent-up serpent-power coiled at the base of the spine. Meditation on the macrocosmic, followed by meditation on the microscopic, represents the cyclic involution and evolution of consciousness that creates, at progressive levels, higher and higher states of illumination through successive "rebirths." Japa unites one with his/her ishta, freeing the sadhaka from the forces of karma. "Voluntary rebirth" is represented by the final offering of one's meditation to mankind. One returns to the world to embody the sanyasin ideal; that is, the self-renounced servant-of-the-god-in-man. The stage following meditation, wherein one does holy work, is preparation for a return to the circle and reentry into the center of the focus of spiritual identity.

This is clearly an esoteric interpretation. Or is it? The devotee's attention is directed toward a divine object. But in what does the object consist phenomenologically? Bhakti is theistic, and its tantric undercurrents, polytheistic. The attitude toward the object, or objects, is that of devotion *to* God in the sense usually meant by Christians. "Faith" (belief *in* God) is taken for granted by the Hindu devotee. To paraphrase Ramakrishna, "Why praise the glories of God?" To the Vedantist there is little need to attend to the details of the characteristics of the divine focus because the divine has no choice but to comply, as it were, because of what it is. It is in the *presence* of the meditator before the shrine, but it is also "evoked." For the devotees, the pictures and statues take on life, and interaction occurs. The God *acts on* the devotees. That experience, variously termed the "vision of God," "samadhi," "union with God," is always potentially available in the interaction context, so its power *must* be controlled. To put it rather crudely, it would not do to have the disciples "realizing God" in just one sitting. The genuineness of the experience is adjudicated by an authority.

That authority is the Swami, whose integration of mysticism and asceticism lessens the possibility of imbalances occurring in either direction on the parts of devotees. Mystic union perennially made a part of this world through service is represented in the nondualistic advaita Vedanta, the religion of Brahman. And this system underlies the tantric system. Above the dieties in the Temple shrine is the Sanskrit OM, the *sound* Brahman. "Brahman is everything, Brahman is all this."

It boils down to this: So what if you have a vision of God? Why should you not have it? But God is "all this," too. Do your work; keep the company of the seekers of God; meditate; surrender. Don't be too preoccupied with visions. If you are, it means you "took your ego with you." It is this last thing that is at the heart of the phenomenology of meditation. The surrender is in the *doing*. One does not *propel* oneself into the act egoistically, but is *drawn* by the power of the focus to vairaghya (renunciation). The entire process, from stage to stage, interiorizes the experience of the meditation until at last one *is* the shrine on which sits the divine incarnation. This is why the *Veda* ascribes no particular characteristics to the jivanmukta (the soul freed from samskara), and why Church Universal prescribes no uniform lifestyle other than that of renunciation. Formal renunciation is, they say, no mere "status." One does not become a sanyasin in the same way that one becomes a lawyer. A sanyasin is not really "here" in the sense that *we* experience ourselves in waking consciousness. Rather, what the sanyasin has done is to manifest not-being-here *outwardly,* by "realizing" his reality (which they call "atman") within. Is that reality a particular kind of *sensus nouminous* to which the adept has access using the meditative frame of reference? Whatever the answer, Vedantically, there is only God; or put another way, God is One.

NOTES

1. The flavor invoked here is intentionally a blend of Sartre, Husserl, R. D. Laing, and a Vedantic epistemology similar to that of Deutsch (1968: 9-65). Add to that my own inclination toward a cognitive sociology and five years of meditating something like this daily.

2. "When something is subrated, one believes it to have a lesser degree or kind of 'reality' than that which takes its place. In terms of subration, one's experience dictates that the more something is capable of being subrated, the less reality it has, or the more reality something has, the less capable it is of being subrated" (Deutsch, 1968: 17).

11. THE MASTER'S BIRTHDAY

As has already been explained, Sri Ramakrishna is a prominent feature of the religious definition of the situation at the temple and in the lives of the devotees. To do full justice to the sociological implications of Ramakrishna's charisma would require a much more extensive elaboration of the historical, social, and existential roots and impact of his prophecy, were we to pursue it on a purely horizontal level. However, inasmuch as the birthday celebration of the Master contains all of these ingredients within its phenomenological scope, I will here use the blending of my own experiencing of the event and my reflexive representation of that experience to reconstruct a facet of the essential meaning-complex surrounding the god-man.

The direction toward which the analysis of meditation was heading in the previous chapter is the Master's position at the apex of all spiritual activity and thought at the temple. Meditation, undertaken initially as a device to induce enlightenment, or at least to propel the sadhaka on his or her transcendent way, ultimately stands to become an ideology of worship. Clearly, worship as an act (e.g., as work) is simply a more vertical or phenomenologically concentrated form of karma yoga. Indeed, this karma yoga of worship is a kind of world-experiencing frame under which the experimental investigating and blending of the four yogas can be subsumed. While bhakti would appear to harbor the essential meanings of worship, especially in its more ritualized contexts at the temple and in the devotees' homes, more importantly, worship compels the worshipper toward a particular way of doing things which, as a bhakta, one is wont to do—namely, attempt some sort of ongoing communion with the divine. In bhakti yoga, the more emotional side of religious expression is called for; in karma yoga, the more rational and this-worldly. In the temple, worshipful attitudes taken toward the Master involve a synchronization of these two apparently contradictory orientations. Moreover, jnana, the path of wisdom, is blended in as the sadhaka attempts to realize through direct intuition of the worship's meaning the essential spiritual wisdom contained or evoked in the act of worship. And raja yoga is implicit throughout, because worship, intuition, and acts of devotion require and perhaps promote concentration and other mental states said in yogic lore to increase the likelihood of divine realization.

Keeping this in mind, together with the fact that worship has differential contexts because it varies both with the object of worship and the location of the event in the lives of the faithful, it will be useful to the discussion to show how Sri Ramakrishna is worshipped at the yearly public event held in his honor. In the final chapter, which focuses on worship's underlying, determining form, and mode of expression, I will concentrate more on the inner aspects of temple religious experience. Now my purpose is to round out the general set of practices and beliefs as they relate to the character and context of the Ramakrishna imagery as expressions of the cult's (and movement's) core elements and raison d'être.

In everyday temple life throughout the year, the devotees are steeped in the imagery of the Master. The Swami's stories and teachings, the devotees' devotions, Vespers, and all the rest continually evoke the special qualities of the charismatic hero. With the arrival of the Master's birthday comes a climax to the day-to-day experiences that have been so carefully collected during the year. But far from being a singularly religious event governed by strict requirements of rite and theology, Sri Ramakrishna's puja contains contrasting elements of humor, detachment, serenity, and sobriety—a unique commingling of the spiritual and the worldly that lend the cult, the movement, its institutional variants and the situation their special flavor.

According to temple doctrine, the object of this worship, Sri Ramakrishna, practiced what they call "universal religion" in his lifetime, and thereby reached the goals of the major world religions. Far from being a sober, stern, "Jesuitical" guru, an image traditionally and popularly associated with the leaders of whatever Eastern group one wishes to name, Ramakrishna found the world a delight and encouraged experimentation and direct realization as means to the highest truths of religion. The spirit of the puja bearing Ramakrishna's name—whose ways of realization are said to be the ways of God Himself—is that of *vijnana.* Jnana means wisdom, ajnana means ignorance. They stand for "knowledge of the one" and "knowledge of the many," respectively. Vijnana, on the other hand, means "a fuller knowledge," "to love God in different ways after realizing Him." The devotees and the Swami—especially "intimate" devotees—no doubt feel the powerful spirituality of Thakur (a name for Ramakrishna that means "living god"), and they behave accordingly during the puja in his honor. On this day, he is addressed directly, and the focus of religious expression becomes sharp.

People are arriving in droves by now. Women are carrying in food and sweets. Men hang onto their kids. The monks appear in their inevitable dark suits issuing orders and adding chairs to the auditorium. Devotees are hurrying about setting places at the tables in the library and assembly room. The tanpura sounds weird no matter what I do to tune it. My attention (and the tone) wanders every time a few more people enter the temple. Finally, the other devotee and I give up, having decided that the tanpura will have to do as is. Just then the Swami enters clad in his robes and asks to hear the result of the tuning. To my great relief, the strings are in tune. "That is very nice," he says. "The Master will be pleased." The Swami is, by contrast to everyone and everything around him, serene, almost indifferent, and he is most engaging. His coming in just now has an impact on the several members of the chorus, who are gathered around the tanpura. His entering brings about a change in the direction of the situation. It lightens things up, and we remember what the occasion is, getting instantaneously high.

Now there is silence in the foyer of the temple auditorium. After a few moments, a woman asks the Swami, "Why do we forget what we are supposed to be doing so easily?" She asks it in such an urgent fashion that I recognize the motivation immediately: It is: Do anything, say anything to keep the Swami around and to make the experience last. Swami is frequently asked to put everything straight. Even when he is around, though, we easily slide back to the down spiral. "Do not feel this way," he answers her. "This is all His *lila*, His divine amusement. The Master always used to say, 'Be cheerful!' " He turns to leave, but hears an atonal twang issue forth from the tanpura as I give its strings a final test. "So He still wants to play?" he asks. We all laugh.

A woman enters the foyer. "Oh," he says to her, "the money is on my desk in a yellow envelope. [She purchases his groceries for him.] Take it and get those things on the list we made." "Yes, Swami," she replies in a cultivated, courteous manner.

Then another woman enters the foyer. "How nice that you have come, Mrs. _____ . Is Mr. _____ here?" She answers: "No, he has to work as usual, but he sends you his greetings." "Very nice," he says.

Then—to all of us standing or sitting there in the foyer—we include inner-circle members and these two transient members, "This is the *real* birthday of the Master. The *public* celebration we shall have on Sunday. Then there will be lecture and puja, of course . . . a little refreshment." When he's rapping like this, he seems to be indrawn, yet there is the apparent happening in monologue form. "Today this is just for a few close devotees of the Master." These women who don't know him will take the comment as flattery. The Swami continues: "I shall offer some flowers, incense, and food to Him. . . . A little light and some *Ganga*. Devotees shall sing." He points at his chest. He's like a little boy bragging about some deed that he is about to do. "And I shall be the Minister and make a speech." The chorus cracks up. The two women aren't sure what the laughter means, so they try to disengage themselves, even though he isn't quite through yet.

"My guru used to say that 'The Master is living here with us right now; one day you will see Him,' " he continued. "But people will think, what are they talking about? Who is this Ramakrishna fellow? Perhaps he is like these Hare Krishnas who are either singing and dancing or else selling something. So we are celebrating this birthday two times, you know. We can say today, 'Oh, Master, let us feed you and sing to you.' Tomorrow [Sunday] will be more scientific. We shall say: 'Oh, Ramakrishna, you certainly were an interesting fellow. Let us listen to a lecture.' " The foyer is filled with laughter. The two women, at first nonplussed by the candor of the Swami, join in the fun and exchange knowing looks with the musicians. The Swami exits the foyer. We attend to the placing of the instruments. The women take seats in the auditorium.

In spite of all the activity outside in the foyer, in the Swami's kitchen, and in the library, the temple is completely quiet. Usually when more than twenty people are in the place a number of position shifts, sneezes, whispers, shoe-removals, and clothing adjustments create a kind of ambience that is somewhere between muffled relaxation and stifled tension. Now more than forty are inside, and it will be some time before the function begins. I repair outside to catch a glimpse of things from another angle and at the same time to see whether there are any last-minute duties to perform. The Swami finds me standing with my hands in the pockets about to say something to a devotee. (Bad form, to be sure.) He calls me by my Sanskrit name and tells me to follow him to the library. I do so. "Get _____ and _____ . More chairs are needed in the assembly room. And put some chairs around the table in my office. They will be for the visiting swamis." The visiting swamis are from two other Church Universal temples, and are arriving outside at this moment. "Here they are," one of the devotees calls out from the front door.

Two cars have pulled up out front. Black-suited novices step out and assist the four ochre-clad swamis from the cars. Two are American; two, Indian. Devotees, amid much excited clamor, line the walkway leading to the front door. There follows a spate of short greetings and exchanges. The Valley City Swami addresses the two Indian swamis in Bengali. They stop and in turn touch a hand to his feet and then to their own foreheads. He is their senior, so this is a form of patrimonial salutation. I try to get the brigade together to set up the folding chairs, but the draftees don't seem interested. "You will do what I asked?" the Swami says to me. "Yes," I reply, and make the rounds again, this time with better luck.

In a few minutes most of the chairs are in place and the swamis and devotees have gone into the temple and are meditating. I am asked by one of the women devotees to carry out and set up the coffee urn. "OK," I say, and follow her to the Swami's kitchen. "Be careful. Hold it this way. Watch the cord. Can you make it?" several women say to me. I answer: "Yes . . . right . . . OK." By the time I make it into the temple, the Swami is already sitting down before the shrine, having made an opening statement to the crowd. The musicians are poised to begin. One hands me the cymbals, and the tanpura starts to drone. Gliding in right behind me is another member of the chorus. As she sits, we begin our song, on time and in tune. It is what would be called another close shave. "All part of the fun," as the Swami might say.

The Swami continually reminds us that his ritual worship is his own invention. His poise and concentration are truly artful, and his manipulation of the objects used in worship—flowers, incense, burning camphor, and so on—lend an aura of simultaneous naturalness and ritualism that vividly illumine the enactment of the overlap among the cosmic, natural, and human orders. Today in his worship of Sri Ramakrishna, assisted at various points by the visiting swamis, he creates an attitude, posture, and focus that display all of the major Vedantic themes for which Ramakrishna is credited with having reestablished. Yet the puja is decidedly, consciously simple. Between songs by the chorus, the Swami chants and makes offerings. At the end of the flower offering by devotees, where people come in twos to bow before the shrine and place flowers on a brass tray, the swamis and novices mount the platform in front of the shrine and chant several Sanskrit hymns to Ramakrishna. After one more song by the chorus, the Swami tells everyone to go to the library and assembly room for prasad.

The festive character of the occasion fully emerges once the food is being served. Young women bring in trays of food to the devotees and guest swamis. There is much relishing of the Indian dishes and sweets, and considerable animated conversation goes on as the swamis circulate from table to table. After some hefty second helpings, people clean up their places, take leave of the swamis, and go home. A few hang around afterward, taking care of loose ends.

I am back into the folding chair routine, this time with more help than is really useful. Chairs are clanging and banging, and the volume of conversation increases to compensate for the noise. I notice that people are breaking into clusters of three and four to talk about the event and what they have gained from attending it. Among them are those making plans to travel semi-caravan fashion to Bay City where the Valley City Swami will perform another puja to Sri Ramakrishna later in the day. The Swami asks me if I would like to accompany him. "Yes," I reply with pleasure. "Fine. Then you ride with _____ . You are responsible, and I entrust these two boys to you."

They are in their twenties. One lives on the grounds already, the other is contemplating renouncing, as entering the monastery is called. "You are not to engage in worldly talk with Dr. Damrell," he admonishes my passengers. "His mind should not be brought down. Say your mantra instead." After setting up a later meeting time, I locate my wife and we take leave of the Swami.

"Taking leave" means formally engaging the Swami and then letting go, as it were. Outside, or in the presence of the "public," taking leave simply means saying goodbye and exchanging niceties that are sometimes accompanied by the familiar Eastern way of honoring another person. One stands erect before the Swami, puts the palms together in prayerful attitude, and delivers a short bow from the waist. The stylistic variation on this gesture-laden encounter is great: some do it with a perfunctory élan; others put a great deal of drama into it. Initiated devotees who are meeting privately with the Swami, however, are occasionally allowed to touch their foreheads to his feet, a ritual known as "taking dust" which is at once a kind of "blessing" by the Swami and an acknowledgment of the devotee's respect for his sanyasin role. An intermediate form of "taking dust" (which can serve as a greeting or as the taking of leave—not to mention as a blessing and honoring) is sometimes done by visiting swamis and Indian devotees. In this instance, the person bows low before the Swami, touches his shoes with the right hand, and then touches the right hand to the head.

(American devotees usually refrain from this practice, probably because the Swami has discouraged it saying, "Let the Indian devotees feel at home. You [Americans] do not need to do such a thing.")

On this occasion of Thakur's birthday, "taking leave" is more special than usual, the Swami having absorbed himself more fully in the Master's teachings via his conducting of the puja. He is in his living room. Most of the "public" have gone. Monastic members are in their quarters or attending to work. A few close devotees are seated on the floor and on his couch. Several women are in the kitchen finishing up the dishwashing. My wife and I enter the room after being announced by a devotee.

"Come here," the Swami commands. We sit at his feet. I remove his shoes. He gestures for me to massage his feet. As I do it, he says, "You are the Master's very own. It is not my dust you are taking, but His. He never let anyone call him guru or *baba* [father]. You see, he was a really clever fellow. Now, go ahead." In turn, we touch his feet with our foreheads. As we rise he pats our heads with his hands, saying, "Jai Ma, Jai Thakur," with each pat. We stand up, our hands in the supplicant's posture. He says, "Go home."

As we turn to leave, he calls out, "Wait . . . have you forgotten your mantra?" I pretend to look for it in my pockets. "It's around here somewhere, Swami," I say. Everyone laughs. "Accha," says the Swami. We remain standing at the door as silence comes over the group. "Go home," he says again. "Can't we stay for just a few more minutes?" my wife asks. "All right," he says. We sit down and watch others take his dust. Each devotee is in turn blessed and given encouraging words. Shortly, the Swami lapses into a serene mood. His eyes are glistening, watery. A young man comes forward and begins massaging his feet. The Swami begins: "Thakur had a vision once that the OM above the shrine was a great vat of spiritual dye used by the Lode to make the devotees into so many exquisite pieces of cloth, each with its own particular beauty. He always used to say that to talk about God was one thing, but to realize Him quite another. One cannot talk when that realization comes. But who would preach to the public if we were to merge in that highest state? So we must go on doing His work and practicing the presence of God a little bit here and there."

There is silence followed by the opening of the door. Two young apprentices enter. "What do you want?" the Swami asks them. "We want to listen," one replies.

"What is the use? The mood is broken now. Why do you come in like thieves, making little noises?"

"We're sorry, Swami," the other says.

"Never mind," he says, getting up. "All right, go home," he tells the group. A few turn and leave after bowing with hands folded in front of them. A few others, myself included, linger on. He scolds the apprentices some more for barging in. Then he tells me, "These two are very restless. The slightest provocation on anyone's part will set them off. Better we should all ride down together to Bay City. That way I can keep my eye on them. Is that right?" he says to the oldest one. "Yes," is the reply.

An hour and a half later we get into the temple's white Chevy. The Swami rides shotgun. He and the driver, the older "restless" apprentice, are in the front seat, on either side of the younger apprentice. In the back seat are myself and two monks. "Before we leave, we shall take the name of Mother Durga," he announces. "OM, *Durgayai Namah. Accha,* let us go."

Fifteen miles from Valley City, we encounter bumper-to-bumper, stop-and-go traffic. The monks are upset because of our not having left earlier. "And if we are late, what will happen?" one asks. "Then your puja will simply have to begin without you," the Swami says facetiously. "Go faster," he tells the driver.

"Yes, Swami," the driver says, stepping on the accelerator. The traffic thins out as we pass by the grassy hills of the valley's edge. We are silent.

Trying to make chit-chat, one monk says in a somewhat authoritative manner, "This looks something like Bengal, wouldn't you say, Swami?" "Yes, yes," replies the Swami in an indifferent tone. After a few attempts at conversation, the monk realizes that the Swami isn't paying attention. A rather embarrassing silence ensues. When we get to Bay City, one monk advises the driver to avoid the nightclub strip that lies between the highway and Bay City's Church Universal temple. The Swami says: "Yes, it is good to keep in mind that seekers of God should avoid contact with worldly places so far as possible, but what is more important is that monks learn detachment." Everyone laughs nervously as he gestures to the driver to continue on course. Passing the strip, no one says a word and all eyes are fixed straight ahead. The Swami laughs at our somber mood. "Is this not the Master's birthday? Where is your gaiety?" "We're happy, Swami," says one of the apprentices, "We just don't know what to say." ". . . or how to act," says the other. "Then keep quiet and sit still," says the Swami, and we all laugh.

At last the car pulls up in front of the temple. A waiting novice opens the Swami's door. We all get out, and the driver takes the car to park it nearby. I accompany the monks, apprentices, and the Swami, plus the welcoming committee, up a long flight of stairs. Three-quarters of the way up, the Swami turns to me and says, "You cannot go in. Only monks can enter the monastery. You must go in through the front entrance to the temple. I will see you later. OK?" It is not OK, however. I am taken utterly by surprise, but am in no position to protest against this discrimination against a householder devotee. In Valley City, I frequently enter the monks' quarters and have eaten with them on several occasions, so I did not expect to be denied entrance to Bay City's monastery, not to mention to be rather summarily dismissed by the Swami.

"Is there really such a rule against non-monks entering the monks' haven?" I wonder. "No doubt there is such a rule. Or maybe this is a test to see if I will do what the Swami has asked. If a chela can't follow simple instructions, how can he or she be prepared to realize God?" Or so the dialogue with myself goes. At any rate, I am disturbed by this incident.

After cooling off and collecting myself, I enter the temple. It is a huge room with high-arched ceilings that extend outward from the focal point, an elaborate, imposing shrine which houses life-sized images in bronze of Buddha, Christ, Sri Ramakrishna, Sarada Devi, and Vivekananda. I am one of a crowd of perhaps two hundred. As I attempt to meditate, I keep thinking of the incident on the monastery steps. Throughout the puja, the invocation of the god-man is for me infused with alternating currents of anger, hurt feelings, and internally generated rationalizations aimed at smoothing the whole thing over. At the end of the puja, when the devotees are offering flowers to the deity,

I have nearly succeeded in chalking it up to my own misunderstanding of the event. But then I notice two male novices from the Bay City monastery as they approach a young woman who is about to step up on the shrine's platform. She is a member of another Hinduesque sect. She is clad in saffron robes, and she appears to be about seven months pregnant. Her bare feet are the issue. The two novices officiously tell her to put on her shoes before approaching the shrine. (A rule against bare feet, too? In Hindu temples in India, only bare feet are allowed. And in Valley City the Swami doesn't seem to promote either position.)

By now my sociologist's curiosity is aroused, so after the prasad has been served and eaten and devotees are filing out, I approach one of the apprentices who had scolded the young woman: "Did you tell that person to put on her shoes before offering a flower?" "Yes, I most certainly did," he responds with still more pointed officiousness. "Swami says they are to wear shoes. This is not India, no matter what costumes people wear. This is not Hinduism. We are following the norm of the American culture." He is bristly, defensive.

Another Valley City devotee, a psychologist, hears my failure to reply, and says, "Don't lecture him [meaning me] on culture; he is a sociologist. I say a flower offering is a flower offering—bare feet, sandals, or combat boots." He and I laugh, but the novice is not amused.

"Listen," he retorts, "You wouldn't believe what people wear in here. They don't have respect for the Lord. Swami says the very least they can do—the very least—is to wear shoes." "And what do *you* say?" I ask him. "I say good evening to you, sir," and he walks away. In light of this new situation my anger and miffed feelings seem rather funny to me. There is room for contrast even within the "movement." In Valley City, few such tensions could arise, the Swami being much more liberal about the distinctions between monks and laypersons, about proper dress in the temple, and about the religious presentation of self.

The psychologist devotee and I wait nearby to help the Valley City Swami into the car. He comes out of the temple accompanied by the Valley City monks and the two apprentices who came to Bay City with us. As the last monk gets into the back seat, he leaves his hand hanging onto the roof of the car, and the Swami shuts the car door on it.

The monk yells. The sound of his hand being pinched between the metal door and the frame is sickening. Unaware of
the accident, the Swami wonders what the yelling monk is up
to. "It's all right, it's all right," says the monk. "Accha," says
the Swami and gets into the car. I start to get into the back, but
he says, "You and those boys [the apprentices] will go with
Mr. _____ [the psychologist]." By this time I have no particular feelings about how I get home, but I ask myself whether I
might have said something on the way to Bay City that caused
the Swami to evict me from his company. Just then my favorite
officious apprentices from Bay City emerge from the temple
carrying overnight bags. The Swami says to me, "They are
coming to Valley City for a few days. Please come tomorrow to
the public worship and sing songs to Thakur. He is very pleased
with you. [Pause] All right, I shall now take the name of the
Divine Mother. [All close their eyes.] Om Durgayai Namah.
Accha," he says to the driver. The car pulls away. Mr. _____
takes me by the arm and we round up our two charges and head
back to Valley City. The women in Bay City have sent a plate
of prasad home with me for my wife and son, a charming and,
under the circumstances, utterly unexpected gesture.

On the way home, we are careful not to rattle the apprentices
with too much worldly talk, but the conversation turns to the
incident of the barefoot "nun" who was told to put on her
shoes. We are both baffled and not a little annoyed by the
haughtiness of the Bay City apprentices, and the gambit afterward, we decide, was plainly inexcusable. Then from the back
seat we hear some soft chanting as the two try to drown out our
vibes. Finally, we are all silent. Shortly thereafter I find myself
chanting the mantra and thinking about the god-man Ramakrishna and his amazing family. "And just what is my place in
this scenario?" I wonder to myself.

My immersed yet critical posture has its counterpoint in the
attitude of the two apprentices accompanying us back home.
They in effect avoid such controversies through their situational
use of meditation. While they appear to have been moved to
interiority by the puja, their mood seems coincident with
Mr. _____'s and my critique of Christianized Hinduism.
Thus, this vignette illustrates something about my perspective

that differentiates it from the scene to which I am attempting to give some sociological moorings.

The predominant social fact of that scene is the institution. But the aggregate experience of that fact by the devotees, and by me as well, is something larger than a purely structured, or even negotiated, reality. It is something that the people there appear to take for granted even as they somehow negotiate it in spontaneous fashion, while I, on the other hand, can occasionally find myself manipulating an oblique glance at it. Which means, I think, that the peculiar ambience of contexts such as Sri Ramakrishna's puja—with all its serenity and abrasiveness—derives in part from the fact that Ramakrishna's charisma has not been totally rationalized. In fact, it appears to defy rationalization, because for all its routinized equilibrium it is nevertheless a fragile reality. Doing a sociology of Sri Ramakrishna's progeny requires that one be particularly aware of the fact that his "presence" is still "felt." Young persons enter his order on receiving the inner call, and old persons undertake lifelong sacrifices in promoting and supporting the order's work in the West. If I were to analyze the phenomenon structurally, it would be at the expense of discovering the meanings of the existential certainties of the actors' religious reality-constructions, meanings which pervade and animate their world-experiencing life in its subjective and collective manifestations.

Thus, I have tried to give an impression of the sense in which temple life involves an ongoing dialogue with Thakur's very personhood, and this aspect of the religious experience is given an open presentation on his birthday. The drama of Hindu worship lends personified and personalized imagery to the devotees' relation to the god-man. Those central to the experience have access to the power of his spiritual nexus. My own access has been based mainly on my association with the Swami, the initiation into sadhana that I underwent, my meditation, and so on. But there is another mode of participation that enables me to experience Ramakrishna's characteristic playfulness up close. In the next chapter, I describe my role as cymbal-player and singer in the temple choir. The description of Vespers will provide, I think, a deeper look into the phenomenon.

12. VESPERS AND DEVOTIONAL MUSIC

A very important event in the life of the cult in the Church Universal temple is the Vespers service held on Sunday evenings. Although Vespers is advertised in the monthly bulletin distributed to the public, it is usually attended by only about fifteen people, including most of the residents of the temple and the laypersons who live nearby or who make the trip from their homes for the ritual. Sometimes students and Indians who live in an adjacent university town attend Vespers, but their participation, as usual in all "public" functions, is peripheral. To a core group who congregate at the shrine during this time, Vespers is central to the spiritual life, because it is a source of the central experience of the religion of devotion wherein a special kind of communion with the divine (Sri Ramakrishna, Holy Mother Sarada Devi, Brahman, the Self, or whomever) occurs.

The ritual surrounding Vespers consists of meditation in the temple, followed by the Swami's offering of flaming candles made of camphor to various forms of god as well as to the formless Brahman. Then hymns are sung, usually in the manner occasioned by current Hindu style, wherein the Swami, accompanied by harmonium, tanpura, and assorted rhythm instruments, sings each line of each devotional song solo, and then repeats the line, accompanied by the chorus of devotees and monastics. Exceptions to this style are the hymns which make up the main purpose of the event. These hymns—two to Sri Ramakrishna as incarnate god, and the other, an excerpt from the *Devi Mahatmya* (or *Chandi*), a classical Hindu scripture extolling Mother worship—are sung in unison in Sanskrit during the beginning and end of the services. After the last hymn (to Holy Mother), there is another fifteen-minute meditation.[1]

When Vespers was initiated by the Swami in 1971 after his return from India, I lived near enough to the temple to attend Vespers regularly and was asked, presumably because of my musical background, to play cymbals in a kind of ensemble consisting of the aforementioned harmonium and tanpura, and a violin. The "cymbals" are actually small Tibetan gongs in a bell-like shape. Made of cast bronze, they are hand-tooled to an A #440 C tone. They weigh roughly eight ounces each and are secured to the hand by means of looped and knotted leather thongs that protrude from a hole in each center. Learning how to play them became a main preoccupation of mine after I was asked to. This afforded me both a permanent role in the social scene and a "place" in front on the platform during Vespers.

The seating arrangement at Vespers is as follows: Two old monks and the Swami sit at the foot of the shrine, in which are installed, beneath the symbol of Brahman (Om), the pictures of Sri Ramakrishna and Vivekananda and likenesses of Buddha and Jesus. The Swami sits to one side and faces the center of the platform on which are seated the monks. Six inches below is another platform on which is seated the ensemble and four or five of the laypersons and apprentices who make up the rest of the chorus. Seated in the auditorium chairs below the platform are other members of the temple cult, plus those who attend only occasionally.

People begin filing into the temple around 5:30 p.m. and are usually all in their places meditating when the Swami enters at 5:45, followed by the two monks, at 5:50. The Swami (after anointing himself with Ganges water and lighting incense), lights candles on the shrine and sits for a period of time doing japa, repeating the mantra. He usually offers food, flowers, perfume and water, and then lights the camphor-wick lamp.

Rising to his feet, he holds a bronze bell with his left hand formed into the appropriate *mudra* (power-position), and holds the lamp with its five burning camphor wicks toward the shrine. Then for a solid minute-and-a-half or so he rings a bell with a rhythmic turning of his left wrist, and waves the lamp in circles before the shrine. The religious interpretation of this act is as complex as any in Hinduism, so the idea that it is an "invocation" of the deity will have to suffice.

Vespers is really a service conducted *unto* the guru of the religious order of which Church Universal is a part. The main hymn, *Kandana Bhava Bandhana,* by Swami Vivekananda, is an evocation of Sri Ramakrishna. Around the temple, Vespers is often referred to as "Kandana," so central is the avatara hymn in this event. Vesper services are fairly much alike, I am told, in Ramakrishna Order institutions in India, and are considered to be an act of devotion to the living representation of their departed guru's divinity. I was told by an old visiting swami that there are no traditional breath stops, and that the hymn contains numerous mantras and occult formulae, and is itself a means to spiritual realization. "By controlled singing of the hymn, one can raise the kundalini [the latent yogic power in the spine] and attain samadhi," he said. Thus, the singing in Vespers is an essential form bhakti yoga takes on, and is a part of the core spiritual practices of aspirants.

There is a quality to the singing at Vespers that sheds light on the social characteristics of the event. Most of the members of the ensemble observe no formal cues while singing with one another. This works well in the songs in which the Swami sings first and is followed by the chorus, because he is imitated, as it were. But in *Kandana Bhava Bandhana,* things happen. Since the cymbals must keep a steady rhythm throughout the hymn, playing on the first, fifth, and seventh beats of a slow, ten-beat cycle, and since no one listens to the cymbals, the voices move in waves and surges around the beat. After many practice sessions and numerous attempts on my part to occasion some sort of recognition of the fundamentals of music performance, I have come to the conclusion that the event is so much a personal act of worship for the participants that any sort of collective effort is impossible. The pronunciation of the Sanskrit words, I am told by the Swami, is, however, fairly good, which indicates that *he* is listened to, at least.

For a whole year of Sundays, when it became painfully apparent that I could not carry the beat alone, the Swami began thereafter, with his left hand, while the other hammered out the melody on the keyboard, to strike the appropriate rhythm on the harmonium's top. For the next two years, a rapport system was introduced whereby he could look at me in a certain way and I would be able to judge whether I was too loud, too soft, too slow, or too fast. For a couple of years, the Swami's comments after Vespers would include mention of how my cymbal-playing fared. Occasionally he would call my playing a "massacre." Once he said that I had practically killed him with an out-of-time beat. His kundalini was far up his spine, he said, and when it rushed to the base on being zapped by a misplaced beat, he was snapped back to the plane of mundane conscious-ness. He indeed gave a visible twitch when I hit the cymbals in true arhythmic fashion, and I knew I was in for some criticism. His reference to the kundalini, however, was the only "occult" one he offered concerning Vespers.

Once it had occurred to me that since there was a yoga of sound called *nada yoga,* perhaps it was through sound that the hymn was capable of producing enlightenment in the singer. "No, it is bhakti yoga," the Swami told me. "Why bhakti yoga?" I asked. "Because it is Sri Ramakrishna's hymn, and we are his devotees," was his reply. From this point it became clearer what bhakti yoga means. In the context of Vespers, bhakti is singing hymns *to* God, not just singing hymns *about* God. And the God is *present,* having been invoked by the ritual offering of lights. The occult nature of the hymn is accessible by means of the proper devotional "attitude," as reflected by the spontaneous singing of the praises of the divine.

The translation of the hymn bears out the statement that it is essentially devotional, and in its rhythm and melody, structur-ally—that is ritually—so. Another hymn, also sung in unison, was introduced later. It is called *Bhava Sagara,* and likewise evokes the presence of the "deliverer from evils of transmigra-tory existence."

Bhava Sagara usually follows by a minute or two the main hymn, *Kandana.* Its rhythm structure is such that improvisation

is allowed the cymbalist, and it is characteristically the lighter
of the two "tunes." Following *Bhava Sagara,* the two old monks
leave the temple via a door situated to the side of the shrine.
Those remaining on the platform usually then sing three songs,
Ramakrishna Govinda Narayana, Tumi Brahma Ramakrishna,
and one from the repertoire of about twenty or so that the
chorus has learned over its four years of singing. The final
hymn, *Sarva Mangalamangalaye,* is sung with harmonium
accompaniment only, the rhythm being a spontaneously emergent part of the expression at the moment of its voicing.

For fifteen minutes after the closing notes of the last hymn,
everybody does japa. Then the Swami rises from his seat,
collects his ritual objects, and exits from the shrine area. He
returns shortly with a damp cloth, which he uses to wipe the
hardwood floor in front of the shrine. When this is over, he
leaves and people rise, fold their meditation shawls (if they are
wearing them), return the musical instruments to their proper
places, and adjourn to the library where the Swami gives a short
audience and passes out prasad. It is an understanding between
the Swami and the devotees, worked out over a period of years
and numerous coaxings and hints on his part, that "idle chit-
chat" will be conspicuous by its absence, that everyone will
attend mentally to the purpose of the function.

The meditation periods during Vespers would appear to be in
the first instance, prefatory, and in the second, climactic. Precisely when the first meditation starts after the adjustments of
instruments, seats, music and bodies is never clear. Eventually
the temple is stilled, though, and, inevitably, within fifteen
seconds, the Swami walks in. People can be heard clearing their
throats and rustling their music after *arati* (the light offering) is
performed and the Swami seats himself before the harmonium.
The meditation that precedes this involves getting ready to sing,
or, "coming down to a singing plane," as one devotee put it.
The link between the parts of Vespers is internal. One's intimacy with the deity, or, in a general sense, with spiritual
experience, is achieved through on-going repetition of the mantra, a sound-particle, as it were, of capital "T" truth, a "piece of
God." The Swami has initiated nearly all in attendance at
Vespers with mantras plumbed from the spiritual lore of Sri
Ramakrishna and his disciples. Since a mantra is customarily a

secret possession of the individual, I will not describe mine beyond saying that I was intrigued by the similarity between the two root sounds, and sounds that are made by the cymbals when struck in a special way. Since the mantra is the essence of the preceptor's teaching, it is a cognitive and ontological constant. Suffice it to say that the repetition of a mantra is the mainstay in the continuity of the religious experience. People periodically reach into the cloth bag containing their mala (rosary) and perform japa. After the singing, japa appears to sustain the mood.

In order to teach the group songs for Vespers, the Swami calls the devotees for rehearsal sessions in the temple library. There the group of seven to ten people gather around the pump organ and hear the Swami's instruction on Friday nights. He passes around photocopies of the words and music (which he himself has written down), tunes the group's voice to the appropriate pitch, and proceeds a line at a time with the lesson. As the group becomes familiar with the standard Vespers songs, others are added to suit mood and occasion until, over a period of five years, the group has built a repertoire of around twenty hymns. Because the rehearsing and "performing" of devotional music are important features of religious feelings and attitudes, I will discuss these contexts briefly in their relation to the social reality of temple life.

Up to the time of the initiation of the Vespers singing, the only public performance of music at the temple consisted in traditional, Protestant, Sunday organ music, provided by a long-standing lay member, guitar-accompanied solo singing, occasional appearances of violin or vocal soloists, and infrequent offerings of chants by the monks and the Swami. Except for the latter, all music was decidedly Western. At semi-private events, such as the Saturday night class on the teachings of Sri Ramakrishna, the Swami was once in a while coaxed into singing a favorite song of the Master, or a song associated with the Vedantic and bhakti traditions. About a year after Vespers was instituted, a group of six people, including myself, began providing musical accompaniment to various sorts of religious functions and temple activities. The addition of the music has cast the outline of these functions into somewhat sharper Hindu relief, providing a less Protestant atmosphere and a more clearly bhakti definition of the religious situation. Thus, it has had a bearing on the dynamics of the cult.

The group gathers around a long table arrayed with Vedantic and other periodicals, women on one side, men on the other. The Swami sits at the organ near one end of the table. He usually warms up the voices by playing key notes in whatever song is being learned or rehearsed at the time, intoning the Indian scale names for the notes. At times he asks individuals to sing notes and corrects their intonation or elocution. When he is satisfied that the group is singing more or less together and/or on key, he introduces the song. Occasionally he will tell us to listen carefully while he sings it through once, but more often he will simply start with the first line. Then the group tries the line, accompanied by the Swami. Five, ten, a couple of dozen times, the group will sing the line, while the Swami listens, now and then interrupting to correct meter, pronunciation, or intonation.

Since there are no harmonies in Indian music, all songs are sung in unison, the men singing usually an octave below the women. The aforementioned method of the Swami's singing solo followed by the group is used in every song. Early in the formative days of the singing group, the Swami would break off rehearsal if things didn't go right. Sometimes this happened because the "mood" was wrong, say, when people acted casually toward the event, or engaged in "idle talk." As the group became more familiar with what was expected of it, the context became conspicuously more religious. That is, rehearsal was not just a going over of the music, but a part of the religious practices of the devotees. I don't mean that "rehearsals" are solemn; rather, they are "serious," something more than mere esthetic expression, which is not particularly high on the scale of values.

Music clearly provides access to the central elements and dynamics of Hindu bhakti in the absence of closer cultural contact. To sing the words and provide one's own vocal inflections and rhythmic and harmonic variations lends a participatory air to a religious expression that is in part, because of the Swami's role as chief purveyor and ritualist, a spectator activity. During rehearsals and lessons around the pump organ, the Swami is clearly offering himself as an object to be imitated, at least on the level of attitude, if not on the level of mannerisms, accent, and so on. His holiness is itself a kind of lesson. At nearly every function, of both a public and a private nature, the typical member forms a part of an audience whose collective religious response is contained in a meditative composure, attuned to the Swami's presence. The hundred or so chairs are, on Sundays, filled with people who exhibit varying degrees of absorption in meditation or some kind of silent prayer or who look at the Swami with seldom-blinking eyes. Though it *looks* like a "church," with rows of chairs, carpeted aisles, hard-wood elevated altar, pulpit, organ, ushers, and preacher (albeit ochre-clad), the place of worship is viewed as a "temple." Members enter it conscious of its "spiritual vibrations" and take their seats. Usually they sit facing forward with back erect and eyes closed. Hands are folded in the lap or slipped beneath shawls to hold the japa beads. Some people sit less still, but if eyes are open they are generally focused on the altar or the Swami. There is a conspicuous absense of note-taking, as such occupations are believed to interfere with absorption into the spontaneous consciousness emergent in the event.

Besides the ushers, the only people who break from this general meditative mood and posture are the musicians, who can come down from their meditation in order to set up instruments and arrange places, and who, in the course of singing, are provided an outlet for an expressive religious sentiment, which temple-going is not. Except at Sunday Vespers, when the assembly is invited to sing with the ensemble, the audience shows little or no overt response to the music. There is no toe-tapping or other obvious audience interaction with the musicians' performance, although the comments I have received about the music (ranging from favorable to the opposite) indicate, in some cases, that the music has added a dimension to temple-going that has somehow qualitatively enhanced the listener's sadhana, either by getting him high or "causing the mind to take refuge inside itself." Many people have indicated they chant mantras and/or a few hymns, having gradually acquired them after being exposed to these musical interludes. Thus, I would interpret the popularity of music and its use in bhakti as being a function of the participation it allows in the "real thing" found in Hindu culture.

At the same time, the music is in tension, more or less, with the subdued atmosphere constituted out of a rational Vedantic frame of reference, and the churchly valence of the surrounds. Many of the people regard themselves as advaitins—that is, non-dual Vedantists, who subscribe to the Shankaracharya interpretation of the world as maya (illusion) and the individual soul (atman) as identical with God (Brahman).[2] For them, bhakti constitutes a continuing, mild embarrassment, if not an occasional scandal. They find it uncomfortable to listen to the music except in an evaluative way. Not that Vedantists cannot appreciate the cultural value of doing Indian music, or even the esthetics of it when everything goes right; to them, the whole shrine-directed musical thing smacks of dualism, of *belief in* God. And "Hinduesque" artifacts—like sitting on the floor wrapped in a shawl, or touching the forehead to the shrine floor before singing—smack of credulity, unless the doers are Indians, in which case one can be more tolerant, the latter having the Swami's implicit approval by virtue of his Bengali origin.

What I am saying though, in describing rehearsals and musical performances, is that the Swami legitimates Hinduization, as it were, by leading the group in singing. The attitude toward the music that he has endeavored to instill in the musicians is one of devotion after the bhakti model, an attitude that is routinized in the ritual behavior of temple musicians in the Order and is a continuing feature of Hindu lore and religious experience as carried on by Vedantists.

In addition to there being an upsurge of interest in Hindu devotional music on the parts of otherwise Christian, or non-dual, oriented members, it has also happened that the group, under the Swami's direction, has given performances at events attended by members of Church Universal temples located in other cities. The effect on mood has been the same at these events as at the temple in Valley City; there is a more vertical direction to the religious feelings of the members, and a lower Christian valence in the definition of the situation. People feel freer to vary the usual audience participation motif of sitting perfectly still, and when more than one swami is present, and they interact with one another, the outcome is still less predictable, with the increase in humorous exchanges and extemporaneous devotional acts being quite apparent.

A DAY AT VESPERS

I arrive for Vespers puffing from the Valley City heat and traffic. I spend a few minutes in the washroom trying to dry myself off. Perspiration and meditation don't mix. My shirt is wet and my previous shower's effects are fast wearing off. I splash water on my face and wipe my neck, arms, and forehead with a wet paper towel. This is no state of mind to be in for singing *Kandhana.* It's twenty to six. Swami will arrive in five minutes. There's barely enough time for me to locate the cymbals, sort my music, and take my place before the temple shrine.

The cymbals aren't where they are supposed to be. Perhaps someone has already picked them up, thinking that I am not going to be there. Panic. I recall once how I thought so and so had picked them up, and so and so thought I had picked them up. Halfway through *Kandhana,* Swami looked at me and asked with his eyes, "Well, where are the cymbals?" I just shrugged and looked stupid, and sang the rest of the songs with self-activated mental vise-grips around my windpipe. Nerve-wracking stuff. So I enter the foyer of the auditorium. The cymbals are in their cloth bag on the desk where one of the devotees sits when books and incense are being sold after Sunday lectures. I remove my shoes without touching them with my hand (hand-foot contact is proscribed, since it is believed to cause a special kind of pollution that renders everything about the person unholy). I drape my shawl around my shoulders and proceed to the shrine. The devotees are bunched together, leaving me no room. This happens so much that the Swami from time to time has to remind people where they sit, and where the harmonium is to be placed, and so on. I say to one of the men, "Scoot over, please," and he does so automatically, as does the next devotee and the next in a chain reaction. Nobody breaks the meditative posture, however. The silence contains us, rather than our quiet creating silence. I sit down, shuffle my sheet music, remove the cymbals from their bag, and hold them up to the Master's picture in offering. Then I put them down and unfold my japa bag. Shortly after I begin doing japa, the Swami enters. He chants and anoints his head with Ganges water, and then lights candles. Then he sits in meditation for a while. The atmosphere is utterly consummating of the prefatory acts that have led us here. This is sometimes referred to as a deep meditation, or a heavy meditation, etc. There is total quiet. Everyone on the platform in front of the shrine seems especially serene. This is a great relief to me. My body temperature has leveled off at a tolerable height. I drift in and out of the mantra's orbit. The sound of Swami putting away his japa beads opens my eyes, and I see him on his knees lighting the camphor lamp. He picks up the bell and rises to his feet. His eyes are intent on the shrine, and the ringing bell is on the fine line between agony and exquisite pleasure. He waves the lamp in a broad arc and in elliptical circles before the shrine. At the end of the ceremony, without breaking the steady rhythm in which he rings the bell he puts down the camphor lamp and picks up a flower, which he handles in a similar fashion as the lamp. Finally the bell-ringing stops, but not the ringing in my ears. It feels as though the vibrations have entered into the very fabric of the shrine and its attendants. The air veritably shimmers with the after-image of the piercing sound. Then the Swami positions himself behind the harmonium, which is the signal for the tanpura to begin its drone.

Kandhana is slow. The cymbals seem like lead weights. Without looking at me, Swami indicates that I am blowing it. His left hand comes down on top of the harmonium to pound out the beat. I am convinced that in the several years that the Vespers service has been a part of temple life, no one pays any attention to how the music sounds. The tanpura player sings behind every note. I strike on the *matra* (beat) and her voice resonates a split-second later. Sometimes her voice sounds like an echo of the other voices. A male devotee sitting to my left sings sharp and rushes the beat. No matter how steady the pulse is, he is rhythmically all over the place, and the sharpness to his tones stretches the overall tone pattern which invariably hovers around flatness. We are only on the fourth verse and I am dripping wet again. My breath is completely gone, as is my concentration. My voice cracks. I miss a beat altogether, and the Swami gives a slight twitch. The guy next to me has practically finished the line and there are two beats to go. It is an exasperating session. The thought that comes is this: Relax, it's all you. Everybody else is into it. Flow with it.

We go into the cut-time verse and chorus. It is all under control once again, except the tanpura is going flat. I try to direct my attention elsewhere, to the god incarnate! This is what it is about, after all. I feel a rush of despair and self-loathing. Here I am mimicking the religion again, trying to form the music into something that I have decided is where the music should be at, criticizing people on technical grounds when their love-act is a manifestation of sincerity and virtue. *Kandhana* ends. I make pranam. There is a gap of some two minutes. Then Swami begins *Bhava Sagara.*

This song is easier; so why does it sound so bad? I'm at it again. Evaluating, criticizing, attempting to control the situation. I do a few rolls on the cymbals between verses, and create a new fixed pattern for each line. The group is sounding better now. My breath is not quite so thin by now, as I've gotten a second wind. The Swami's face is radiant. He is lost in the song. He pumps the harmonium and lifts his face up to the shrine, singing for all he is worth. The energy is infectious, and the group causes the pulse to surge and drag. I am losing it again. I try to play louder, but this just causes the tanpura to be louder and the violinist to scrape harder at the barely hit notes. It is a tenuous balance at best that has become a horse race. I decide to win it and mentally deal with the absurdity. If there is a god here listening to this, would our folderol be amusing, or just rather banal? *Bhava Sagara* finally ends with a proverbial whimper. What next? This is where the Swami seems to evaluate how we are all doing spiritually, not necessarily musically. If we sing *Ramakrishna Govinda Narayana* and *Tumi Brahma Ramakrishna,* chances are the singing will last for quite a while. The first of these "swings," as does the second, although in a more subtle way. Both have fixed beats, but because Swami precedes the group on each line, his meter and tone can be imitated. Thus, the group gets it on and the atmosphere becomes enlivened, charged up. Then it ends. There will be no Shiva or Krishna songs today. Swami goes into the a cappella hymn to the Divine Mother. We sound like a junior high school summer vacation chorus. I am embarrassed by the way I hit the high notes. It is cheating to slide into them, but my breath has disappeared and I am drowning. At last we agonize toward the end. Then there are a solid fifteen minutes of meditation. My legs are killing me. A bead of sweat on my neck feels like a fly is circumambulating my vertebrae. Now I have a headache, too, and my lower back is telling me to ease up. I feel the creases of straining muscles mold my face into a contorted grimace. "Better luck next time," I say to myself. Finally, the Swami rises from his seat, puts out the candles, places a few flowers into a basket, and exits the shrine. The sound of running water can be heard. Shortly he returns with a wet cloth with which he wipes the floor in front of the shrine. My body is in the meantime telling me to faint, scratch, cry out in pain, and to relax—a maelstrom of messages to brain-central. The Swami leaves, and I am feeling exhausted as the devotees gather themselves up and leave the auditorium. Better luck next time, indeed.

Getting from the temple shrine to the library where the devotees will encounter the Swami involves exiting, complete with making a final pranam, folding one's meditation shawl, putting on the shoes, and generally collecting one's balance without breaking the continuity of the mood that has been established at Vespers. Conversation is usually avoided, although several members frequently discuss mutual goings-on despite the annoyed expressions of the others who are trying to "stay high" by continuing silently to repeat their mantras. Once inside the library, the Swami appears to assess the quality of the mood attained by the devotees. Occasionally he says that the mood has been "broken" by people in too big a hurry to leave, or by errant cymbal players who botch the job, or by his own claim of not feeling up to a spiritual discourse. When this has happened, people take their prasad (usually cookies offered to the Master), and leave, sometimes displaying a tad of polite upset over having to get back to the world so soon. When the Swami does give a discourse, it varies with the mood and the occasion, and lasts until precisely seven-thirty, unless he can be persuaded to sing or chant a Hindu song or verse, which takes ten to twenty minutes more.

The Swami's discourses tend to be informed by the "spiritual mood" induced in the course of the meditation, ritual, and singing. By "mood" I am not sure what I mean, because there are no displays that signal its appearance. People are being quiet, and they look somewhat pained when others disturb the quiet. They generally sit quite still, but look neither benign nor "charged up." Some of them do look poised enough to appear in control of an undifferentiated nervousness that sometimes pops out between parts of the event, a nervousness that is more or less present at *all* events. Japa tends to allow a lot of flux in the definition of the situation between the final meditation and the meeting in the library. People go hither and yon—rarely directly to the library. The student who has been given a room beneath the temple goes to check on his pot of cooking lentils. One of the women devotees hurries about distributing paper napkins. A few men head for the basin to wash their hands. Other devotees examine the bookcase and write down titles. Everyone else finds a chair, usually the same one each time. Then the Swami appears with the plate of prasad, having donned his Western clothes after the service. The mood is characteristically dependent on a kind of nascent spontaneity that is expressed in the interchanges between the Swami and the group at this time.

"Oh, so you are here after all," he says to me, apparently not having paid attention to my presence at Vespers, though I sat four feet away from him. "The cymbal was very nice. . . . This is Dr. Damrell," he says to the group (I have been among them for five years, so they certainly know who I am). "Professor [sic] Damrell plays the cymbal very nicely. He has a keen musical intuition." The group utters a nervous agreement.

"And your violin on *Bhava Sagara* was very sweet," he says to a woman devotee. "You have practiced?"

"A little," she says.

"A little won't do, you know, but then you have many worldly duties."

"Yes," she says.

"Yes, indeed." Then he turns to the group and says, "Mrs. _____ is a very good mother who keeps a difficult job and who comes here for . . . how long?"

"Nine years," she says.

"Yes, nine years," says the Swami, and the group gives another nervous titter of approval. "Do you have a pet dog?" he asks her.

"No, Swami," she answers.

"Accha," he says, "dogs are a distraction."

As the prasad is handed out he talks to individuals or addresses the group as a whole about various matters of a spiritual nature. Many times he has talked about his experiences with his gurus in Belur Math in Calcutta during the twenties and thirties, or he will address himself to a parable from Hindu mythology or a verse of a famous holyman or Indian poet. The point of emphasis is inevitably phenomenological, in that it forges a link between the goal of spiritual practices (such as that of devotional singing) and the focus of the immediate context in the library. The meeting in the library is the culmination of the enactment of the establishment of communion with the deity, which brings the core of that religious experience to the existential level, and to the brink of rational discourse. As the Swami is fond of saying, quoting the *Veda,* "Brahman is this." That is, wherever you are *is* the Reality. The objects of ritual and of worship are not symbolic of God; to the worshippers, they *are* God. As we eat the prasad, we are taking food given *by* God. And the food itself *is* God. The eating, the eaten, and the eater are Brahman. Phenomenologically, then, the devotee eats the leavings from God's plate of food, prays for a vision of the face of God, and the faces around him or her *are* God. The devotee sings a hymn to God, and the hymn is God. The devotee meditates using a "particle" of God, and his meditation *is* God. Vespers, with its concentrated focus, infuses the situation with this "fact."

The point I am trying to make through the evocation of the image of the devotee's fusing of himself with the object is that "God" is a felt presence in the interaction between the devotee and the phenomenological object of the situational focus. In the Church Universal, this presence, the object of religious attention, and the mood that lingers once the attention becomes more dispersed, is termed "spiritual truth," "Reality," Brahman, God, the atman, the Master, or a variety of other names denoting a transcendent "suchness." The contrast between the state of consciousness attained at Vespers and that attained. when engaged in the affairs of everyday life is the contrast between what the Swami terms the spiritual life and the world. He enjoins the devotees to attempt a synthesis of the worldly and the spiritual by "living in the world as a mudfish," as the Master used to say, "whose scales are always shiny despite their contact with the silt at the bottom of the river."

The practical level of everyday living is the testing ground for the experience attained in Vespers through devotional songs. On a mundane level, it could probably be said that singing a twenty-minute song without taking a deep breath can be the basis for "learning" a kind of autonomic composure. If one can sit still while ostensibly slowly suffocating, one can endure quite a lot. But when taking the others into account, the attainment is attitudinal, and is based on the compelling logic and imagery of the ritual and its prime purveyor, the Swami, who never appears superconscious, or affects a wise gait or stance, who displays no preacher's self-induced confidence, but is only himself. There is only Swami, and it is increasingly clear that he is "embodied" holiness.

Which brings me to the consideration of the social dynamics of this event. The mere arrangement of places, the setting of times, and the routinization of interaction, plus a little singing, ritual, and meditation, are not sufficient to produce the felt religious effect. The catalyst is the Swami, whose charisma defines every aspect of the situation for the participants. By charisma, I mean the authority that is invested in his very being. This authority is partially rationalized, in the sense that he is a certified senior monk in an established monastic order. To his credit is a forty-some-year sadhana. His robe signifies the nearest thing to godliness that can be among incarnate beings, so obeisance is expected, though never solicited. The Swami, however, wears the robe only on special occasions, and seldom outside the temple grounds. It is plain that he needs no robe, as his authority is derived, as some would say, from the state of his spiritual enlightenment. Not that he makes any claims about having attained a higher state, but his manner of exposition, his bearing, is authoritative.

To put it crudely, he obviously practices what he preaches. He *is* his own teaching. But he has no throne, wears no flower garlands, poses as no one's guru, and avoids crowds. Indeed, there is a fundamental point in this fact, which sheds further light on the meaning of the Vespers service. The truth according to Vedanta is not different from itself. This does not mean that the truth is common sense, or the natural attitude (à la Husserl), but that it needs no special window-dressing. It is self-evident once ignorance is removed, and the sanyasin's occupation is the removal of ignorance.[3] Ignorance is phenomena, the flux of events and things. Meditating, doing japa, singing, partaking of prasad, are all means to dispel ignorance, to ground one's perception in noumena. Religious objects—including gods—are not the end, as they are themselves phenomena, albeit provisionally elevated to accomplish a spiritual "task." The end is the unification of the Absolute with the relative, which comes on the realization that "Thou art That." Vespers is an evocation of "That," and it is the central purpose in the mind of each participant, which is enacted through private devotional communion. Music helps to make "That" *this,* the reality at hand, and in the course of doing it, the god becomes "Thou."

But not everybody in the cult plays musical instruments or sings devotional songs. Indeed, it would appear that these are "assigned tasks," like everything else done by the devotees. In other words, participation in every "cult" event is by invitation, because, as the Swami often says, the devotees are of "diverse temperament." My analysis of the Vespers ceremony, together with the vignette describing my own inner struggle, details the participation-criteria of a central cultic event or context. Another such event that I participated in is described in the next chapter. While maintaining the perspective of cultic involvement in the construction and realization of the Vedantic spiritual focus, I will describe the contours of religious experience within the idea of worship as karma yoga, the path of action.

NOTES

1. Mother-worship is discussed further in the final chapter.

2. Advaitic "prejudice" against devotional practices is strictly an unstated affair, the great Shankaracharya himself permitting worship and other acts. Bhaktas sometimes refer to advaitins as "dry," while the latter term the former "emotional"—all out of range of the Swami's hearing, of course, since such invidious pronouncements are forbidden.

3. That is, by stages the sanyasin is said to illumine the seeker by removing the latter's self-created delusion about the permanence of the world and the nonexistence of the Self.

13. THE PATH OF HOLY WORK

Another of the paths to spiritual realization endorsed by the cult is that of karma yoga (yoga of action). This may seem incongruous because in much of the Vedantic literature, including formal Vedanta philosophy, the state of union with the Absolute is characterized as freeing the yogin from all action. Much imagery surrounding retreat from the world is built up around the theme of the dispassionate yogin who has stilled his mind to such a degree that not only does he not act, but no mental processes arise which would present him with the possibility of action. Moreover, the reclusive character of cult monastic life reinforces this.

Yet, woven throughout the fabric of Hinduism is the central thesis of the so-called "Bible of Hinduism," the *Bhagavad Gita.* This work is among the most widely disseminated in Indian thought, and its injunctions and prescriptions for living are followed by the majority of Indians who still count themselves among the "orthodox" or "modern orthodox." In this section of the epic poem, *Mahabharata,* the spiritual preceptor, Krishna—represented as an avatar of the preserver deity Vishnu in the form of the "divine attraction"—instructs his disciple, Arjuna, a prince and leader of an army, in the art (yoga) of action.

The historical ramifications of the ethic of renunciation of the fruits of one's labors (and ultimately of one's own thought and being) on Indian culture are, of course, felt in the Vedanta temple community. In addition to Krishna's word, there is a more modern—and more appropriate—model, Swami Vive-

kananda, who is enshrined in the temple alongside Ramakrishna, Buddha, and Jesus, Sarada Devi, and Mother Jagadhatri
(Kali, as the protectress). Vivekananda is, in a sense, the father
of modern Hinduism. He provided Indian thought with its
modern rational and ethical moorings and was, of course, in
addition to being the founder of the Order, a composer of
hymns and verse, a teacher, writer, world traveler, and renun-
ciate. And it is his gospel of action, illustrated by principles
found in the *Gita* and in his writings, that members of the cult
evoke to explain the everyday meaning of "doing-in-the-world,"
a pun the subsequent explanation will hopefully justify.

The Ramakrishna Order has a slogan and a symbol, both the
creation of Vivekananda, which suggest the manner and degree
to which karma yoga and the holy work it enjoins are close to
the central meaning cult life has for the members. Renunciation
of action; worshipping God through the service to man; spiritualizing the world—these are a few of the watchwords signify-
ing a special union between the world of everyday life and the
spiritual world as portrayed in worship. Right action is worship,
Vedantists say, just as the highest knowledge is also the highest
love and the highest awareness. It was Vivekananda who synthesized the different yogas (perfected by his Master, Ramakrishna) into a single ethic that rationalizes work in the world
alongside spiritual endeavor.

In the cult, Vivekananda "stands for" the Ramakrishna
Order, the group of swamis dedicated to spiritual realization
and the relief of the masses' suffering. Sarada Devi represents
karma yoga; her duty in life, as Sri Ramakrishna's companion,
was to perform essentially worldly tasks associated with the
care of the teacher and his disciples. Jesus represents the Western spiritual ideal—his main imagery is mystic and is drawn from
the Sermon on the Mount. Mother Jagadhatri, a form of Kali as
the protectress, provides a link to the Hindu spiritual tradition
of Mother worship which Sri Ramakrishna rekindled. Finally,
Sri Ramakrishna represents the savior, the charismatic yogin,
who, though the ever-pure avatara, undertook spiritual practices
for the purpose of showing mankind the way to godliness.

When one performs selfless work in the cult's meaning of
the term, one enters into special communion with the divinity of Sri Ramakrishna. One's ishta (chosen spiritual ideal or

model) may be some other divine personality, but one performs *work* for the Master. Because Sri Ramakrishna is seen as Krishna incarnate, the *Gita* injunction to "offer everything to Me [Krishna]" is often expressed. And, because Ramakrishna is Brahman, the Vedantic absolute, the same sense is conveyed in the nature verse from one of the *Vedas* that is chanted by the Swami before the Sunday lecture.[1]

> May Brahman protect and nourish us both the speaker and the listener. May we be strong in limb and character. May our study of the Vedanta be fruitful. And may we cherish no ill feelings toward anyone. Om. Peace, peace, peace be unto us all.

Because of my commitments to graduate school, and, later, various jobs, I was not able to contribute much labor to the maintenance of the several acres surrounding the temple, which devotees and monastic members have made into an expansive garden with parklike trappings. What work I did do, however, can be mentioned here in the context of explaining the inner meaning of holy work for the cult members and its outer correlates with their behavior. While I was working I noticed how others approached what they were doing and the forms interaction took in the work context.

It is clear that the three old monks, the apprentices, and the Swami regard what they do every day as "work." They rise early, and after meditation and prayer and a light breakfast in the kitchen off the monks' quarters, they then go their various ways to undertake or accomplish whatever tasks are before them. The monks, with the help of men devotees, have done much building around the place since I first came. Two houses were built, and major expansion of the monastic quarters is under way. In addition, a large room, formerly headquarters for the workshop, was converted into what is called the Assembly Room. Its tile flooring, cabinets, and ceilings—every detail down to the picture-frames surrounding portraits of Sri Ramakrishna's disciples were done by the monks and the devotees. Only the wiring was contracted, because county ordinance required it. In addition, the grounds have been gradually transformed from a weed-patch to a rather pleasant arboretum.

This is not to say little had been going on before I arrived. The entire temple complex was already built and landscaped. A workshop and gardening shed, driveways, trees, and a parking lot had been put in over the years. During an annual membership meeting, I was surprised to hear that during the first planting of the temple flora, 30,000 plants were installed. The place, though located in a middle-class suburb, is natural enough that wild ducks visit the lotus pond, and pheasants, birds, snakes, lizards, and sundry mice live undisturbed on the grounds. In addition to numerous varieties of flowers, there is a vegetable garden, a walnut orchard, a rose garden, a garden for flowers grown for use in worship, linden tree-lined driveways, and extensive lawns, all well pruned and manicured. At the back of the place is what is called *Santodhyan* (Saints' Garden), which contains statues of Krishna, St. Francis, Guru Nanak (founder of the Sikh religion), and Shankara, seventh-century saint, mystic, and philosopher, whose nondual advaita system forms the basis for the cult's philosophy of Vedanta. (The Ramakrishna Order claims Shankara's *puri* order as its roots.)

Only once in five years did I hear the Swami ask for volunteers to work in the garden, and he did so jokingly during an annual meeting in early 1975. A young man, presumably a relative newcomer, had asked the treasurer, who had just read his report, to explain the meaning of the apparent budget deficit. (It had occurred because the Church had taken the owner's depreciation allowance.) "Is this place going to be able to remain here? I mean, what I want to know is whether you're in trouble." The treasurer then painstakingly tried to explain the ins-and-outs of property value and depreciation. "So everything is all right, then?" the young man asked. "But we do need help in the garden," the Swami interrupted, "there are more weeds than the devotees can manage to pull," a comment the audience found riotously funny.

All of the work done by devotees (that is, by nonmonastic members) is, as they say, "a labor of love." Persons desiring to contribute to the garden are assigned specific tasks by the Swami, and they work there when they can spare the time until the job is done. When I volunteered, I was assigned to pulling weeds and otherwise helping to maintain the area known as the "Krishna Pond," which consists of a small, moat-encircled island in a corner of the property. In the island is a cement base on which will stand a statue of Krishna that has been commissioned by the Church. I did work at the pond on Saturdays and during the week when I had a day off from time to time. Later on I was assigned, along with my wife, to two flower beds, where altar offerings are grown. Preparing soil, providing plants, watering, and weeding were done under the watchful eye of the Swami, who commented now and then on the progress or lack of same in the beds, and related the work to our sadhana in short conversations in the garden.

Tools were provided in the workshop. Despite the apparent crowdedness and disarray of the shop, "each tool," a monk told me, "has its special place." Nothing was to be left lying about; and things were to be returned in the condition I had borrowed them. A washroom was available for men devotees, and one for the women. I could do as much as I wished or as little, but nothing was to be undertaken without prior approval of the Swami. And most important of all, I was not to promise more than I could deliver.

Some of the work going on at different times includes such things as extracting crabgrass, cleaning muck from the bottoms of the lotus and Krishna ponds (which the Swami himself often does, clad in undershirt and *dhoti* rolled to his waist), painting, mowing lawns, and so on. The attitude of the workers is inevitably industrious, if somewhat nonchalant. On Saturdays in summertime wheelbarrows are pushed to and fro, ladders are climbed, weeds are formed into impressive piles. Despite the dust and heat, there is much activity and some conversation. It focuses for the most part on the immediate task at hand, or on the religious meaning of the task, or on what Swami says, does, or presumably thinks. Working at the temple is practical experience in karma yoga, it is said. Devotees offer their work before starting by prostrating before the shrine and mentally giving up the benefits to be accrued from their efforts. When the work is done, they return to the shrine to offer thanks for the opportunity to work, or to offer an apology for having done so little.

My big chance to do some work of a special sort came unexpectedly during a conversation with the Swami and one of the monks. I had been pulling weeds near the beehives when I saw the Swami talking with a woman devotee and a monk. A sort of wooden tower had been erected around what was once an incinerator. The woman devotee was in the process of planning some lettered panels which would contain the name of the garden and assorted religious slogans meant to evoke the spirit of the place. The monk was offering esthetic hints, when the Swami called out to me, saying, "Come here. A sociologist's opinion is needed." I came over to the group and listened to the discussion. "This monk tells me he is a 'poet.' It is too much for my brain. Can you be a 'painter?' " "Why not?" I replied, thinking there was some touchup work needed or something like that. "Then you shall paint the flag that goes on top of the staff that this poet is going to make," said the Swami.

Despite mild protests on my part, it was decided that I would paint the emblem of the Ramakrishna Order on some sort of flag. It would have to be visible from the ground, and strong enough to withstand the elements. And I was to get it done in time for the arrival of a visitor, a high-ranking Swami in the Order, who was planning a stopover at the temple, which gave me three months to finish.

In line with my perspective at the time, I saw this as the opportunity to do karma yoga by undertaking the task somewhat ceremonially and by suspending doubt in the commonsense definition of the process. I treated a "flash" I had on how to do it as the "yogic" solution. The moment the Swami announced that I would be its painter, the flag—enamel emblem on painted and shaped sheet metal—appeared in my mind, together with the way the emblem could be re-created. Find a likeness of the emblem and photocopy it. Make a transparency. Then, using an overhead projector, trace the outline on the sheet metal, paint, and finis. The problem was, I couldn't paint. Nor did I have a copy of the emblem. It took a month to round everything up and convince myself I could do it.

Selecting the paint was a lesson in itself. The Swami informed me I was to consult with a particular monk (the "poet") on the matter. For hours, the monk and I pored over his charts and guides on paints. His complete patience with and interest in what I saw as utterly trivial was at first astoundingly beside the point. I was anxious to get on with it, as time was running out, but he would have nothing of hurrying. Before the emblem could be traced, the sheet metal had to be painted. Somehow I managed to cut out a fair likeness of a flag, with pendants, with tin snips. Getting paint to stay on it required that the metal be scoured and re-scoured to remove its galvanized finish. Thus, the monk and I pondered the problems of color, strength, and adhesiveness. We settled on a light green that had been used to paint the drains on the temple eaves. Then I coated it with a special enamel, also green. Two more coats readied it for the tracing.

While running around trying to locate a good likeness of the emblem, I secured the overhead projector, an easel, and the paints. When I had exhausted myself searching for a suitable picture, the Swami finally gave me a color picture of the emblem. It took hours of mucking about with the copy machine and the transparency maker to produce a likeness that would lend itself to being projected.

Two days were required to do the tracing. The flag kept slipping off the easel little by little, and before I noticed this, I would have several unconnected sections that made the image of the emblem look melted. Finally, though, it was done. Throughout my work I repeated the mantra the Swami had given me.

After a few false starts I completed the design in one continuous sitting of just two hours' duration. Painting was just a matter of filling in the picture, which I outlined in black. Repeating the mantra as I painted, I studied the symbolism of the design. There is a circle formed by a cobra with its hood raised over the top of a sun that shines on a churning ocean. Before a swan riding on the waves is a red lotus. Sanskrit lettering appears beneath the cobra. Its meaning is usually given as: Through devotion (symbolized by the lotus) the individual soul (symbolized by the swan) will conquer samsara (worldly existence symbolized by the ocean) thus awakening latent yogic powers (symbolized by the cobra) and enabling him or her to partake of divine knowledge (symbolized by the sun). It represents the synthesis of the yogas described earlier.

I "saw" this symbol outlined in the work habits of the devotees. Their pre-work offering was the red lotus; the work itself was the ocean. By concentrating on their work, they aroused the cobra of psychological insight. Finally, their outcome was knowledge (knowledge of, not knowledge about). The latter is there, to be sure. Every nook and cranny of the place, every bush and curb is known in intimate detail. Moreover, the cognitive mapping of the place by the workers is expressed in enormous verbal detail. Then there is the vertical knowledge—a kind of experience that has as its focus no particular object.

The painting of a flag, like the planting of a flower bed or the exposing of the roots of the walnut trees when there is danger of their rotting, is action done with a high degree of sensitivity to the underlying processes that are involved. The external details (such as selecting of paints) are a device to arrest one's attention. They provide a grasp on the immediate act. Concentration and dispersion make the act automatic, freeing the mind for its vertical climb. At the summit is the lotus throne of Sri Ramakrishna, who accepts the offering and enters into communion with the devotee. Not that all work is explicitly for Ramakrishna *himself,* as it were. Ramakrishna is also a *representation* of Brahman, the undifferentiated Absolute. Brahman needs no intermediary, so to speak, because the work, too, is Brahman. The ongoing simultaneity of these two foci shape the course of holy work and ground it in the sense of place and history that has grown up around the temple. And they allow for work to be done by those whose understanding is not great, but whose backs are strong. No one just goes to work, even if it is a one-time thing. Each bit of work will be laid out in detail. Those who can't, or won't, do what is specified don't last long as gardeners. But there are many projects, changes being made all the time, and there's always room for one more or less.

In the course of painting the flag, it occurred to me that I had only traced the emblem on one side. But, as I was practically exhausted by the job, and slightly unnerved about working in a new medium, I utterly put the blank side out of my mind. While waiting for the paint to dry, I became increasingly excited about the prospect of presenting the thing to the Swami. I was amazed that the paint job looked as good as it did. From a distance of ten feet it didn't look altogether unlike the likeness I had copied. Up close, of course, there was evidence of my lack of technique with the brush, and a few inevitable blobs and slips. Nevertheless, I was quite pleased with my own accomplishment when I unveiled it for the Swami.

He was happy to see something recognizable in a piece of painted sheet metal, and praised my resourcefulness and steady hand. Then he turned it over. "But of course it is not yet finished on this side," he said matter-of-factly; and, handing it back to me, he walked off. The idea of rounding up the projector and tracing the emblem, to say nothing of the outlining and painting all over again, boggled my mind. I tried a quick out: "How about if I paint a silhouette of the headquarters of the Ramakrishna Order on the back?" The Swami paused, turned around, and then remarked, "You may do as you wish." I knew at once that there was no choice. I had to round up the projector, set up the easel, shake the cans of paint, etc.

Painting the emblem the second time gave me pause to consider where karma yoga had eluded me the first time around. Somewhere in between selecting the paint and handing it over, I had put my claims on the act, deciding how far I would go with it, and how much I might be able to learn, enjoy, etc. Karma yoga required a different kind of attention than I was familiar with paying, so I merely "indulged," as Don Juan might say, in making the flag, in doing a "good" job (Castaneda, 1974). The second time around, I concentrated just on the flag, and, in so doing, found many ways to correct for my lack of technique. The flag and I were constant companions for six days, sixteen hours a day. I felt a part of it, having been drawn there by the underlying power in an act defined as selfless work.

When I delivered the thing to the Swami for the second time, I was hard pressed to conjure up any feelings of completion, let alone of accomplishment. My previous feelings of pride had been both conspicuous and premature, so I was attempting to be a little cooler. "Is it finished?" the Swami asked.

"Yes," I answered.

"On both sides?" the Swami asked, somewhat skeptically.

"On both sides," I said.

"Accha," he said. "Then take it to that 'poet' and have him mount it on the flagpole."

That was that. Multiply this times the adobe wall that was constructed by the devotees, the earth fence that was created on three sides of the property by the devotees, the planting of this tree or the resurfacing of that floor, and one arrives at the first quantum for a generic feature of cult life, the power of holy work. The temple appears stable; things change, but slowly. There is an ongoing world of purposive activity viewing itself as having transcended the benefit of the outcome of such activity.

NOTE

1. This is the "Peace Chant" from the *Yajurveda,* quoted freely from Sambuddhananda, (1971; p. 55).

14. A VEDANTA PILGRIMAGE

To the Hindu, pilgrimage is a vital part of the spiritual life. Places of pilgrimage abound in the subcontinent. Whoever can make a pilgrimage will attempt to do so.[1] Its import will be felt for the duration of the pilgrim's life and the experiences had there woven into his very existence. Among Hindus in the United States, there are Indian and American pilgrimages. It is the latter that will concern us here.

The present chapter describes a "pilgrimage" attended by me in May 1975, in an improvised spiritual setting. My purposes at present are to explain the meaning of the pilgrimage to those present and to place the event within the context of the wider social world at the temple.

The pilgrimage began for my party at 6:30 a.m. I had been invited by the Swami to attend an event of some significance to his order and to spiritual seekers at the temple. It was an event in honor of a now-defunct monastic retreat in the remote hills, a place that was founded in 1902 and operated until 1926 or 1927 by a direct disciple of Sri Ramakrishna, who had spent nearly two years getting the place under way. His return to India and his subsequent death saw the Order placing another of its swamis in charge, an arrangement that lasted 25 years. In 1927, the ashrama had been abandoned due to fires that destroyed several of the main structures the group had erected. Because of the general remoteness from Church Universal temples, plus the availability of other land for much the same purpose, the place was never rebuilt. This May day in 1975 was meant to be in honor of the spiritual heroes of the past whose lives give the present seekers inspiration in their various ways of pursuing the goal of "God-realization." Thus, the pilgrimage was in itself a potential spiritual experience, and the more receptive the pilgrim, the more likely a spiritual outcome would occur.

The Swami arranged to send three female devotees and one male devotee in my van to the site. Prior to leaving Valley City, I was presented with a map, and an admonishment to carry water, adequate clothing and anything else my riders or I might need for the four-hour trek by car.

On the way to the old ashrama, I tried to gather a sense of how my riders defined the situation. Rather than question them, however, I chose to simply allow things to follow a natural course, which is how I have generally approached such matters in this study. The conversation was light and casual, centering on various topics Vedantins are wont to discuss when they get together for a religious happening. The topics ranged from the health, well-being, and spiritual state of the Swami to the latest temple gossip, plus assorted tidbits relating to the life of meditation led by the devotees. The one male passenger sat in the seat opposite mine, and as I drove, we talked about various groups and the way they define religious experience. This is a favorite topic of conversation among Vedantins, because it enables them to demonstrate their skills at pluralizing the world's religions according to Vedantic philosophy. During one particularly engrossing exchange, I drove past a turnoff point along the route, and as a result made us so late in arriving that we missed all but the last few minutes of the puja conducted by the Valley City Swami.

When we arrived at the pilgrimage site, we found a hundred or so people gathered around a shack that I later learned had been the meditation hut of the ashrama that had once been there. It was a ten-by-ten, one-room building, the inside of which was decorated with the usual objects that are appropriate to the worship of Ramakrishna, Sarada Devi, and, of course, Swami Vivekananda, to whom a woman devotee in New York had given the land for the retreat in around 1900. On the floor in front of the makeshift shrine sat the Valley City Swami. To either side of him sat swamis from other Church Universal temples. A "visiting swami" from one of the Order's Indian missions was photographing the event.

As my party came upon the scene, I was struck by the contrast between my own mood and that apparently attained by the assembly. I was somewhat tired after the long drive, and I noticed that my salutations to other devotees went pretty much unheeded, as their attention was focused on the ritual, mine on finishing the journey and finding a way to get into the event, if only to rest. I wanted to talk and greet people—a natural impulse, or so it seemed to me, considering the expectations I had built up about the event at the Swami's and others' behest—but they were into meditating, into being "indrawn." I felt myself subduing the impulse to walk about taking in the scenery and the vibes as I might have done under "ordinary" circumstances. Suffice it to say that I tried to look like I had not just arrived (late) to something that could be pretty easily unbalanced by an unscheduled intrusion. A few annoyed expressions greeted my entry. The people I had brought in my van disappeared into the crowd. I sat down in the grass and awaited my turn to enter the hut and make pranam before the pictures of the holy personages.

I noticed the variety of people present—older devotees; young, hip-looking Americans; short-cropped, novice monks and nuns from the monasteries and convents operated by the Order in the area; Indian couples; and assorted middle-aged men and women. All directed their attention to the meditation hut. People removed their shoes at the entrance and slipped into the shrine in twos, and, after making pranam, came out again, and were followed by others. After most of the crowd had saluted at the shrine, the swamis and novices made their way to a large circus tent that had been erected for the event. The devotees followed en masse.

The shrine itself was a source of contrast. Outside the vast expanses of fields and hills dotted with scrub oak, wildflowers in myriad colors displayed nature's spring intensity. Grasses waved in the breeze as if on fire. Inside, another kind of intensity had been created by the focus of the worshippers. Burning candles and incense, flowers arranged in vases and bowls, offerings of food and water, together with numerous likenesses of the cult's heroes were conspicuous for their im-

peccable, yet somehow spontaneous, arrangement. On the outside, there was the macroscopic; on the inside, the microscopic.
In the Vedantic frame of reference, this scene was symbolic of
Brahman and atman: The former, "Absolute, Infinite, Fathom-
less"; the latter, the communing individual soul. Below the hut
was the tent. It was really spectacular—twenty-foot ceiling,
seventy feet long by forty wide. At one end stood a portable
podium with built-in public address system. Behind the podium
and to one side sat the swamis in their ochre robes. Devotees
and *brahmacarin* made places for themselves on the grass
"floor." Rugs and blankets were spread about and people sat
cross-legged in relative silence, awaiting the first speaker.

The first swami to speak announced the day's program and
gave a brief history of the place. Then he asked everyone to
meditate. During the meditation, I noticed the impact of the
engulfing silence that was punctuated now and then by the calls
of meadowlarks and the flapping of the tent in an occasional
gust. Nature and the group's focus created a solitary mood of
quiet reflection in the assembly.

The end of the meditation was signaled by the first swami,
who entoned, *"Shanti, shanti, shanti."* Then he announced a
group of American women to whom he had taught several
Sanskrit chants. Their offerings were first translated and then
sung a capella in unison. The chants evoked the spirit of
renunciation of worldly life and extolled the virtues of spirituality through a life of devotion, meditation, holy works, and
acquisition of knowledge.

Following this, the Swami from Valley City spoke about the
meaning of pilgrimage for the spiritual seeker. Some places of
pilgrimage, he said, are readily accessible and are places where
religious practices are being actively pursued. Others, like the
present one, involve visits to remote places connected with
religious history and mythology. At these latter sites, a spiritual
atmosphere remains where holy people had once conducted
religious pursuits. The swamis and devotees connected with the
place had infused it with spirituality. "It remained," he said,
"for the assembled pilgrims to imbibe the vibrations of the
retreat and enhance their own progress toward the goal [of
realization]." He described how the hardships endured by the

original founders, and their pioneer spirit, gave the retreat area its special significance. After his talk, lunch was announced.

Tables containing breads, salads, desserts and assorted Indian dishes had been set up some fifty yards west of the tent near some of the remaining huts. A large motor-home was used as a kitchen for the preparation of food. Before everyone queued up to be served, the swamis stood before the tables and blessed the food by chanting mantras. The introspective mood of the crowd grew, and there was very little conversation. People gathered in small groups and ate in silence.

After lunch, knots of people followed the swamis and brahmacharis around to various places of interest within the retreat. I listened to a description of the life of meditation led at the ashrama next to the fallen remains of a gigantic oak, underneath which the founding swami had conducted daily lessons in the inner life. Pictures of the once magnificent oak surrounded by meditation platforms were set up on an easel. Devotees listened intently to the "tour," taking in as much of the atmosphere as possible.

Some distance away from the tent, on a high hill to the south, devotees gathered to hear about special worships, involving a sacred fire, that were once conducted there. The relics of two of the swamis who had lived at the retreat were implanted under rocks on the top of the hill, thus adding considerably to the reverence the devotees felt during the brief visit.

When nearly two hours had been passed in looking over the grounds, the group assembled again in the large tent to hear devotional singing and more speakers. The Swami from Valley City had arranged to lead a chorus of singers, including myself, in several Sanskrit hymns. Harmonium, tanpura, tabla, and cymbals (the last played by me) accompanied the singing. Songs to Shiva, Sri Ramakrishna, and the Divine Mother were sung over a period of about an hour. During the singing, from my vantage point in front of the throng, I noticed the mood of the group was gradually changing from one of introspection to one of celebration. By the time the music ended, a climax of sorts had been reached. People showed expressions of conviviality and joy, along with reverence and piety. There was much enthusiasm being displayed by the time the next speaker was announced.

The visiting swami, who had earlier taken pictures of the event, spoke about the different attitudes toward spiritual life that had evolved in the course of human history. As he spoke, I glanced occasionally at the swamis, who, engrossed in meditation, added a vividness to the speaker's descriptions of Vedic India and its emphasis on other-worldliness. Saffron-colored robes and erect postures provided a powerful contrast to the fields of grass being combed by the breezes. The crowd again became reflective. Occasionally the speaker's voice was punctuated by a bird's call.

The final speaker was a head swami of a temple located in a university town. He spoke about the personalities of the founders and latter-day ashrama residents, attempting to evoke the character of their religious life by describing events some of them had recorded in journals and books later published by the Order. After his talk, the words to a hymn sung in all of the temples of the Order were passed around.

I had the cymbals in hand and was invited to sit with the swamis and accompany the hymn. The Swami from Valley City sat opposite me and played the tabla. Afterwards the group was silent for a full five minutes before anyone moved. Finally the silence was terminated by the soft chanting one of the swamis. People got up and slowly filed out of the tent, moving in small clusters toward the eating area for a final snack before leaving for home.

This last segment of the event was clearly one which provided a kind of cloture to the experience. The swamis were overheard talking to devotees about how they might use the pilgrimage to their advantage, and people spoke with one another about how their spiritual sentiments had indeed been aroused by the visit. Then people began moving toward their automobiles, which had been parked in neat, if improvised, rows some distance away. I bade the swamis farewell, taking the dust of their feet, as is customary in such circumstances. Then I rounded up my passengers and started homeward. During the trip I noted again the mood of the group. Each spoke in turn about highlights of the visit and attempted to synchronize the pilgrimage with his or her own particular spiritual disposition, and with the teachings of the Swami, Sri Ramakrishna, and other divine personalities.

When we got to the temple in Valley City, we were greeted by the Swami, who had arrived ahead of us. He thanked us for attending and wished us well in our efforts to integrate the pilgrimage into our spiritual pursuits. After some light conversation, we took his leave and went home.

The pilgrims I talked to before, during, and after the event described the situation in terms of their own metier. Some described its meaning in historical terms, expressing a continuity between present religious pursuits and those in the past. Others made comments of a personal existential nature: The event had occurred at a time when just such a thing was needed to overcome an obstacle or to underscore the significance of some aspect of their religious pursuits. Still others described how the pilgrimage had effectively diminished the apparent contrast between spiritual and everyday, worldly life.

In terms of the context in the lives of members of the Vedanta subculture—a portion of which was in attendance—the pilgrimage was clearly of a world-constructing character. It was a one-time affair, but just the same it aroused in those who attended, both the horizontal and the vertical focus of the group. On the one hand, it was historical: Past personalities, past events, and a location not now in use provided a ground for the traditional and a link to the cult's roots. On the other hand, the event was itself a spiritual experience in which the pilgrims could participate: The evocation of gods in the ritual worship, meditation, the partaking of prasad, listening to the discourse of holymen, and singing hymns formed the immediate divine focus of the experience. Together, the historical and the experiential provided a unique commingling of cult and culture, of a special kind of religious life and its dynamic movement in society.

NOTE

1. A few devotees from other Church Universal temples with whom I am acquainted have made pilgrimages to India to the birthplace of Sri Ramakrishna. Insofar as I know, none from the Valley City temple has taken this trip, probably because of lack of funds, and the Swami's view that such "orthodox" practices are in fact luxuries and not a real necessity for the aspirant.

15. SOCIAL REALITY, SPIRITUALITY, AND SELFHOOD

In order to tell what temple life is like and to shed some sociological light on the "phenomena," both religious and social, of which temple life is the expression, I have purposely avoided overexplaining or overdescribing what seems to be there. Yet the analysis has been complex and perhaps not always directed in a straight line toward the point, so it is appropriate that a number of patterns be drawn out of the interwoven elements of social life, the religious experience (which members call spiritual reality) and the self who is engaged by and influenced by such experience.

The "problem" that the spiritual life of the temple is intended to solve is that of "separation from God," to use the common bhakti metaphor, or, put Vedantically, that of "ignorance, caused by the superimposition of the many upon the One." The lives of the temple's heroes are so many testimonials in action that lend potential "ultimate" significance to the petty hassles and disappointments, as well as the real problems and hardships, faced by ordinary people. The specific spiritual practices enjoined by the Swami and taught to individuals are the legacy of exemplary spiritual livelihood as it has been amassed by the "saints, sages and seers" in the movement's historical past. The problem with a catalogue of the temple's sacred lore, or with getting a frequency distribution of spiritual experiences had by members, is that they present the practices as a curious hodgepodge of arbitrary, arcane religious usages, which one apparently familiarizes oneself with and in whose use one gradually becomes adept. I have tried to avoid this kind of problem by showing the context of the practices. Now, it is surely time to describe what the practices "do." What does a person who is no longer "separate from God" or who has "renounced ignorance" look like?

One of the things to be said before I attempt an answer to this question is that it is not the place of the investigator to comment on the truth value of the religious claims of his or her subjects. But because the claims made on behalf of the avatarhood of Ramakrishna and the relevance of Vedanta to today's world are largely a matter of social or cultural expression (rather than of intellectual expression), my description of the setting may appear to endorse them. Were I to point out where disparities arise between the members' claims and the "facts," the temple might not come out looking so good, but there still would remain a kind of implicit, *seeming* endorsement of this kind of religious life, because getting close to it gives temple life a human quality that more or less cancels out its strangeness. At any rate, describing it normalizes it and minimizes doubts about the people's sincerity. They are perhaps a little strange, but it is *harmless* strangeness. So long as we don't feel the wrath of the gods imposed on us by Vedantins (were they to do such an unlikely thing) or have to be confronted by evangelical Brahman-freaks, their brand of difference is permissible, and sociology of the sort being done on them by me might appear to help both the public and some of its far-flung sectors along the precarious path toward actual cultural pluralism. Needless to say, however, for their parts Vedantins may view my efforts with their characteristic impatient neglect. After all, they expend much effort making the temple look like it belongs where it in fact is, in middle-class America, holding its own as a religion. Then along comes a sociologist who addresses the side that the churchly, denominational, democratic, modern Vedantic Hinduism eschews—namely, the occult, the mystical, and the rest of the stuff that attracts far too many would-be mystagogues and spiritual pretenders to the temple gates and prevents potentially "good" Vedantins from coming. My point is that it is precisely the neat fit of the exotic religious concepts with ordinary theology, of the wan indifference toward people and the emotionally charged concern with holy company and spiritual relationships, of the seeming "dorkiness" yet intellectual and commonsense astuteness of the people that constitute their religious norm. Whoever Ramakrishna was, it is far from "normal."

Which is not to say that it is another exotic religion into which we have peeked for obvious scientific (or at least classificatory) reasons. What is of interest here is how several phenomena interact, and how a world is created and maintained for a milieu of people living in a set of circumstances in a certain time-frame. It is a world that largely contrasts with what we call everyday life, and it is now appropriate to show how that contrast appears in the self of the seeker. The assemblage of details on sect organization, a general historical overview, some interactional tidbits to flavor the data, together with an ongoing analysis of the experience called religious by the members, have framed the world of the spiritual seeker and given a sense of how that seeker creates, even as he or she is contained by, that world. What remains is to discover therein a theory of the seeker's selfhood, and of the manner in which the commingling of religion and identity is positively correlated with the phenomenon of "religious experience."

It has been hard enough to describe what is meant by the religious experience because it arises out of a perfectly aligned and coordinated organic social whole that is being spontaneously constructed ex nihilo with each successive situation. That is to say, one does not have at one's disposal a fixed cultural reference point such as would be the case if the temple were in India. As it is, its Hinduisms are the tip of a vast spiritual-cultural iceberg. The discovery of the depth loci of the entire temple complex requires more than a few hints about Hindu origins, or even of a fixed, recurrent pattern. Precisely what is Hindu and what belongs to a local variation or an ad hoc improvisation is impossible to determine, not only because of my own lack of firsthand experience in a Hindu culture, but because the embeddedness of personal style in cultural patterns renders the one a part of the other. There is no thread one can grasp in order to unravel the warp and woof of personhood and culture, as it were, because it is a tightly woven fabric in temple life. What I have tried to do is reproduce parts of the tapestry selected from various essential places. The selection of the places in the weaving has been mediated to a large degree by the subjects' own characterization of the experience that life in the temple enables them somehow and in varying degrees to approach. That characterization on their parts is in a way a "replication" of this study. They, too, are continuously assembling a display taken from the overall tapestry. And this is a clue to what the religious experience is to these people.

I think first of all it is a kind of selfhood, a kind of identity that is difficult to explain because it is not always in equilibrium and does not appear to have continuity in the way that selves normally operate. The multiplicity of selves becomes diminished under the force of temple life, and another set of foci arises in the person. These foci are urges, both discernible and otherwise, that propel the person in the direction of transcendence.

Vedantins pretty much see themselves as members of a kind of underground spiritual network, if the term "underground" is not too political to use in speaking of their mutual reference world. Perhaps "subculture" is a more appropriate term, since what they do is not illegal or immoral; they do it in secret because they value it—the more rare (not "secret" per se), the more valuable is the "commodity." And the cherishing of it creates a kind of spiritual economy. Human qualities seen as spiritual become highly prized, which, when competed for—their value implying scarcity and, hence, uneven distribution among members—yield a political economy of sorts. The politics of being a yogi, then, forms a locus for sociological analysis because it is a function of the yogi's being-in-the-world, albeit a special, highly personalized one.

On entering the community, one can't gain a position by acquiring a command of cult lore or Vedantic philosophy. Erudition per se goes fairly well unnoticed because of the Swami's intellectual and moral domination of the setting. Of course, there is in use among members a wide assortment of informal measures by which individuals judge one another's attainments, but these tend to exclude purely intellectual things while at the same time maintaining a certain minimum standard. People are judged superior spiritually on the basis of how well they assimilate the Vedantic spiritual life into their character, demeanor, and being. There is continual reference to the *gunas* (modes of being) and their characterization by Krishna in the *Bhagavad Gita,* which gives the scene a *Vaishnava* quality at times. Everything is said to be pervaded by the three gunas. That which is characterized by inertia is *tamas.* That which is characterized by activity, restlessness, and the like is *rajas.* That which is light, self-contained, and so on is *sattva.* A "satvica" person is spiritual. A "rajasica" person is intellectual. A "tamasica" person is immoral. Vedanta philosophy, with its usual concern for the transcendent, also refers to *turiya,* which literally means "the fourth"; that is, the stage *beyond* the gunas, or "limiting adjuncts" of phenomenal life, known as Brahman. Turiya is called "the fourth" because it cannot be called by name with any accuracy. Vedantins strive for "the fourth," for turiya, and they do it, they say, by increasing their "satvica" traits. Persons who *do* this, or who try to do it, attain high standing in the Vedantic temple community. Not that certain people have "gone beyond the gunas," but rather they display equanimity, reasonableness, fortitude, etc., and have a record of consistent performance of the participation-criteria in temple social life. How they display it is to be economical about *their* spiritual life, and about spiritual life in general. In part, to keep quiet and stay in the place that one's being there by the grace of the Swami establishes is to be a good Vedantin. Veterans of the temple have a very reserved, but at the same time commonsense, business-like manner when dealing with what is euphemistically termed "the public," meaning not a few of the general membership as well as veritable strangers. They affect virtually no mannerisms, unlike novices who seem to exaggerate their gait, stance, and bearing in various situational contexts, such as when elaborately saluting before the shrine, and hence calling attention to themselves. The ideal Vedantin is the opposite of the noticeable American yogi—beturbaned, berobed, or whatever. He or she is strictly low-profile. If someone is heard espousing Vedantic principles or alluding to *Upanishadic* verses and the person is not the Swami, chances are it is somebody new on the scene allowing to prevail over the enforced silence the expressive urge to display his or her new-found inspiration. Otherwise, it would be a chance hearing of an exchange between two or more veterans of the scene who are clarifying a point that has been in the process of being clarified for years. In sum, the longer one has been in the scene, the more economical one is in the expenditure, as it were, of spiritual commodities. Perhaps this is the sociological meaning of the folk dictum, "silence is golden." The well-placed remark, the appropriate display of "indifference" in a situation in which common sense would expect the opposite reaction, the consistent appearance of forthrightness and solidity—all these make one a candidate for high status-honor. Yet, there is no opportunity to display status-honor, so the yogis must be content to utilize its impact as part of the struggle to "go within."

Of course, there is a kind of impasse here. Say somebody wanted to prove to the Vedantic community that he or she possessed spiritual qualities or powers. What would be involved? The best way to do it would be to delve into the practices, into meditation, worship, spiritual work, study, and so on. In addition, one would have to become devoted to the ideal, Sri Ramakrishna, and live for service to others. One would have to become utterly moral, self-abnegating, pure, etc. Daily practice could harbor no secret motives, because (it is said by yogis) they cannot remain a secret for long, turning up as they do as "aberrations" in the mind or about the character of the individual.

What one would have in such a person would be a genuine spiritual person, not a fraud, because although the person's motivation to become a star in the temple show was behind the initial involvement in spiritual life, this merely displays a latent spirituality, members say, which becomes fully manifest once the person is totally absorbed in spiritual practices. Weber, who had a good eye for logical consistency, noted that when the yogis were able to manipulate gods, the gods' days were already numbered. In Vedanta, such manipulation is entirely appropriate to gods, who are, after all, incarnate beings subject to decay, and, possibly, manipulation at the hands of the "all-wise yogin" (1958: 159). This is where the doctrine of grace comes in, a doctrine that must be described as the self of the yogi is analyzed. For Vedantins, it is the service of the "true Self within" that constitutes the highest form of human endeavor. Devotees are people who allegedly do this. Spiritual persons (yogis) are people who demonstrably do it. Worldly people are those who allegedly or factually don't.

It is important to point out that nothing will help one get the experience of transcendental awareness, the highest state attainable by human beings, but as the Vedantin says, it is already available to one. The Swami told me one day:

In vain one searches for external means to have a glimpse at capital "R" reality. Knowledge, meditation, conversion, "acceptance" of a Christ, a Krishna, or a Buddha, rituals, holy service, and all the rest are of no avail in the pursuit of cosmic consciousness. Cosmic consciousness is! But you fancy instead that *you* are. You are located in a particular place and a particular time. When you think, ideas seem to come from the mental complex which you take matter-of-factly to be the mind, intellect, intelligence, ego, and so on. It is all I, I, I, I. My body, my mind, my life, my world, my grace, my dis-grace. But on the cosmic plane, that is, with the conscious awareness that the same Being dwells in all matter, space, energy, and time, there is no separation between me and you, or between my desires and their object, or between a perceiver and the perceived; there is only the One. That One is called *Tat,* That. It is also called Satchidananda, meaning Infinite and Absolute Being; the Infinite and Absolute Consciousness of that Being; and the Infinite and Absolute Bliss arising from the Infinite and Absolute Consciousness of Infinite, Absolute Being. All this is within, if you would but examine your experience. Transcendence is with us all the time. But this is obviously not sleep, because one might just lie down and go to sleep in order to experience it. And it is not a mirror's image, or the child's coming, or even one's own experience of life. All these are gauged by some external source: A shiny object, a birth, life itself with its shortcomings and advantages are the measure of our experience of them. And the perceptual apparatus is the medium of that experience's transmission. One thing is dependent on another, so all of this is irrelevant to that highest Truth, which depends on nothing. Whether men and women seek it matters not one whit. Those who do are of course "blessed," for they uphold the truth in its human expression. But even they cannot characterize it beyond saying that it is like no other, without a second.

This is, of course, a familiar theme nowadays, and it invites a sociological question: How is it that people are differentially endowed with the desire for transcendental experience? The correlates of the desire involve an obvious specialization of interest and social function on the parts of those who seek to satisfy it. The Eastern "way" is obviously different from the "way" most familiar in the West. And by "way" we mean the way to transcendence, which is not always the goal of religion or even the exclusive property of religious people. Being infused with this, the yoga scenes are liberal, heterogeneous. From the Indian perspective, *everything* that is, arises from a fundamental misidentification of its essential identity with the unitarian being of Reality on the part of a perceiver.

Put metaphorically, a desire for food is really an underlying urge for transcendence that is inappropriately channeled through the sense organs by the deluded ego perceiving the self as an experiencer of "hunger." A sexual desire is a desire to re-establish the unity lost in the creation of a desirable object. All objects of desire are merely reflecting the ultimate desire known primordially as the desire for a cosmic consciousness. This is a desire that permeates the mind so thoroughly that we automatically transfer it to the world's contents by our perceptions. Life in the temple is designed to alter the perception by transcending the perceiver and perceived. This one does by attempting to know the True Self, the Vedantic catchall for God, Guru, Reality, Brahman, etc.

The Swami has characterized Vedantic spiritual life as a means of "changing one's psychology from within," with a set of devices and aids. Indeed, this is probably the clearest way of formulating what one is doing by carrying on a program of religious activities as taught at the temple. Whatever input comes to the senses, one attempts to "harness to the wagon" of the sadhana, or, put another way, one renounces them, "chasing away the worldly." One lets them "flow through" one and keep on going. Using pranayama, one breathes them away, as it were, by controlling the breath (and hence the reactions and impulses), and remaining calm. "Vedantic inquiry [meditation] is a thorn," the Swami told me, paraphrasing Ramakrishna. "It is used to remove another thorn that is stuck in one's toe. The world is the thorn in the toe, inquiry the thorn-tool used to remove the first. Once the job is accomplished, both are discarded." What this means is that one gives up everything on reaching dhyana (the state of meditation), including the *act* of meditating. The act is an end in itself only insofar as it stands for dharma (holy duty). Thus, the Swami says, Sri Rama-krishna, though he was an avatar—meaning a full incarnation of God in possession of all the attributes usually pertaining thereto (except the miraculous)—performed sadhana, underwent auster-ities, and did japa and the like "for the sake of devotees," but not so much to set an example as to serve as a vehicle. It is he who "catches" the samsaric flotsam and jetsam. He is there in sound form, blocking the door into the inner world of the devotee's consciousness. Traditionally, this function is per-formed by the guru, although at the temple every effort is made to remind the disciple that Thakur, and not the Swami, is the real guru.

He told me: "This Thakur was a clever fellow. Words like 'Father,' and 'Teacher' pricked his flesh like sharp pins. He used to say, 'She [the Mother] is the guru. I am her child. I am not anybody's guru. The mind is the guru.' " Nevertheless, using his teaching, one sweeps the room clean and constructs the cogni-tive and ontological edifice for eventual occupation by the main object of the quest, the "experience of God." Meditation is both the stage and the script for the enactment of the human-divine dialogue. It is that dialogue, a feature of life since the earliest peoples, about which the sociology of religion is now able to inquire in a more direct fashion than previously.

It is not a matter of why people believe in God, but how they put themselves spontaneously into devotional acts. It is not whether spirituality is real, but what spiritual identity is made up of. What is the spiritual selfhood that the people in the setting I have described allude to and perhaps occasionally experience? What ultimate sorts of concerns are being expressed in the religion, and with what do these concerns resonate in everyday existence such that reasonable people attempt to "renounce," "undertake sadhana" or any other such term denot-ing both the symbol and fact of being in that comparatively rare place? Quite a few people really do define themselves as spiri-tual seekers in spite of their apparent pretenses—that is, they are trying to act in a certain way because somehow they have come to feel that they must (or they choose to) act that way. People are seldom relaxed or casual around the temple (Swami excepted; it's his house). Instead, they look as though the capacity to spontaneously project themselves into situations had altogether been omitted from their socialization. People normally have fixed expressions on their faces, although not dour or serious or sober. They might, for instance, have on a face that "radiates joy" or is "indrawn," or any number of other types. It is just that the faces are maintained with just a bit too much regard for how they should look, but definitely don't look natural. I have noticed that there are many rules governing what may or may not be touched, who may enter what part of the temple, when one may come and so on, but they are more or less understandings worked out in rather awkward interactions, not theological utilities.

The rules of access and passage are apparently unsystematized, although their invocation or justification may make them appear simultaneously rational-legal and divinely sanctioned. For instance, no one ever told me not to enter a certain sacred area of the temple (the flower room), yet I "knew" that it was inappropriate for me to go there. I once started to enter the hall leading to it thinking that it was a hitherto-undiscovered way to the side parking lot. Halfway to the flower room I realized it was not a course I should pursue. The "vibes" told me. An alarm went off, and I took the shortest course backwards. But before I could leave, the woman who was doing the worship at that time, who had been preparing offerings for the evening service, stepped into the doorway and said, "Uh . . . your shoes?" in a very complacent tone that was too direct to be really complacent. She had heard my feet trampling the rubber runner covering the high-gloss hardwood floor. I recalled at that instance that I had listened to myself enter, too. The *sound* signaled me that it was inappropriate for me to be there. Walking down the hallway felt rather like walking on a table or the roof of a car—or something not ordinary like a floor or the ground. Not that there is anything mystical in this. On the contrary, my purpose has been to try to show the "insanity" of place, to use Goffman's (1971) term.[1] That place is where floors don't feel like they should be walked on, and where conversations never seem to be *about* anything. It is where the same man stands near the same door every Saturday, where the people (or a goodly seventy-five percent of them) greet me in exactly the same manner every time, whether I see them first in the temple and a few moments later in the garden, or after an absence of a month. To learn what this fixedness is about, what the lack of spontaneity means, one must know how a place functions as a transmitter of messages regarding proper comportment.

The temple is indeed a place apart from the world of ordinary waking consciousness. Its life is decidedly, categorically, an "inner" life of pursuit of the Self. The members' concern with and grasp of the world as we purport to know it is even more fleeting than I have been able to evoke in the preceding pages. Paradoxically, then, the religious, monastic mold into which the temple is cast by my cataloguing, classifying, and defining operations, is only a tentative construct and not a true image of the impermanent yet complex "reality" that I encountered there. The image I have tried to create is still rational and sociological, but hopefully somewhat more evocative than a (merely) objective account. It is an image based on the datum that describes how the members of the temple cult, and to a degree the members of the general "congregation," spontaneously invoke, and habitually reinforce, the simultaneous simplicity and complexity of the "religious." They do it by being Vedantins, yogis, but being yogis is easier for them, I think, than I have been able to demonstrate. And as for interpreting what being a yogi means: On the one hand, this kind of "behavior" may be seen as a purely adaptive response to special conditions—perhaps social, perhaps psychological, perhaps economic, but more than likely a combination of all three. On the other hand, it is an improvisational projection of a self into a certain kind of existentially grounded event for which no prediction is forthcoming, and the outcome of which cannot be known except that it does occur intuitively, or by some other subjective method. My observations have been directed toward "filling in" what really cannot be described. Not that "it" is a secret, although there is a certain amount of secrecy, too. It is just that the "truth" of Vedanta is inexpressible, and that it *is* occult, though not a secret! Thus, my observations—the data— are units of my experience assembled in a way that will give an impression of this inexpressible thing as others might have it impressed on them in situ—without substituting the items I have used to reconstruct the picture for the essential phenomena that in reality find expression there in the tapestry of temple life.

The god-man in Christianity, Jesus, is in perpetual (that is, chronic) tension between his natural self and the god in him. This object of duality and opposition, in a word, of worship, has an analogue in the image of Ramakrishna's fatal illness. Here, too, is a model of tension, between avatarhood and mortality. Yet Ramakrishna's tension was itself natural. Avatars come and go. In Indian religion, this is taken for granted. Thus, his dying was simply natural, and his state of consciousness indicated his utter equanimity. Externally, one could say that Ramakrishna is like Jesus, that he, too, "bore his cross." But he is worshipped as the yogi/god-man, the prophetic exemplar, not as the dying body. Ramakrishna was content to *be* God. Jesus' way was to force the issue and die crucified.

What I am saying is that the Indian way is profoundly different from the Christian way, and this difference appears in Vedantins. Vedanta is much more relaxed about religious meanings and religious conduct than Christianity. Now this may appear to be a contradiction, because Hindus seem so preoccupied with rules. But their order actually conforms to the natural, not the normal. The rule is "within" and depends on no external authority. What I have tried to describe is how the normative is really fairly loose, given the monastic setting and the polar tensions between the Western and Eastern definitions of the situation. Indian religion, and especially modern Vedanta, is concerned mainly with experience, and only offhandedly mentions rules. There is no Vedantic morality, although the *ethic* is a kind of humanitarian conservatism. And many people in the group have, it seems, simply grown up Christian in this otherwise non-Christian environment.

The self that Vedantins construct is different because its normalcy and normativeness have diminished. This means that its capacity for multiplicity has been rechanneled. What remains of long-term Vedantins' former selves—the viable, responsive, multiple, rationalistic selves—is a multilayered construct attuned to several levels of consciousness. First there is consciousness of the underlying One. Next comes Guru/Avatara/Ishta/Inner Self. Then there is holy company. Then there is the world. Then the ego. Their tensions and social armoring relax with time, and they go from the dualistic interpretation of the universe as tension-model to the universe as One.

It is implicit in the foregoing analytic description of temple life that the strivings—moral, spiritual, intellectual—of individuals to create a synthesis of the gospel of withdrawal and realization on the one hand, and the gospel of action and service to others on the other, are in reality global in their proportions because they are determined by Hinduism's situation with respect to its history and present evolutionary stage. One popular idea of the meaning of modern Hinduism arises from Weber's description of Hindu culture as a static order unreceptive to the rational economy of worldly works, and which, unlike the Occidental world, where the ethic of capitalism gave rise to modern society and its citizen-members, remained essentially feudal and ignorant of science.

Weber's view is not entirely wrong. Modern Hinduism, particularly under the influence of Madame Blavatsky's Theosophy and the respective pan-Hinduism and neo-Hinduism of the *Brahmo Samaj* and the *Arya Samaj,* two influential nineteenth-century Indian religious movements, is often syncretistic, perhaps a bit too blatantly so in view of their claims to wisdom. Attempts to justify Hindu custom in the modern world of nineteenth- and early twentieth-century Bengal seem today to have given a decidedly inauthentic cast to the character of *all* the movements that contributed to the rise of the Indian nation. Their religion is just an apology for a worldly demand—nationhood and the transition to modernity—which they cannot yet understand because of their failure to assimilate a modern world view. Anyone who stands out as "Hindu" is necessarily "infantile"—thus Shils' impatience with the Indian intellectual's propensity to merge his higher levels of abstract thought (required to carry forward the sciences) in Brahman, rather than attending to the practical matters of theory-building (Shils, 1961). This viewpoint says that India will have to give up Hinduism in order to "make it" as a nation.

Thus, much of modern sociological Indology has devoted itself to discovering the evidence of India's going in one direction or another—either toward or counter modernity. Recently, however, a few investigators have looked more closely at the total situation and have discovered that the modern and the traditional in India exist not only side by side, but in situ, as it were, in a harmony that with our penchant for viewing history as a replacing of the traditional by the modern in an inexorable, if awkward, forward lurch, we might miss, or at any rate, misunderstand (Singer, 1972). How can the desire for contemplation and the "sublimated intellectual ecstasy" that characterizes its goal exist in a situation demanding service to others? Vivekananda, of course, gave Hindus the idea that "others" were a form of the divine, and, hence, service to them was a kind of holy act. But are not acts, even holy ones, disavowed in Vedantic thought? The *Vedas* themselves are divided into the jnana and the karma portions, the former with their philosophy and refined spiritual insights being ultimately contrasted, in invidious fashion, with the latter which are composed of rituals (that is, actions or works). Does not Vivekananda's declaration of the sanctity of holy action create a theological burden of proof for the modern believer that previously was a taken-for-granted truth by virtue of the hierarchical nature of Hindu sacred knowledge? Traditionally speaking, of course, actions are permissible. But can they be an end in themselves? Orthodoxy says, "Impossible." Thus it would appear that Vivekananda has done what Marx said religionists in the modern era are wont to do when their gods are losing their power to the scientific ethos—namely, create a religious rationale for something that has purely social meanings. From this standpoint, Vivekananda's gospel of action appears to be just another way of putting off a confrontation with the fact that the old tradition has lost its way in the morass of social changes taking place with the advent of rational industrial and bureaucratic power. The distinction between jnana and karma becomes in reality a distinction between those privileged to know and those who must instead disqualify themselves from candidacy for godhood by their mundane involvements and pursuits—a hidden endorsement of caste!

Yet, Vedantic thought is both other-worldly and modern, while avoiding syncretism. The Ramakrishna Mission's work is a fact exemplifying the plausibility of the gospel of action, as are the Vedanta temples outside India. And yet the movement as a whole retains its vertical direction and neo-Orthodox Hindu demeanor. Vivekananda's sanyasin ideal is the answer to the jnana-karma paradox, and as I have tried to evoke through a series of sociologically weighted descriptions of temple life, that ideal has many facets that give it a complex character.

The cult member is the person for whom the multiplicity of selves has become a burden. Under the Swami's tutelage and through self-effort, this multiplicity is compressed, as it were, into fewer and fewer dimensions. Besides creating a *monad of selfhood,* there is released into the immediate social surroundings a cumulative psychic tension which the members utilize as a barometer of the spiritual. The higher the tension, the higher the mood and the greater is the diminution of the ego-self. Old "selves" fall away. But they are not replaced by new "selves," but rather by the rituals, mantras, "insights," and other elements of Vedantic spiritual culture. Where one once had a facet of an old (worldly) self, such as a role, one develops in the cult a spiritual analogue that wraps the person in a cloak of potential spiritual power. Again, the index of that power is the tension which gives the temple its peculiar ambience and fills the members with the expectation of imminent realization. Public functions and private cult-rituals simultaneously enhance and provide an outlet for the cumulative effects of the tension created by putting the ego into vertical perspective. Where there were old "selves," there is now the Self, awaiting its chance to illumine itself to the not-yet-ripe ego-remains of the seeker.

Short of a further elaboration of this theoretical statement, a demonstration follows.

NOTE

1. See especially the chapter entitled, "The Insanity of Place."

16.   A DEMONSTRATION

I told the Swami about my having written a book about religious life at the temple and about the "Hindu religious experience." As soon as I had put it to him in this manner, I knew that I had entered into what—for the devotee, the field researcher, or whomever—must remain a no man's land. He answered, "Of course you do not know what is Hindu and what is not. Sister Nivedita went to India with Swamiji and lived among the people for many years. In fact, she became a Hindu, as her writings testify."[1] My researcher's sense of accomplishment for having done a sociological study on this unexplored social world having been thus dismissed, I sat in his office rather uncomfortably for a few minutes until saying, "I don't know when the book will be finished. It is being typed now. I will give you the manuscript when it is ready."

"Accha," he answered.

As I was leaving, I added, "I want your permission to publish the book, because I don't feel I should say anything about this place without your knowing what it is in advance. If you disapprove of something I've told about temple life, if I've presented facts incorrectly, or drawn erroneous conclusions from what I've observed, you may feel free to withhold your approval to publish, and I will abide by your wishes." Again he said that what is at his temple is not Hinduism, but rather the Vedanta of Swami Vivekananda.

"It was Swamiji's idea that the American character and temperament were unsuited to Hinduism, so he presented Vedanta as a scientific religious system." He then added: "Come to the shrine at noon and sit with me in meditation on the platform."

"All right," I answered.

Then, as I was about to take leave of him, he asked me: "Are you free this evening?"

"Yes," I replied.

"Then come to the temple at seven-thirty for a *private lesson.*"

I was delighted. "Splendid!" I exclaimed, and then took the dust of his feet.

While the fact that I had told him about the book made my encounter with him special, the impending "private lesson" intrigued me. I was rather curious about his apparently innocuous way of putting it. On the one hand, he was saying that he was giving us (my wife and myself) attention, which would be a kind of gesture intended to reward our diligence. On the other hand, I felt that he was implying that there was "something special" in store, and this idea became more and more viable once I was outside.

This particular encounter had been similar to others that have implied a subtle change in our relationship. Where there was once a certain amount of ritualized, or at any rate formal, distance between us, which, when momentarily abandoned, inevitably gave our encounters an enhanced, spontaneous quality, now there was a more or less continuous intimacy. I had come to regard this new "relationship" (if it is anything that can be so captured by this rather crude, overused term) as an especially rare phenomenon.

He seems content to be himself around me, while for my part I am content to sit quietly with him, discussing in turn worldly and spiritual matters. If he is in a teaching mood, I listen, and, on occasion, ask questions (although my questions never seem to be entirely appropriate). Or he may want to play with my son, making a great game of following his explorations of the Swami's apartment. Or he will ask for an account of my latest feats at the university.

My attitude is being guided in these contexts by something I read in Shankaracharya's (1960) *Quintessence of Vedanta,* where it is said that the only action known to the sanyasin is that of service to the guru. It is not that I have become a sanyasin, or that the Swami is my "guru." Rather, I have come to view contact with him as the occasion for the learning of a graceful, dignified way of being-in-the-world. "In return" we bring the Swami small tokens, such as canned milk, certain fruits and vegetables, and so on. And we work in the garden when we can, pulling weeds, pruning, watering, and planting. But we neither give gifts as "disciples," nor does he accept our offerings in the name or role of the guru. When we ask to be able to give more, he tells us that the sadhu's way is like that of the bee gathering honey. "The flower is not drained of all its nectar. Just a little is had from here and there. And in this way honey is made. So only a handful need be given, and only what one can afford to give." Thus, there is no "price" on the teaching. Indeed, what can be the payment for having learned how to effect a quiet moment, the sharing of which serves to affirm a mutual ideal, and in the name of which all of it (religion and life) goes on?

As I prepared myself for the noon meditation he had asked me to attend, I continued to ponder the anticipated "private lesson" that would come that evening. Just before twelve, people were filing into the auditorium. As I was entering, I heard a young woman say that the Swami had on the previous day kicked everyone off the shrine's platform because they were distracting him from "going deep," as he had put it. My mood was somewhat agitated, and I became momentarily unsure of whether the Swami had meant for me to sit directly behind him (i.e., on the platform), or generally behind him (i.e., on the floor in front of the auditorium's front row of chairs, or in a chair). Thus, I became uptight. After some five years of going there, I expected that I would be able to treat meditation in the temple matter-of-factly, but I found myself unable to decide what to do. I was saying to myself at the time, "If I sit on the platform, my mood may bother the Swami. If I sit off the platform, then perhaps I won't be doing what I think he told me to do, but has told the others not to do."

At first I sat on the floor below the shrine platform. Others were already seated there by this time, so I simply joined them. After adjusting my position and going through the preliminaries to doing japa, I realized that something was wrong. Actually, it was more like a strange feeling of being out of place, a feeling somewhat akin to what I had experienced as I stood on the hallway floor leading to the flower room, a floor that was not "conditioned" to receive shoe-clad feet. Moreover, the feeling came in the form of a recollection of the Swami's exact words instructing me to sit *with* him on the platform, and partly the feeling was a sensation in my stomach that called forth a hazy awareness that I should immediately move. At any rate, after first taking notice of the sensation, and wondering briefly what to do, I found myself sitting behind him on the platform. Without a break in the stream of my meditation I sat for nearly an hour. So far as I can remember, I was not even aware of such involuntary responses as swallowing and minute muscular movements. I did not feel that I was holding myself still. Yet, there was a kind of self-possession.

This was a different sort of experience. I had had it before, and it is alluded to in the descriptions and analyses I have presented of different aspects of temple religious activity. But for the most part, I had rather automatically equated meditation with getting to some plane of heightened awareness from which one must re-enter the world, not as a mode of reality that is present all the time, a reality to be had without necessarily bringing the mind under purposive control. Meditating finally seemed like a natural thing to do. There were limitless ways of experiencing the awareness that accompanies meditation, it had occurred to me, and all of them are formed of natural phenomena, accessible to ordinary human consciousness.

As I sat in meditation a number of ideas came to me in a spontaneous manner. One comes from the *Upanishads.* It is that there are no external characteristics which can give one a clue as to whether a person is a knower of Brahman. "The wink of the eye" contains the fleeting image of the elusive atman. Yet, for one who has found the atman, no particular criteria apply. These impressions brought on a feeling of being wide awake, a feeling that was peculiarly free of the usual accompanying bodily sensations of vigor and drive, or of mental moods, such as alertness. I use the term "wide awake" because the second spontaneous thought that occurred to me contained the image of the "awakened one," the Sanskrit meaning of the term

"Buddha." He awoke from the ego-dream, yet his experience was neither an experience of quiescent interiority, nor of the anesthetization of his world-experiencing life. Vedanta calls this state, the state beyond waking, dreaming, and deep sleep, turiya (the "fourth"), which is the unchanging witness to the fluctuations of the other three.

Apprehending this notion in my meditation is not the same thing as "realization," but I nevertheless experienced it as an exquisite, joyous process. Then, for a while, I had no feelings or sensations. I flowed with a kind of directionless current as an undifferentiated cypher. Very gradually I became aware of a soft buzzing that seemed far away. The longer it went on, the more I was able to focus on it, and, eventually, the more I was unable *not* to focus on it. At last, my spine felt like it was being cut in two by what sounded suspiciously like a chain-saw. It was one in fact! I was snapped back to my ordinary waking state and began wondering what would possess a monk (of all people) to cut logs in the walnut orchard during the noon meditation. Then a wave of compassion swept over me. I opened my eyes and saw the Swami as a yogi without a quiet cave in which he could search for God. But he didn't budge or otherwise indicate that he even noticed the saw. Perhaps he didn't need a cave. I recalled how during one of his Sunday lectures it suddenly began to hail and the temple thundered under the deluge of the golf-ball-sized stones. The audience became very restless, and there was some laughter. The Swami simply continued talking as though nothing extraordinary was happening, and he made no reference to it. He gives lectures, in other words, with the same degree of concentration as he applies to meditation. He calls this kind of nondistractability "steadfastness," a word that seems most appropriate.

All day after the meditation in the shrine, its effects lingered. I examined word after word in a search for an appropriate label for what perhaps couldn't even be called an "experience." It was an "altered" state of consciousness, to be sure, but its parameters were unclear to me. I didn't feel "high," for one thing, yet experience per se seemed more compacted and intense. Moreover, my life, including the sadhana and all the rest, seemed to be drawing to some sort of conclusion.

This entire sense—a mental cum experiential development, which had been set in motion by the Swami's promise of a special lesson—triggered a sort of mood in me, and I became preoccupied with an attempt to put some kind of existential cloture around it. My ongoing intellectual convolutions, which had come to represent a kind of sociology of knowledge of Vedanta, seemed for the moment beside the point. The intellectual/rational/cerebral infrastructure of my cognitive apparatus had been "subrated" by a set of energies and thoughts that eluded classification and codification. My former common sense seemed somehow more problematic than usual. In its place stood a most "uncommon sense" that I could not feel completely sure really existed, although it was *real* enough at the time.

Overall, a greatly exaggerated state of inner attentiveness and self-preoccupation was produced in me. By the time of my arrival with Linda at the temple for the lesson, I was feeling amused about the air of contrived aloofness I was displaying. Beneath the surface I was very afraid that in my state of mind, even the gentle civility taught me by the Swami would fail me and turn our forthcoming encounter into a disaster. Nevertheless, I resigned myself to whatever would happen because in a last-minute ego-play, I managed to become self-assured that nothing of significant moment could happen, because, after all, *I could not be moved by it if I chose not to be,* a feeling that I had had the first time I entered the temple and met the Swami.

In spite of all that had transpired since that first meeting, I did—or rather I believed I did—retain in the face of a powerful de-socializing process my firm, if unarticulated, belief in the "how and what of things," to employ Alfred Schutz's phrase. I felt I could imbibe at will the cultural expressions, in both discursive and nondiscursive forms, that gave substantive focus to the very moods, feeling states, linguistic utterances, interactional sequences, and essential meanings that constitute the very essence of Vedantic spiritual life, a life with a more or less provisional reality, when compared with my own. But on the other hand, the Swami's enactment of Vedantic reality was itself immovable, and the lesson, I understood, was to be a demonstration of the interface between our two world views.

The Swami was talking to a young man, a stranger, outside the temple when we arrived. The lawn was being mowed by a devotee. A child, the devotee's daughter, clung to the Swami's leg as he explained to the young man that the temple was presently in recess, but that services were to resume in two weeks. The Swami told us to wait for him in the library. Once inside, we sat down on a bench with our backs to the old pump organ on which the Swami plays the melody lines to the songs he teaches to the devotees. We watched him talking to the boy, a student majoring in ceramics. Finally, the Swami entered the room. "It is too loud in here due to the lawn mower. Come, we shall have a spiritual lesson in the garden. It is a nice time for walking."

My wife and I followed him in silence to the entrance of the part of the property known as the Garden of the Saints. The light of dusk played on the myriad shades of green. Bright flowers glowed in pastel hues, and the dry coolness of the evening carried the fragrances of the blossoms to us. An organ-throated bullfrog sounded like a ship's buoy groaning in the Krishna Pond. In spite of the placid surroundings and the gentleness of the Swami as he led us to the asphalt path that stretches like a half-buried snake through the garden, I still felt uneasy and preoccupied. I knew that I was not in any way prepared for a "lesson." I was remorseful of the fact that all throughout our association I had downplayed the real significance of knowing a sanyasin, in spite of having consciously "suspended" my understandings about religion and having been "open" to its central experience. Vedanta was indeed a steep path after all. I had mounted it, leaving a part of my own world behind, but having told Swami about the book, the experience I had had during the noon meditation and my subsequent paranoia convinced me that I was more interested in protecting what remained of my slowly dissolving, worldly frame of reference than in being given a demonstration of Vedantic reality.

"Do you see all of this? It is just a show, the Lord's own maya. That Cosmic Intelligence is just beyond, and it peeps through now and then. The lesson has begun!" He said this in a soothing tone of voice, but with mirthful excitement in his eyes, and he moved his left arm gracefully as he spoke, punctu-

ating his talk with sweeping gestures. It was as if the entire
garden was specifically arranged so that he could display the
world's artificial character, although the garden has a naturalness that has been intentionally preserved.

I felt utterly heavy. I was unable to go on and wanted to
excuse myself because I sensed that I would ignore his teaching
again, blotting out the feelings that were coming on, rationalizing the evidence provided by my senses, and holding onto
ego-satisfying aspects that could be put in another sociological
report. But at that moment he touched my arm and this whole
feeling of ennui and loathing just disappeared. I was amazed.
My attentiveness came back momentarily as I heard him say,
"To know what the world contains is one thing, but to know
what the world is and what is beyond the world is quite
another. The two most important ingredients of knowing are
viveka [discrimination] and *vairagya* [renunciation]," he said.
"These enable one to *see.*"

We started walking again, and, after going a short way along
the footpath, he stopped. He touched my arm and we stood
still, waiting to hear more. Again the feeling of heaviness came
over me as I reflected on what was taking place. It was indeed a
demonstration, and I did not want to witness it, as gentle as the
instruction was. All of my prostrations, study, and meditation
had amounted to an act, something that seemed directed
toward anything but a spiritual quest for my own "True Self." I
was incapable of giving up my life, which is what it then
dawned on me the sadhana amounted to. If I could "spiritual-
ize" my worldly self, fine, but sloughing off my old self in favor
of a new spiritual self was too much to ask. I stared at the
asphalt path and then felt the Swami's hands pointing my face
in the direction of the Krishna Pond.

About fifty yards ahead, I "saw" a most curious thing. My
entire perceptual frame of reference faltered momentarily and
the objects within it became, as it were, frozen; as if someone
had stopped the projector, leaving a fixed picture on the screen.
At the same time, it looked like a sudden wave of heat had risen
from the ground, giving the atmosphere a sort of translucent,
smoky appearance. Everything wavered in the twilight. My
equilibrium nearly failed, and I felt the urge to change my
position, but I wanted to take in what I could of the experi-

ence, so I didn't move. As if to pacify me, the Swami touched my arm again, saying, "He is known by giving up our reliance on the senses and the mind. The Master (Sri Ramakrishna) used to say that one should first realize God, and then let other things come in. It is that God, the 'One Without a Second,' that we pursue here."

Normally I would have remained silent, but a question forced itself on me and I couldn't help saying what I did at that point. Haltingly I asked him, "But how can you tell when what you see is Real? I mean, when is the world the One, and when is it maya?"

His eyes widened until I expected they would pop right out of their sockets. "A good question!" he exclaimed. His joyful mood put me more at ease. I recalled other such moments with him. Many times we had meditated together, taken tea in the kitchen and walked around the grounds. He said, "The awareness grows through the exercise of *creative imagination*. We shall practice *de-creating* the world." He then took hold of my head with his hands and turned me around so that I was facing the rear of the temple. Again my perception changed and the translucent wave rose from the ground. He watched my face intently. My wife looked on in apparent understanding of what was taking place, but I recall thinking that she must have been somewhat puzzled by the whole situation. Of course, it was indeed special to be treated to a walk and a few well-chosen spiritual words, and what was being said by the Swami was not very different from what he had told the devotees countless times before. For me, however, the character of the event was entirely extraordinary. Seeing the things I saw changed my way of being-in-the-world. It was as though I had entered into another mode of experience, wherein and wherewith it was altogether commonplace to be shown the transparency of the otherwise solid mass of the world. Again he touched me on the arm and my mind became distracted from its normal operations of world-construction. As I took in the astonishing sight, I heard him say, "With creative imagination one pokes a hole through the world and discovers Brahman."

The garden was perfectly still. Then, as the bullfrog once again took up his refrain, we proceeded along the path, stopping at a place where a large, cement statue of Krishna, commis-

sioned by the Church, will stand. On either side of the cement
platform that will one day support the sculpture are two gigantic wisterias. He approached one and held a long, leafy creeper
in his left hand. As he nestled into the plant, which seemed to
be embracing him, he said, turning around to face us, "I call
these wisterias by the names of Sri Krishna's favorite devotees,
Lalita and *Vishakha*. . . . From the *Bhagavatam,* you know," he
added. "Can you hear them crying for their beloved?" We remained silent. He turned and addressed the plants: "When will
He come?" (There had been a great delay in acquiring the
statue, a delay that caused the Swami some consternation.)

"It is Sri Krishna's play," my wife said.

"Truly, truly," the Swami said in a sad tone. But then his
mood changed again, and, turning to me, he said with a look of
utter guilelessness on his face, as if he were telling me the
equivalent of "the world is round," "I always feel the plants in
this way . . . I touch them like this" and he touched "Lalita"
again with his hand "so that I might know them." There was a
lengthy pause. Then he laughed, saying, "Creative imagination."

But my heaviness was coming back as he took my arm and
the three of us began to walk along the path once again. In the
distance, I saw the statue of Shankara that sits on a small hill
amid well-tended flowers and shrubs. A fear of great intensity
gripped me. I was not ready for Shankara or his nondual
teaching. Although my perception had already been altered, the
change was something that still contained the elements of a seer
and the thing seen. In the highest Vedanta, these elements
disappear. I was satisfied with the intellectual knowledge that:

> The Supreme *Atman* is unique. There is nothing else like unto it. It
> is non-dual. That is why there cannot be any qualities which differ-
> entiate the *Atman* from other objects. The unreality of the world
> would render all such differentiation invalid (Shankaracharya,: 128).

A demonstration was out of the question, but it seemed
imminent. I recall being amazed at my recklessness. I had
blundered into a situation that taxed and finally exhausted my
capacity to resist being drawn into its peculiar vortex. Just as I
was ready to excuse myself from the lesson, the Swami changed
directions, saying, as he left the path and headed toward the
duplex occupied by a monk and a lay worker, "Let us see if

Mr. _____ is available. We shall go and sit in front of his statue of Shiva Nataraja. Have you seen that statue?" he asked me. I said, "Yes," and noted that he was looking at me very intently. "Then let us continue the lesson," he said, satisfied that I was not going to run away. As we approached the house, I was wondering what I was going to do with the rest of my life, which seemed somehow to be at a point where such a decision was called for.

Mr. _____ graciously received us at the door and we repaired to his front room, sitting down on his Danish modern sofa and chairs. If my fear of approaching the Shankara statue was real, I was terrified of facing the bronze "Lord of the Dance." In this form, Shiva is in an awesome posture. And there is great symbolism surrounding it (O'Flaherty, 1973). The Swami patted me gently on the head and made a gesture intended to make me look at the statue. As I had feared, the flames surrounding the dancing god actually appeared hot. The patina on the bronze looked like an unearthly kind of skin. The demon on whom Shiva's foot is resting appeared to grovel in a kind of perpetually agonizing ecstasy. Then I became the statue, which is to say that my sense of self merged with the god, one of whose names the Swami had given me. It was an experience not unlike meditation and it continued until I had a very profound shock. I could hear someone chattering about a statue of Hadrian that had recently been discovered near Jerusalem by a vacationing stockbroker using his metal-detector. How foolish it sounded. I was disgusted with the thought of someone wasting the interlude with the Swami with such drivel. Then I realized that *I* was the speaker! I had been simultaneously engrossed in both the statue and the "conversational" monologue. My first thought was that I had gone insane. Everyone was looking at me like I was crazy. "I *am* crazy, aren't I?" I offered.

The Swami and the others roared with laughter. "Not exactly crazy," he said with glee. "But almost, just like the rest of us. You see, we are devotees of God. Sometimes it is possible to remember that peace of Brahman, but usually we cannot; we forget, thinking we are perfectly sane, although of course. . . ." His voice trailed off and he stood up. "Let us go. Thank you, Mr. _____ with your fine Nataraja, for the excellent lesson."

I followed the Swami and my wife down Mr. _____'s driveway to our next stop, the house called "Sarada Cottage" where Mrs. _____ lives. I was temporarily relieved that the lesson appeared over, but then the Swami and my wife began talking about the unused television set that sits in her living room. "It is seldom turned on because the view from this cottage is so nice. Television requires little creative imagination." I felt completely defenseless, but I was now unafraid. Mrs. _____ was sitting at her kitchen table looking out the window. The Swami and she continued talking about the view. I looked and saw the driveway, a small gazebo, and shrubbery. In the distance lay the rear parking lot of the temple. We listened as the Swami described how the transition from day to night brings a corresponding change in the person's mood. "Is that not so?" he suddenly asked me, grabbing my hand. As I started at his unexpected question, the view shifted, and once again the world momentarily froze, then wavered, and finally returned to its original contour. I felt relaxed, and we remained in our positions for some time until the Swami moved to leave, commenting again in a matter-of-fact tone about the pleasant "view." "Sometimes when the lights are off," Mrs. _____ said as we were going out the door, "I am sitting here looking out that window, so don't hesitate to call on me."

"Accha," said the Swami.

We walked in silence as he led us back to the temple by a route that made our itinerary of the evening a complete circle of the temple grounds. When we returned to the place outside the library where he had been talking to the stranger earlier, he told us to sit down in the wicker chairs. The lawn was finished, and the devotee who had mowed it, together with his wife and daughter, joined the Swami, Linda, and me. We sat quietly for a long time in the settling darkness. Finally I asked, "What are you thinking, Swami?"

A few moments later he answered, "Whenever I think of a saying from the *Upanishads,* or when I think of Thakur, or of the Divine Mother, or of the Self, I imagine that all these ideas are coming from the mantra, the name of God. This is what is meant by 'creative imagination.' Previously, as a novice, and later as a young sanyasin, I would think of these things in order to induce a higher state of consciousness. Now I see that the mantra contains them all already. They are not different from the mantra. Whatever is—*Veda,* Vedanta, guru, god, the Self, the world, the Reality—is contained in the mantra."

It was then that I recalled how in the garden and in the houses of the devotees I had said the mantra to myself and had found that it had seemed to be the one constant in my shattered impression of the world that had remained intact. The Swami continued, fixing his gaze on me, "You should say your mantra constantly, as if your life depended on it, which it does, of course, as you well know. Is it not so?" he asked.

"Yes," I said. There was another long pause, punctuated occasionally by the little girl's restlessness.

Then the Swami spoke again, still looking intently at me: "When you meditate in your ashrama, fix your mind in the Supreme. Do not think of your wife or son. Do not think of your job. Let the mantra be your only thought."

"Easier said than done," I said.

The Swami gestured for me to keep quiet, and then continued: "So you find it difficult to give it up all at once? You are afraid?" I shook my head in the affirmative. "All right, then," he said, "You may go slowly, having a few enjoyments along the way." He pointed an admonishing finger at me, saying, "But be ready to give them all up at any time, and if you do not do so now, how will you be any more willing later? You and you alone must decide how it will be. This is the meaning of the sadhana." There was a pause. "Accha," he said, and we took his leave by touching his feet with our foreheads.

The next day on the way out of town I stopped by the temple to thank the Swami for the lesson. He was in an entirely different mood and made no reference to the previous day's events except to say that the key to understanding lay in vairagya and viveka. In case I was putting a kind of ultimate significance on my experiences, he told me that he himself was "truly an advaitist [a nondualist]," and didn't care much for "visions" and the like. "All of the higher states are on the way to that highest reality, Brahman. At the back of every experience of the god with form there is that Eternity. Who can understand this?" What he had said at the beginning of our association finally made sense to me. I would begin with bhakti and later on study jnana. Vedanta contained both approaches within a single focus.

Exoterically, the religion is "scientific," in the sense of being based on experience, inquiry, rational procedure, and so on. Esoterically, it is amethodic, transcendental, mystical.

There's nothing more to analyze, having drawn this subjective line. Vedanta has become a part of my reflexivity, which is a peculiar circumstance for a sociologist who has attempted to "creatively imagine" a grand chunk of social reality. But then, isn't social science itself, to paraphrase Andrewski (1972), a special kind of sorcery, a "transmografication of elements?"

I suspect that much of what I have understood about Vedanta has been distorted by my presentation, and much of what Vedanta is about still eludes me. Here and there some outlines of its religious "factors" emerge. True, as the Swami said, what goes on at the temple is not Hindu per se, but then just what is, if this is not? And if it is not Hindu, then what is it? My meta-theory of religious experience is based on a single datum, my subjective determination of the "reality" of Vedanta, as the cause and the locus of my experiences as a seeker. While my cognitive way of grasping what is there gives the religious an appearance of having an evolution and a being that lies beyond the experience of it, I cannot say that this "appearance" is "God," in the semi-abstract Judeo-Christian sense, let alone "Brahman" in the Vedantic sense. As subjective as it is, "my" sociology still won't allow such a statement, just as it cannot prove the falsity of religious claims. What it can do, and what I have tried, as it were, to "let" it do, is perform a governor's function on the spiritual machinery of Vedanta, slowing it sufficiently so that its constitutive processes can be treated sociologically. The remains of my sociological imagination I am now attempting to reconstruct under the influence of an evolving thought: Science and sociology *are* the *Veda,* the sum of knowledge. Vedanta is a way of being herein discovered through a cognitive sociological way of knowing. All have been affected by their having been commingled. For my part, I anticipate the opportunity that the next act in the unfolding drama will bring.

NOTE

1. See Further Readings.

17. EPILOGUE: The Divine Mother

The temple is a place where a certain kind of experience is sought, specially prized, used, and delineated. What is called "the religious" has a variety of approaches and expressions— almost as many as there are members of the Church Universal— and an equally variable context. Although I have used a cognitive perspective in exploring various facets of this experience in my ethnospiritual undertaking, obviously sociological language is inadequate to generate much in the way of an "ultimate" explanation of religion or even to match the subject matter of Vedanta. Indeed, I have not even used all of the tools available to me as a sociologist, but what tools I have used and the manner in which I have employed them suggest a possible valuable role for a cognitive sociological approach to religion which has as its object of analysis the subjective experience of the devotee of religion. What, the cognitive sociologist asks, is the character of the fit between the observable or experiential features of the "religious response" and the devotee's claims on the one hand, and the compelling internal logic or rationale of the religious meaning on the other?

   The foregoing chapters have explored several directions in which a cognitive sociological perspective can travel, given certain factors bearing on the observer's situation in the field. In my own particular case, direct observation of the setting of the

Vedanta religion would have precluded my being admitted to the core religious practices and everyday meanings supplied to them by the members of the temple cult. In doing the study, I more or less became a Vedantist, but at the same time I remained a sociologist. This is different from the process whereby a researcher temporarily adopts a role-playing stance in the everyday affairs of his or her subjects, then abandons the role once the study is completed. I never had a role as such in temple. It is, after all, an impenetrable reality-construction which has only on rare, unpredictable occasions admitted me to its inner life.

Without a doubt, I have not exhaustively elaborated on its lifestyle in its fullest and richest detail, nor have I given a full hearing to sociological explanations of religion that perhaps invited inclusion here and there. My only excuse for not doing an "interactional" or "structural" analysis of the social world of the temple was that I would thus be confined to the grosser and peripheral kinds of data. Thus I am perhaps less than convincing. Although I attempted to *present* Vedanta, because religion, I am convinced, is presentational, it remains ambiguous, a fact that is true to its structure and its interactional realm. What religion is beyond this, I cannot say, but my account of it as something special to those who somehow have it is, as the data reveal, valid in a special sense. This book, in concentrating on the interaction between identity and cult, and on how the temple members regard the religious experience—*and on how I regard their regarding of it*—has shown, too, how religion has its followers to the same extent that they have it. To paraphrase George Cooley, religious meanings, seen as real, have real consequences. And, as Ninian Smart has said, the cult itself is part of the power of the religious, which the analytic descriptions of religious experience in temple life confirm.

Perhaps the final statement to be made by a cognitive sociology of Vedanta will confirm its contribution to our understanding of the religious. It concerns still another dimension of temple life that is not much in evidence on the surface, but harbors the forces that propel the devotees toward the patterns of existence that intersect around the Swami, Sri Ramakrishna, Vedantic inquiry, and the very temple itself. These forces divest the members of worldly involvements and play havoc with their desires. They bid them to meditate instead of doing something else. This is not a process of habitualization or socialization, although for members these phenomena inhere in its nature as an increasing consciousness of its nondiscursive, rudimentary effect. It is an urge, felt as an inner psychic compulsion and an outer manifestation of cosmic force. It determines the context of the religious frame of reference and forms the symbolic imagery from which the contents of the experience of it are assimilated into the self and translated into social reality. This "power" and the ways in which it becomes known together become the fundamental nature of the religious experience. It is present in every context of temple life as the source of all the ideational imagery and, hence, of the dramatic intensity and existential immediacy of the religion. By remaining "cognitive" throughout my encounter with the temple, which has meant, among other things, allowing it to retain both a semblance of order and a special sort of disequilibrium, I discovered an almost totally masked and hidden dimension of Vedanta, which to me seems to contain an essential and final datum on spiritual life, a datum that would have gone undiscovered had I resorted to a traditional way of gathering and analyzing evidence.

What I am saying is that there is yet another pervasive and at the same time less visible dimension of temple religious experience which forms the main determining structure of the in situ Vedanta. The reality that gives character to the forms of religious expression found in the temple, that constitutes the motivating force in the lives of the devotees and the Swami (who in turn measure their lives by its influence and their ability to endure it), is known to all of them by the name, "Mother," a name that utterly belies the ultimacy and awesomeness of its centrality of meaning. Mother is *Power*, and to a yogi, even if he or she has properly renounced all claims to occult powers, Power is everything that is, in the literal sense. In the temple it is said that "Mother" is everything. The reality contained in worship, in meditation, in devotional singing, in holy work, in scriptural study, in worldly, and spiritual life, is the manifestation of Mother's power as Shakti (primal energy personified), who is the complement of the inert male principle, *Purusha*, the primal cause of the universe, symbolized by the meditating Shiva.

Surprisingly, in spite of its seemingly "dualistic" character, the role of Mother worship is extolled in the *Advaita Vedanta* as well, particularly in the *Kena Upanishad,* thus forming a religion within a religion.[1] *Kena* means "by whom" in Sanskrit and the inquiry concerns the question of what impels the several senses to alight on objects, speech to come forth, consciousness to be filled with awareness of self, and so on. The answer is, of course, Brahman, and the message is presented in the terse style of other *Upanishads.*

Then comes a story ostensibly dealing with the demotion of the Vedic gods, *Agni* (the god of fire), *Vayu* (the god of wind), and *Indra* (the chief of gods). They win a contest with opposing daemonic forces, and in their victors' vanity imagine they are the greatest. But Brahman appears before them as an "adorable Spirit," and they inquire one by one as to who it is. The Spirit asks Agni, "What power resides in such as you?" and he says, "I am omniscient because I can burn anything on earth." The spirit replies, "Then burn this straw," which Agni cannot do, so he returns, humiliated, to the other two gods. Vayu is next to take up the matter of the Spirit's identity. On confronting it, it asks him what his power is. He replies that he is king of air and can blow away anything on earth, and, after being shown a piece of straw he cannot blow away, he returns to the other two gods. Next, Indra goes to the Spirit. On encountering the Spirit he beholds her as *Uma,* the daughter of *Himalaya* and wife of Shiva, "wondrously fair." Asking aloud, he says, "Who can this adorable Spirit be?"

She answers: "Brahman! Indeed through Brahman's victory have you attained greatness." So Indra understands that what his and the other gods' attainments amounted to was nothing. It was all due to Brahman. Then the spirit tells Indra that he is the superior of the other two gods because he was the first to know Brahman, but that Agni and Vayu excel above all other gods, because by approaching the Spirit they came closer than any others and now know also. Then Uma tells Indra, "Lo! He is illumination in the flash of lightning and wonder in the wink of the eye. In the motions of the mind, the power that is shown is the power of Brahman; he is the adorable atman in all beings. Meditate on him as the manifestation of Self. Because of Him the mind knows the external world, and remembers and imagines things. He is worthy of supreme adoration, and all will love such a lover of the Lord."

Then the student, who is hearing the story, asks his preceptor whether there is more to it than this. The master replies that the student has been taught the "truly saving knowledge of Brahman which is most secret." The preceptor says: "The foundations of this knowledge are austerity, restraint, dedicated work; the *Vedas* are all its limbs; Truth its abode. Verily, he who has this knowledge is established in Brahman—the boundless, the highest, and the blissful. He indeed is established in it."

Uma's role in the story is clearly an allegorical one, as are the roles of the three gods. Each god corresponds to an aspect of "ordinary" experience. Their cosmic activity is reflected in life as a victory over the senses, hence their "right" to approach Brahman as the Spirit. Vayu, as wind, stands for prana, or the vital force, the outer manifestation of which is breath, and the inner one, mind. Having conquered the mind's main obstacles, it is complacently imagining that it controls the universe (Husserl's natural attitude?). Indra, king of gods, stands for consciousness of the Supreme Self, into which a glimpse has been won by virtue of his mastering of the *Vedas* (absorbing the sum of knowledge). Agni, the god of fire (and, hence, sacrifice, which creates *saman,* speech), is a representation of the sum total power of causal explanations. Agni, of course, was the first of the gods to be defeated by Uma, followed thereafter by Vayu. Indra, because of his knowledge, approached the Spirit, which revealed to him the secret that it was Brahman who was both the victor and the goal of Indra's victory over "ignorance." Moreover, Indra is told to *meditate* on that spirit after it was revealed to him as Uma, the resplendent goddess, standing for the *manifestation* of Brahman's power. In this sense, the goal of the *jiva,* or the individual, after the *Vedas* are known in their totality (an activity enabling one to dominate the gods) is to realize Brahman within *itself* as its very own essence. To the bhakta, this realization comes in the form of a glimpse of the essence as a divine object of religious worship or devotion, a vision of the chosen ideal. To the Vedantin, meaning the strictly nondual advaitin (namely, one who says that Reality is not a constituent of its parts, but is nondifferent from the Self), the central, perpetual, and determining realization is that of the continuous reality of the *vidyashakti* of the atman, the power of divine knowledge made manifest in consciousness as a realization constituting mukhta (liberation in life) for the aspirant.

In other words, Vedantins regard the religious experience as the Mother, the power of Brahman, and this central fact, a given of everyday waking consciousness, is the ultimate phenomenological ground of the temple's spiritual cohesion. This power is in constant flux, and it is referred to by the devotees in their everyday speech. This is "Mother's will," that is "Mother's play," "Mother is compassionate," "Mother is beneficent," "the Divine Mother, whose name I invoke again and again," or simply, "Ah, Mother."

Mother worship in the temple characterizes the goddess's femininity as the complement to masculine inertia, as I said earlier, but more than this it forms the basis for the *subration* of all ultimacy claimed by common sense and the contents of ordinary experience. So long as there is an image of Ramakrishna, there is a gap between the devotee and this object of his or her devotions. Even if one were to perfect and purify the sadhana, one would always be no match for the Master's avatarhood. Being an incarnation of god *and* a practicing yogi simultaneously, Ramakrishna is clearly not of this world and not knowable, except through a trans-divine intermediary. The intermediary is the Mother, the spirit-form of Brahman and its creative power. She, like the power of nurturance and deliverance, manifests in nature and accepts one as one is. She is the link to the lotus throne of the god incarnate, the medium of the experience's transmission and the spiritual message contained therein. Instead of giving the mind credit for all the knowledge it possesses (as in the allegory of the gods), instead of forgetting our mortality, which we are wont to do naturally (the awareness of our imminent death being replaced by our taken-forgranted belief in the infinite duration of our immediate experience of the immediate world at hand), instead of granting ultimate ontological status to that which is (that is, to maya), Vedantins surround it with the imagery and ritual suggestiveness of Mother, in whom they say the ultimate ground of existence is manifested. Temple life, then, is mainly a realization of the meanings of this manifested power, and the religious experience is the individual and collective communion with it; that is, with Her.

The Bengali hymn, Sri Ramakrishna's favorite, that goes "The black bee of my mind is drawn in sheer delight to the blue lotus feet of Mother. . . . My mother's feet are black, and black, too, is the bee; black is made one with black! This much of the mystery my eyes behold, then hastily retreat. [The seeker's desires] are attained in the end; and [the seeker] swims in a sea of bliss, unmoved by joy or pain" is one of several instances of the vertical and pervasive character of the Mother consciousness. Mother's black feet are what one "sees" with one's eyes closed. In the temple, there are other images of the Devi of similarly "natural" form. The hymn sung at Vespers's close, *Sarvamangalamangalaye,* begins, "Oh auspicious one, Thou art the source of all auspiciousness. . . . Thou art the repository of all divine attributes and the support of the three gunas" (which notion, you will recall, figures prominently in the psychology of the emerging spiritual self-identity of the temple member). The Mother is the "remover of misery, the energy of creation, sustenance and dissolution" (references to the cosmic qualities of the gods, Brahma, Vishnu, and Shiva which these energies embrace in the Vedantic system). Above all, the imagery of the Mother and the centrality of her role in the emergence of the religious experience, comes through in Ramakrishna's life as a priest in the temple of Kali at Dakshineswar on the Ganges above Calcutta. That entire experience can be summed up as a dialogue between the priest and the Divine Mother, who manifested herself to him as the god of bhaktas and the Brahman of the jnanis. She is nature as well as consciousness itself. For the mind to be aware of anything requires her creative power, the impact of unmanifest Brahman. She, therefore, is identical with Brahman as the *Upanishadic* allegory discussed above states.

The Mother cements the cult to the movement and makes for continuity between the apparently divergent streams of the modern Hindu religion. When I first became acquainted with the temple's religious life, I regarded the role of Sarada Devi, Sri Ramakrishna's wife, with some puzzlement. On the altar in the temple, she is conspicuous by her absence. (Her portrait is rather on the wall above where the Swami sits when he does the worship.) Yet, my initiation took place on her birthday. I was given mantras which came from her spiritual experiences. I meditate on her picture, along with that of Ramakrishna. But no "explanation" is forthcoming. I said in an earlier chapter that she embodies the ideal karma yogin, the selfless worker. She served the god-man at Dakshineswar and instructed his disciples after his death. Her entire life, like that of her husband, was spent in meditation and devotional self-surrender. Moreover, Ramakrishna conducted a worship to her as the incarnation of Kali, and regarded her as his divine companion and teacher. She has many forms, and her centrality in my initial immersion in temple life is not fortuitous. The temple's presiding deity is a *Puranic* form of the Divine Mother, *Jagadhatri,* the world protectress. Every fall she, Durga, and Kali are worshipped by the devotees. Following these three pujas is that honoring Sarada Devi herself. I will attempt an explanation of their meaning to temple life.

The idea behind the worship of the Mother is, of course, summed up in the Brahman/atman concept. The relationship between Brahman-atman, which does not act, and the creative power (of Brahman) the divine Shakti, which does act, is ritually and dramatically evoked in the pujas. The first puja is a four-day affair that symbolizes the short return of Uma to her native village from her husband's abode in Mount Kailasa. The second day of the festival involves a ritual invocation of her presence in an image (a color photo of a painting). As the major autumnal festival of the Hindus, Durga puja clearly has meaning as a rite of increase and communal well-being based on the harmony between nature and human life. In the temple community, it has an additional, perhaps more important, meaning. It is first and foremost a comparatively riotous affair. After flowers are offered by each Swami, and the food offerings have been removed by the several attendants, devotees literally rush the shrine in their eagerness to prostrate themselves before it, and the usual temple decorum is dramatically broken. Moreover, on the final day of the puja, members are permitted to engage in a ritual act of solidarity. The "peace" attendant upon the Devi's conquest of the demon gods is "called forth" by the Swami and "infused" in a brass pot containing specially perfumed and prepared water. Then the Swami circulates through the temple audience sprinkling people with the water. He flicks the water

on each member using a handful of leaves and stems he has
retrieved from the pot. There is both a meditative mood and
much commotion as members are hit with splashes of the water.
Afterwards members give each other embraces meant to signal
the end of any hostilities or disagreements between or among
them. All in all the meaning of the Durga puja in the temple
community seems to be embodied in the reduction of tensions
and the release of pent-up energies that are occurring as the
usual temple ambience is transformed from one of contemplative piety to that of festiveness. That sense of release, of good
feelings between devotees, is the Mother-sense, they say.

Durga puja is followed several weeks later by Kali puja, a
somewhat less elaborate affair, but nevertheless vital to the
religious definition of the situation. As in the case of Durga
puja, Kali puja includes music, a ritual worship in which the
goddess is evoked into a form (this time as Bhavatarini) and an
emergent transformation of the definition of the (usual) situation. Cast in a more Vedantic context, Kali puja is an attempt
on the parts of devotees to induce the experience of vidya
(knowledge). Sri Ramakrishna's edicts regarding the primacy of
Kali worship are followed and his perspective dominates the
situation. There is, as I said earlier, a perpetual tension between
bhakti and jnana. Ramakrishna, in worshipping Bhavatarini,
enacted its resolution.

The image of Bhavatarini worshipped by the god-man stands
on a prostrate Shiva, and her eyes are fixed on him. As he
represents the undifferentiated, Absolute Brahman, her gaze
signals her union with Brahman and her nondifference from
Brahman. The puja is a demonstration of this Vedantic maxim:
(paraphrasing the *Kena Upanishad*) Whatever is known is not
Brahman, but by Brahman everything is known. Whoever says
he knows it doesn't. Whoever knows it not knows it. This
contradiction is personified in Bhavatarini as the capricious
savior who is the consort of time and death. She holds in her
hands the sign of forgiveness and a sword. She has subdued
Shiva, even as her manifestation is dependent on him. Just as
Durga's rite has to do with the celebration of her (and Brahman's) victory over the senses and the mind, so does Kali's
celebrate the union of the cosmic processes of evolution and
involution, symbolized by the shakti (primal energy) and

purusha (primal being). This celebration is, hence, a Vedantic recognition of the need for a provisional reality on which to base an inquiry into the nature of Brahman. And the purest form of that reality is Bhavatarini, whom the Master worshipped throughout his life and whom married devotees have invited to their shrines.

Following Durga and Kali pujas there is Jagaddhatri puja which falls on the anniversary of the temple. According to Sri Ramakrishna, she is the "bearer of the universe" who reveals herself to the one who can control the mind. She rides a lion which is symbolic of her controlling power over the elephantine dross of ordinary, waking consciousness. Like the other Mother-worships, this one forms a sort of spiritual matrix about the sources of the temple's ultimate values and meanings. Her domain is the universe and the world (whereas Durga's and Kali's respective domains are—allegorically speaking—in the body and in consciousness). She is the most beneficent of the three forms of Mother, as she accepts all who present themselves in good faith. Taking each devotee as he or she is (in contrast to the gods like Shiva, Rama, and Krishna—not to neglect to mention Sri Ramakrishna—who demand purity and ritual exactitude), she is the presider over happenings in the devotees' lives and in the daily life of the temple itself.

Jagaddhatri is not just a fortuitous addition to a seemingly overpopulated spiritual assembly. Jagaddhatri first appears in Sarada Devi's sadhana. Sarada's mother, it seems, was especially fond of the form of the Mother as the protectress, but found herself unable to afford the elaborate worship that was required to keep the goddess ensconced in the woman's shrine. Sarada thought that her mother's consternation would pass, but she herself had a vision of Jagaddhatri who asked Sarada whether the goddess should move to another village. Sarada the next day secured the necessary materials for the puja, and in later years even went so far as to procure land so that the food for the offering could be especially grown. This tradition, Mother-worship in the form of Jagaddhatri, has been carried on continuously since that time. In the Valley City temple of the Church Universal, Jagaddhatri represents in consciousness a sort of provisional ultimacy of the means of spiritual inquiry. It is a kind of symbolic shraddha (inner conviction) which when evoked in worship conveys to participants in the ritual the sense of the *active* intervention of the divine on the behalf of the Swami, the devotees, and the temple itself. Jagaddhatri holds the lease, as it were, on the spirituality of the temple and is the key to the spiritualization of the devotees' everyday lives. It is she whom they address in the generic way as Mother. "Mother solved the problem for me." "Mother has been kind enough to allow my meditations to be very deep." "Mother has provided insufficient rain." "She died because Mother wished her to." This mother is intimately known and readily knowable provided one has the appropriate medium. That medium, of course, is Sarada, capital G god, in the form of the mantra, the sound Brahman. Her worship is a climax to the annual round of Mother-worship, and it renews spiritual energy and provides new opportunity to express the imagery of her immediate presence, counsel, and companionship, which is the course sadhana ideally takes in everyday life. Sarada is the illuminatory of Ramakrishna and of Brahman, so her worship—which includes her special propitiation and an ongoing, everyday vertical link to the transcendent—is *mutatis mutandis,* a dualistic, non-dual religion. The experience of god as Mother hence is a felt presence of assorted forces that bear on the question of the reality of the objects of consciousness and indeed of consciousness itself. Which is to say that the goddesses, worshipped in the temple at different times, are really there at all times in the devotee's frame of reference.

Or is this not just a poetic way of describing a kind of stylized self-suggestion? Are people in the temple authentically different? My answer is clearly affirmative, although it is, like nearly every other statement I can make about religion, going to have to be mightily qualified. The Indians in the scene seem to know the whole Vedantic experience as a unitary phenomenon, which has continuity without having to be consciously reconstructed in experience. That the Vedantic experience is for them a total reference world, which provides a place in the community formed around the cult objects and the sacred knowledge, is certain. They do not see participation in any other way than a natural outcome of their prior socialization. They are relaxed, poised, and in control. Friendly to the point of graciousness, they nevertheless respect social distances. I think every American in the scene knows the meaning of the rooted character of the Indian presence in the temple setting.

For their part, the Americans are at best able to assimilate only so much of the Vedantic frame of reference. Lacking the cultural foundation for the training in the awareness of the essential nondifference of the Self and God, or of "All is Mother," or of the presence in waking consciousness of the god-man Ramakrishna's image, the experience is fragmented. I would interpret the experience I had by saying that I was not sufficiently bent on labelling a sudden, momentary lapse in the dominion of my common sense a vision of the Divine Mother, though from the standpoint of the reality of cult life this is probably what it was. Indeed one can go further than this: Mother is, as the *Purana (Chandi)* says, "The Devi who exists in all beings in the form of faith, compassion, death, success, grief, anger, beauty, ad infinitum. Her name I repeat again and again."

The devotees in the music group are assembled in the back of the auditorium. The hymn to the Divine Mother is up next. It is extremely difficult to keep in tune, so the group has to allow the Mother to do with it what she will. It is approached with lightness, although it is solemn, liturgical. The same verse is repeated ten times; at the same place each time a verse is repeated, a new attribute is injected. It is a formula that accompanies the worship being done by the Swami. While he is placing flowers before the shrine's images and putting flowers above the frames of Jagaddhatri and Sarada Devi, we are entoning the Puranic portrait of Mother as the simultaneous source and content of experience. The definition of the situation during this singing, and the feelings that accompany it, are similar to the definition and feelings during Mother worship at the four pujas described above. Indeed, that feeling is perpetually felt and the accession to Mother's will in the situation forms the underlying continuity for a cult and the social movement which serves as its vehicle. The temple is the Mother, the Swami and the devotees her children and their playmates.

The reality of the Mother in everyday waking consciousness is both the material and the efficient cause of the religious experience in temple life. Her power has been ritually created, preserved, and utilized through an ongoing discovery and articulation of trans-divine reality emergent in the lives of the Swami and the members of the community. This specially created and existent reality is more than a sum of the objects of religious focus that appear to make it up. Giving it some ultimate sociological import would be inappropriate. Suffice it to say that it withholds at least as much as it reveals about the social creature in that apparently age-old quest for divinity.

NOTE

1. The following rendering of the *Kena Upanishad* has been drawn from three sources: Prabhavananda and Manchester (1968), Juan Mascaró (1969), and Sharvananda (1960).

BIBLIOGRAPHY

REFERENCES

Andrewski, Stanislau. *Social Sciences as Sorcery*. London: Deutsch, 1972.

Berreman, Gerald. *Hindus of the Himalayas: Ethnography and Change*. Berkeley: University of California Press, 1972.

Castaneda, Carlos. *Tales of Power*. New York: Simon & Schuster, 1974.

The Cultural Heritage of India. (Volume I). Belur Math, Calcutta: Sri Ramakrishna Centenary Committee, 1936.

Damrell, Joseph D. *Improvisational Youth Groups & the Search for Identity: A Study of an Urban Religious Sect in the Youth Culture*. Doctoral Dissertation, 1972.

Deutsch, Eliot. *Advaita Vedanta: A Philosophical Reconstruction*. Honolulu: East-West Center Press, 1968.

Durkheim, Emile. *The Elementary Forms of Religious Life*. Glencoe, Ill.: Free Press, 1947.

Goffman, Erving. *Relations in Public*. New York: Basic Books, 1971.

Isherwood, Christopher. *Ramakrishna and His Disciples*. New York: Simon and Schuster, 1965.

Kohn, Hans. *Nationalism: Its Meaning and History*. Princeton, N.J.: Van Nostrand, 1965.

Mascaró, Juan (trans.). *The Upanishads*. Middlesex, England: Penguin Books, 1969.

M (Mahendranath Gupta). *The Gospel of Sri Ramakrishna*. (Swami Nikhilananda, trans.). New York: Ramakrishna-Vivekananda Center, 1969.

Needleman, Jacob. *The New Religions*. New York: Doubleday and Company, 1970.

Nikhilananda, Swami. "Vivekananda," in Vivekananda, Swami, *Vivekananda: The Yogas and Other Works*. New York: Ramakrishna-Vivekananda Center, 1953.

O'Flaherty, Wendy Doniger. *Asceticism and Eroticism in the Mythology of Shiva*. London: Oxford University Press, 1973.

Rolland, Romain. *The Life of Ramakrishna*. Mayavati, Almora, Himalayas: Advaita Ashrama, 1927 (Seventh Edition, 1965).

Prabhavananda, Swami and Frederick Manchester (trans.). *The Upanishads: Breath of the Eternal*. Hollywood: Vedanta Press, 1968.

Sambuddhananda, Swami (trans.). *Vedic Prayers*. Calcutta: Sri Ramakrishna Mission, 1971.

Saradananda, Swami. *Sri Ramakrishna: The Great Master*. (Swami Nikhilananda, trans.). Madras: Advaita Ashrama, 1963.

Schutz, Alfred. "The Stranger: An Essay in Social Psychology," *American Journal of*

Sociology 49 (May, 1944).

Shankaracharya (1970) *A Thousand Teachings of Sri Shankaracharya.* (Swami Jagadananda, trans.) Mylapore: Sri Ramakrishna Math.

——— (1967) *Self-Knowledge.* (Swami Nikhilananda, trans.) Mylapore: Sri Ramakrishna Math.

——— (1960) *The Quintessence of Vedanta.* (Swami Tattwananda, trans.) Kalady, Kerala: Sri Ramakrishna Math.

Sharvananda, Swami. *Kenopanishad.* Mylapore: Sri Ramakrishna Math, 1960.

Shils, Edward. "The Intellectual Between Tradition and Modernity: The Indian Situation," in *Comparative Studies in Society and History.* The Hague: Mouton, 1961.

Shrimad Bhagavad Gita. (Swami Swarupananda, trans.). Mayavati, Pithoragarh, Himalayas: Advaita Ashrama, 1972.

Singer, Milton. *When A Great Tradition Modernizes: An Anthropological Approach to Indian Civilization.* New York: Praeger, 1972.

Smart, Ninian. *The Science of Religion and the Sociology of Knowledge: Some Methodological Questions.* Princeton: Princeton University Press, 1973.

Swahananda, Swami (trans.). *Chandogya Upanishad.* Mylapore, Madras: Sri Ramakrishna Math, 1965.

Usha, Brahmacharini. *A Ramakrishna-Vedanta Wordbook.* Hollywood: Vedanta Press, 1962.

Veysey, Lawrence. *The Communal Experience: Mystical and Anarchist Countercultures in America.* New York: Harper and Row, 1973.

Vivekananda, Swami. *Vivekananda: The Yogas and Other Works.* New York: Ramakrishna-Vivekananda Center, 1953.

Wagner, Helmut R. "Sociologists of Phenomenological Orientation: Their Place in American Sociology," in *American Sociologist* 10, 3 (August 1975).

Weber, Max. *Religions of India: The Sociology of Hinduism and Buddhism.* Glencoe, Illinois: Free Press, 1958.

Wilkins, W. J. *Hindu Mythology: Vedic and Puranic* (Second Edition). London: W. Thacker, 1900.

Zimmer, Heinrich. *The Philosophies of India.* Princeton, New Jersey: Princeton University Press (Bolingen Series), 1951.

FURTHER READINGS

Berger, Peter and Thomas Luckmann. *The Social Construction of Reality.* New York: Doubleday, 1963.

Brahma-Sutra Bhasya of Shankaracharya.. (Swami Gambhirananda, trans.). Calcutta: Advaita Ashrama, 1972.

Campbell, Joseph. *Myths and Symbols in Indian Art.* New York: Pantheon Books, 1946.

The Cultural Heritage of India (Volumes II and III). Belur Math, Calcutta: Sri Ramakrishna Centenary Committee, 1936.

Damrell, Joseph. "Book review of *The Science of Religion and the Sociology of Knowledge* by Ninian Smart," in *Contemporary Sociology* V, 5 (July 1975).

Deussen, Paul. *The System of Vedanta.* Chicago: The Open Publishing House, 1912.

Gambhirananda, Swami. *History of the Ramakrishna Math and Mission.* Calcutta: Advaita Ashrama, 1957.

Garfinkel, Harold. *Studies in Ethnomethodology.* Englewood Cliffs, N.J.: Prentice-Hall, 1967.

Glaser, Barney and Anselm Strauss. *The Discovery of Grounded Theory*. Chicago: Aldine, 1967.

Husserl, Edmund. *Cartesian Meditations*. The Hague: Martinus Nijhoff, 1969.

Laing, R. D. *The Politics of Experience*. New York: Ballantine Books, 1967.

Lyman, Stanford M. and Marvin B. Scott. *A Sociology of the Absurd*. New York: Appleton-Century-Crofts, 1970.

Madhavananda, Swami (trans.). *Bhartrihari's Hundred Verses on Renunciation*. Mayavati, Almora, Himalayas: Advaita Ashrama, 1971.

Nehru, Jawaharlal. *The Discovery of India*. New York: Doubleday, 1946.

Nityaswarupananda, Swami (trans.). *Ashtavakra Samhita*. Mayavati, Almora, Himalayas: Advaita Ashrama, 1969.

Nivedita, Sister (Margaret E. Noble). *The Web of Indian Life*. New York: Henry Holt, 1924.

Prabhavananda, Swami and Christopher Isherwood (trans). *Narada's Way of Divine Love: The Bhakti Sutras*. Hollywood: Vedanta Press, 1946.

Rolland, Romain. *Prophets of the New India*. New York: Albert and Charles Boni, 1930.

Sartre, Jean-Paul. *The Emotions: The Outline of a Theory*. New York: Philosophical Library, 1948.

Schutz, Alfred. *On Phenomenology and Social Relations*. Chicago: University of Chicago Press, 1970.

Singer, Milton (ed.). *Krishna: Myths, Rites and Attitudes*. Honolulu: East-West Center Press, 1966.

Spear, Percival. *India: A Modern History*. Ann Arbor: University of Michigan Press, 1961.

Sri Sarada Devi: The Holy Mother. Mylapore, Madras: Sri Ramakrishna Math, 1949.

Srinivas, M. N. and A. M. Shaw. "Hinduism," in *International Encyclopedia of the Social Sciences*. 6 (1968) 358-366.

Weber, Max. *The Sociology of Religion*. Boston: Beacon Press, 1922.

Woodroffe, Sir John (Arthur Avalon). *The Serpent Power: The Secrets of Tantric and Shaktic Yoga*. New York: Dover Publications, 1974.

GLOSSARY

Accha. An expression in Bengali I take to mean "O.K." or "right on," which the Swami frequently uses.

Advaita Vedanta. Nondualistic Vedanta philosophy evolved from the *Vedas* which holds that the perception of the universe as manifold is a misreading of the one ultimate Reality; the nondual philosophy of Shankaracharya (c. 800 A.D.). According to Sri Ramakrishna (1836-1886), Advaita Vedanta is the final outcome of successive stages of spiritual realization which move from God with form to God without form (i.e., from Ishwara to Brahman).

Agni. The God of Fire, Agni is prominently mentioned in the *Vedas*. In the *Kena Upanishad* Agni represents the sum of the explanatory power of speech which is subrated by Brahman.

Arati. Part of the Vespers worship at the temple in which burning camphor wicks on a brass lamp are waved before the shrine.

Arya Samaj. The name of an Indian religious movement that promoted the return to strict Vedic orthodoxy, including ritualized worship, the upholding of traditional notions of caste, and the disavowal of all European influences.

Asana. As employed in the text, asana refers to the posture of the body during meditation (i.e., seated cross-legged, with back, head, and neck held erect and still) and to the place where one sits for meditation.

Ashrama. A holy residence, such as a monastery or hermitage. Homes of devotees are called ashramas by the Swami.

---

*The Glossary was compiled with the assistance of Linda Damrell. Words are defined according to their everyday use by temple participants. Use has been made of Brahmacharini Usha's work, *A Ramakrishna-Vedanta Wordbook,* Hollywood. Vedanta Press, 1971, and W.J. Wilkins', *Hindu Mythology: Vedic and Puranic,* London: W. Thacker & Co., 1900.

Atman. The Self in Vedanta; God conceived as immanent; the "soul" of the jiva (individual embodied being).

Avatara. Divine Incarnation. Deriving the notion from the Vaishnava religion which states that the undifferentiated Absolute takes on form to establish religious truth, modern Vedantins maintain that Ramakrishna is such a phenomenon, like Buddha, Krishna, Christ, Rama, etc.

Avidya. Ignorance. The result of maya (illusion).

Baba. Father. A Bengali term of endearment sometimes reserved for gurus.

Belur Math. Headquarters of the Ramakrishna Order in Calcutta, built in 1898.

Bhagavad-Gita. (Also *Srimad Bhagavad-Gita* and *Gita.*) Dated between the fifth and second centuries B.C., it forms eighteen chapters of the epic, *Mahabharata.* In the *Gita,* Krishna instructs his disciple Arjuna, a warrior prince, in yoga.

Bhagavan. Personal God, or the Lord. The object of the devotees' devotions.

Bhagavatam. A sacred book of the Vaishnava religion, it is one of the *Puranas* dealing with the lives of Hinduism's ancient heroes, including Krishna.

Bhakta. A devotee of a god; in the temple, a Ramakrishna devotee.

Bhakti Yoga. A form of yoga emphasizing ecstatic devotional practices. Its outcome is the merging of the ego with the chosen ideal (ishta). Church Universal Vedantins combine, as per Ramakrishna's edicts, devotional yoga with Vedanta metaphysics.

Bhavatarini. A form of the Divine Mother Kali, known as the Redeemer of the Universe, who was worshipped by Sri Ramakrishna.

Bhava Sagara. A hymn by Swami Vivekananda extolling the divine qualities of Sri Ramakrishna; it is sung at Vespers in the temple.

Bodhisattva. A nearly emancipated being in Mahayana Buddhism who postpones enlightenment in order to help humankind.

Brahma. The creator in Hindu mythological systems, and one of the Hindu trinity; identical with the Personal God.

Brahma Sutra. Also known as the Vedanta Sutra, it is an aphoristic statement on the *Upanishads* in which the focus is the knowledge of Brahman. It is the root of the philosophical tradition of Vedanta.

Brahmachari. A person who has taken monastic vows in the Ramakrishna Order; one who is devoted to spiritual life and has embraced chastity. Bramacharya is the stage at which such vows or less formal resolutions are taken; literally means "student life," which is one of the four stages of life in traditional Hindu society. The word's plural form is brohmacharin.

Brahman. God as transcendent; impersonal Absolute Existence, knowledge, bliss (i.e., Satchidananda); also referred to in the text as turiya (the "fourth"), a state of awareness beyond waking, dreaming, and dreamless sleep.

Brahmo Samaj. The name of an influential religious reform movement that promoted the worship of the formless (monotheistic) god and rejected the gods of the Hindu tradition, along with caste. Quite a few members of the Brahmo Samaj were devotees of Sri Ramakrishna.

Chadar. A shawl used in meditation by temple members.

Chandi. A sacred book from the Shakta Tantra praising the female form of the Divine; also known as the Devi Mahatmya.

Chela. A disciple.

Chit. Pure consciousness without limiting contents of objects; an aspect of Brahman.

Chosen Ideal. (Ishta), an aspect of God, with whom communion is sought, chosen by a spiritual aspirant. Mantras given in initiation are "names" of this ideal.

Darshan. Paying one's respects to a shrine or holy person as well as the experiences derived from such acts as they are performed.

Deva, Devi. God in male and female form, respectively.

Devi Mahatmya. See *Chandi.*

Dharma. Merit, morality, religion, duty, law.

Dhoti. A cloth wrapped around the waist that hangs nearly to the feet; it is occasionally worn by the Swami.

Dhyana. Meditation, or deep concentration.

Disciple. One who has established a relationship with a spiritual guide.

Durga. A form of Kali, the Divine Mother, who is worshipped in the fall. In the *Chandi* she destroys her enemies, symbolic of ignorance, and bestows love and knowledge on spiritual seekers.

Durga Puja. Annual worship in the fall of Sri Durga. Several worships are conducted at the temple during the five-day affair.

Durgayai Namah. A Sanskrit mantra invoking Sri Durga; frequently used by the Swami before embarking on a trip by car.

Ganesha. Worshipped at the beginning of all pujas as the incarnate remover of obstacles and God of Wisdom, he is believed to grant success in all matters spiritual and worldly. He is the son of Shiva and Uma.

Ganga. The name in Sanskrit for the Ganges River; the water from the river is used by the Swami in ritual worship.

Gerua. The ochre-colored cloth of sanyasins thatis draped in a special way about the body, providing the distinct look associated with Indian teachers.

Ghee. Clarified butter used in worship and cooking.

Guna. The three qualities of personality according to Samkhya philosophy and expounded in the *Srimad Bhagavad-Gita.* Sattva refers to spirituality, rajas to activity, tamas to inertia.

Guru. Spiritual teacher who knows the "spirit of the scriptures," is "sinless," "without desires." The guru assumes responsibility for the disciple's spiritual undertaking. The Swami, as customary in his order, does not allow anyone to call him "guru," though he obviously plays the "role."

Guru Bada. The practice of worshipping the spiritual teacher in living form; common in the Vaishnava, though not in the Vedanta, tradition.

Guru Dakshina. Receiving the blessings of the spiritual teacher, together with his or her taking on the karma of the devotee, especially during initiation into the sadhana.

Guru Purnima. A traditional Hindu ceremony that involves honoring spiritual teachers. In the temple the focus is on the Swami and the heroes of the Vedantic tradition and the Ramakrishna Order. It is conducted in private at the temple on the appropriate calendar day.

Hatha Yoga. The physical culture system used to ensure physical health. Some temple members employ it, but do not consider it to be a part of spiritual life.

Holy Mother. Sri Sarada Devi (1853-1920), wife of Sri Ramakrishna, considered to be an incarnation of Sarasvati, Hindu goddess of learning, or in general, of the Divine Mother Kali.

Indra. Chief of the Gods, he represents self-consciousness in the *Kena Upanishad*. He was the most popular deity of the *Vedas* and was worshipped as the god of the firmament who made the earth fruitful.

Ishta. The Divine Ideal.

Ishta-Nishta. The devotee's Chosen Ideal toward whom (or which) spiritual life is directed.

Jagadhatri. The temple's protectress. She has a place of importance in Ramakrishna-Vedanta as the special focus of Sri Sarada Devi. A form of Shakti, she is analyzed in the Epilogue as the personified power known as "Mother" in everyday life.

Jai. Victory.

Japa. Repetition of a mantra, a name of a god.

Jaya. Same as jai.

Jivanmukta. Liberated individual; one who has had a vision of a god, or else lives "in the consciousness of God."

Jnana. Knowledge of the ultimate reality and the path leading to it.

Jnana Yoga. The form of yoga most often associated with Vedantic inquiry, the principal method of which is to analyze phenomena, rejecting what is transitory.

Jnani. A practitioner of nondual jnana yoga; a knower of Brahman.

Kailasa. A mountain in the Himalayas regarded as the abode of Shiva and Parvati.

Kali. The consort of Kala (time); the "primal energy" in the form of a female.

Kandhana. A hymn to Ramakrishna by Vivekananda said to be a method of liberation which is sung at Vespers; another name for the Vespers service at the temple.

Karma. Action, mental or physical, or its consequences. In the *Vedas*, karma also refers to ritualistic worship.

Karma Yoga. The path of selfless work; one of the four main types of yoga wherein the practitioner gives up all fruits of work to the ishta, regarding the ishta as the "doer" and the self as a "witness" (i.e., as the atman).

Krishna. Hero of the Mahabharata; incarnation of Vishnu.

Kundalini. A word derived from yoga meaning "coiled up" (i.e., like a snake about to strike); a reference to the latent spiritual energy in the individual which when awakened gives the subject mystical experiences.

Lila. Play of the Divine (i.e., the relative: time, space, causation); when an avatar is incarnated lila means that God is playing all the roles in the drama.

Lotus posture. See asana.

Mahabharata. The world's longest epic poem dated (at the latest) c. 500 B.C. It contains assorted paeans to God and represents a kind of compilation of numerous Vedic insights and spiritual truths. The *Bhagavad-Gita* forms one of its parts.

Maharaj. "Great King," a title of respect for the Swami.

Mahavakya. Literally, "great saying." A mantra containing the "essence of Brahman," of which there are four. They come from the *Upanishads* and are part of the Sanskrit repertoire used by the Swami at pujas and in teaching.

Mala. A rosary containing either 54 or 108 beads which is used when repeating the mantra given the aspirant after the initiation.

Mantra. A name of a god, usually one's Chosen Ideal, which is often repeated silently; the essence of the guru's teaching to the disciple; also, a hymn, verse or phrase from the *Vedas.*

Master. A name for Sri Ramakrishna.

Matra. Pulse or beat; as in "four matras to the measure."

Math. Monastery.

Maya. A concept in Vedanta philosophy characterizing the phenomenal world as Brahman's power. Epistemologically maya means "illusion," phenomenologically, maya refers to the mental act of superimposing "the many" on "the one." Maya causes and is the result of "separation from one's real nature," which spiritual life is intended to correct.

Mudra. A term referring to any number of positions into which the hands are formed by the conductor of a ritual; they are said to aid concentration and to release spiritual energies which contribute to the effects of the ritual.

Nada Yoga. One of the subdisciplines of yoga that forms a spiritual path in its own right. In nada yoga the aspirant seeks to realize the soundform of the divine.

Naren. Swami Vivekananda's boyhood nickname.

Nataraja. Shiva as the Lord of the Dance (i.e., the play of the world). He is portrayed with one foot raised (representing spiritual knowledge), one crushing a demon (symbolic of worldliness) while dancing in a ring of fire (nature or the cosmos). Devotees in the temple allude often to the many symbols suggested by this image, and it is on many private shrines.

Neti Neti. "Not this, not this." The method of Vedantic inquiry in which phenomena are analyzed and rejected because of their transitory nature.

Nirvana. The Sanskrit term used by Buddhists to characterize the state of final release from the bondage of samsara (relative existence). Literally it means "extinction" (i.e., of desire).

Nirvikalpa Samadhi. The supreme transcendental experience; identity with Brahman, hence the obliteration of duality. It is above Savikalpa samadhi, which is a kind of experience of Brahman's attributes (e.g., vision of the ishta).

Om-Kara. The sound form (mantra) of Brahman, formed of the letters A, U, and M from the beginning, middle and end of the Sanskrit alphabet. It is a symbol of the Absolute (Brahman) and the personal god, as also the logos. Temple members and the Swami use Om in meditation, chanting, and at the beginning and end of temple events.

Prana. Sum of primal energy, the manifested signs of which are breathing, digestion, etc. It is the force sustaining life, according to yogic thought.

Pranam. To salute the teacher or other holy person by touching his or her feet with the hands and then touching one's own head; to prostrate; to bow in salutation with folded hands (a less formal pranam).

Pranayam. Rhythmic, controlled breathing that accompanies meditation.

Prasad. Food or some other offering to a god or spiritual figure that is partaken by devotees after the ceremony; considered to contain holy power.

Puja. Ritualistic worship.

Purana. One of eighteen sacred Hindu works said to have been composed by Vyasa; they concern the popularized stories of gods and goddesses that illustrate Vedic ideas.

Puri. As used in the text, a "denomination of sanyasins," as it were. One of ten of such monastic orders founded by Shankaracharya, and the one with which the Ramakrishna Order is affiliated.

Purusha. The self in Samkhya philosophy (corresponding to atman in Vedanta); the witness to Shakti's energy and change; the male principle.

Rajas. See guna.

Raja Yoga. The system developed by Patanjali in his Yoga Sutras; the path of mental concentration.

Ramakrishna Govinda Narayana. A hymn sung at Vespers.

Rishis. The divine beings whom Hindus consider the original recipients of the Vedas; Swami Vivekananda is believed to be an incarnation of a rishi.

Sadhaka, sadhika. Male and female spiritual aspirant, respectively.

Sadhana. The path of spiritual disciplines.

Sadhu. Holyman; monk.

Saguna Brahman. Brahman with attributes; "god with form," the obverse of nirguna Brahman, "god without form."

Samadhi. Superconscious reality in which identity with the ultimate Reality is attained.

Saman. The word means "speech," and derives from the *Sama Veda.* See *Veda.*

Samkhya. One of six systems of orthodox Hinduism.

Samsara. The cycle of birth and death which one is bound to repeat until the atman (or Brahman) is known.

Samskara. The effect of a thought or action whose sum is the character of the individual; samskaras are created in this life and inherited from past ones. They must be exhausted before liberation is attained.

Sanatana Dharma. "Eternal religion," (i.e., Hinduism).

Sandesh. A sweet made from milk.

Sanyasa. Monastic life; a tradition of renunciation originating in Vedic India.

Sanyasin. A yogi who has taken the vows of renunciation.

Santodhyan. "Garden of Saints." The retreat area on the temple grounds.

Sarada Devi. (1853-1920) Known as the Holy Mother, she was the spiritual wife of Sri Ramakrishna, who is regarded as an incarnation of the divine Shakti and worshipped accordingly in temple life. Many members claim her, along with Sri Ramakrishna, as a Chosen Ideal (ishta).

Sat. Pure being; an epithet of Brahman.

Satchidananda. Absolute existence, knowledge and bliss (i.e., Brahman).

Sattva. See guna.

Sattvic. A character trait ascribed to a person who possesses a spiritual bearing or manner. The Anglicized Sanskrit term derives from sattva, one of the three gunas. See guna.

Satyagraha. "Truthpower." What Gandhi employed in his acts of civil disobedience.

Shakti. The god of the universe in female form; the dynamic aspect of the total godhead. The vision (or grace) of Shakti is prefatory to the liberating transcendent experience. Shakti is worshipped as Sarada Devi, Kali, Durga, Bhavatarini, and Jagadhatri in the temple.

Shankaracharya. Eighth century philosopher whose advaita Vedanta is practiced in the temple; the founder of a monastic lineage (the Puri) to which the Ramakrishna Order is joined.

Shanti. Peace.

Shiva. God of Destruction (or renewal) in the Hindu trinity, the other modes of which include Brahma (the creator) and Vishnu (the preserver). In temple thought Shiva represents Brahman, the destroyer of the ignorance of relative knowledge. He is also represented as the Supreme Yogi, the Lord of the Universe, and as the inert principle of Brahman in consort with power (Shakti).

Shiva Ratri. A puja in honor of Shiva as the eternally meditating yogi. A shorter version of the traditionally all-night ceremony is held on the appropriate calendar day at the temple.

Shraddha. Faith, inner conviction; also, the power of one's comprehension of spiritual truths which influences the outcome of sadhana.

Sri Ramakrishna. (1836-1886) The inspiration of the Vedantic renaissance who is worshipped as an incarnation of Rama and Krishna by many in India and at the temple.

Swami. "Lord." The title given a Hindu monk.

Swamiji. A nickname for Swami Vivekananda.

Tabla. Two drums, the tabla and baya, played during occasional music offerings by the Swami.

Tamas. See guna.

Tanpura. An instrument with a large gourd which serves as a sounding chamber. It is plucked and its sound serves as a drone accompaniment to singing.

Tantra Shastra. A work extolling worship of Shakti; in the view of *Tantra,* the universe is the lila (play) of Shiva and Shakti.

Thakur. "Living God." A name for Sri Ramakrishna.

Tumi Brahma Ramakrishna. A Vespers hymn.

Turiya. "The Fourth." The state beyond the gunas. A way of referring to Brahman. See atman.

Uma. The first known name of the consort of Shiva (whose other names are Devi, Parvati, Ambika, etc.). She is an ancient form of the shakti principle. She is the daughter of King Himalaya, and, according to the *Ramayana* (the most ancient Sanskrit poem—c. 500 B.C.—that describes the life of Rama, an heroic avatara of Vishnu) Uma is "the most excellent of goddesses." She is the vidyashakti of the jnana yogis, as her role in the *Kena Upanishad* demonstrates.

Upanishads. A sacred collection of Vedic wisdom focusing on the sages of India in quest of spiritual experience. They form the "conclusion" (Veda plus "anta"—"end" or "essence") of the *Vedas,* and so are known as Vedanta. Out of 108 *Upanishads* that have been preserved ten are said by Shankaracharya to be primary: *Isha, Kena, Prasna, Mundaka, Mandukya, Chandogya, Brihadaranyaka, Aitareya, Katha,* and *Taittiriya.*

Vairagya. Renunciation.

Vaishnava. The religion of Vishnu; a sect of Hinduism whose followers worship Vishnu's incarnations (e.g., Rama and Krishna). Aspects of temple life contain Vaishnava beliefs and practices (e.g., the worship of Sri Krishna).

Vayu. Vedic God of Wind, discussed in the Epilogue as a personification of mind and breath, which the knowledge of Brahman transcends.

Vedanta. Essence of the *Vedas,* (i.e., the *Upanishads*).

Veda. The name of ancient Hindu scriptures (c. 4-6,000 B.C.) which the orthodox regard as divine revelation. The four books are Rk, Sama, Yajus and Atharva. Divided into the ritual (karma) and knowledge (jnana) portions, each book contains treatises on gods in the form of mantras and hymns, explanations of ritual duties and rules of conduct, and spiritual interpretations of the former. Finally, each *Veda* has a knowledge portion known as *Upanishad,* from whence derives the Vedantic tradition.

Vidyashakti. Maya in its knowledge aspect (vidya) personified as the incarnate divine Mother (Shakti), which is analyzed in the Epilogue in terms of its natural, social, situational and existential dimensions in temple life.

Vijai. See jaya.

Vijnana. A term that means, roughly, wisdom. In Vedantic philosophy, vijnana refers to the nondual Knowledge of Brahman. Such knowledge is beyond ordinary, relative knowing (the latter being the mere opposite of ignorance, and therefore within the realm of duality or illusion).

Vishnu. The God of Preservation in the Hindu trinity, he is said to pervade the universe. Though invisible, he incarnates whenever a world calamity occurs or when the gods need help. Some *Puranas* describe ten incarnations, others twenty-four. Among those worshipped in the temple are Krishna and Ramakrishna.

Viveka. Discrimination.

Vivekananda, Swami. (1863-1902) Head disciple of Sri Ramakrishna, founder of the Ramakrishna Order and the introducer of yoga and Vedanta to the West. He is a "patriot saint" of modern India and considered to be one of the architects of the renaissance that led to the ouster of the British Empire.

Yoga. In general, the term refers to "union with God." Specifically it refers to the system of Raja Yoga developed by Patanjali (4th century B.C.).

Yogi, Yogin. A practitioner of Yoga, a knower of Brahman.

Yuga. An age. The present age is, according to Hindu mythology, the Kali Yuga, the age of unrighteousness and moral decline.

ABOUT THE AUTHOR

Joseph D. Damrell received his Ph.D. in sociology in 1972 and has since held academic appointments on two campuses of the University of California. He is currently an Associate Editor for *Contemporary Sociology: A Journal of Reviews*, published by the American Sociological Association, and is engaged in two field research projects: one on the youth culture, and the other on the social worlds of musicians.

NOTES

NOTES

NOTES

NOTES

NOTES